ESSENTIAL VULNERABILITIES

SERIES EDITOR

John Russon

REREADING ANCIENT PHILOSOPHY

ESSENTIAL VULNERABILITIES

Plato and Levinas on Relations to the Other

DEBORAH ACHTENBERG

NORTHWESTERN UNIVERSITY PRESS • EVANSTON, ILLINOIS

Northwestern University Press
www.nupress.northwestern.edu

Printed in the United States of America

10 9 8 7 6 5 4 3 2 1

ISBN 978-0-8101-3563-5

The Library of Congress has cataloged the original, hardcover edition as follows:
Achtenberg, Deborah, 1951– author.
Essential vulnerabilities : Plato and Levinas on relations to the Other / Deborah Achtenberg.
pages cm. — (Rereading ancient philosophy)
ISBN 978-0-8101-2994-8 (cloth : alk. paper)
Includes bibliographical references and index.
1. Plato. 2. Lévinas, Emmanuel. 3. Other (Philosophy) 4. Self (Philosophy) I. Title. II. Series: Rereading ancient philosophy.
B395.A27 2014
184—dc23

2014007867

CONTENTS

ACKNOWLEDGMENTS

This book is the accomplishment of many years' different endeavors and shows the impact of people who have influenced me in many different periods of my academic life and career.

I first read dialogues of Plato in high school English. That study, among other things, led me to attend undergraduate school at St. John's College in Annapolis, Maryland. The influence of that institution, and those who shaped it and carried it on when I was there, is never missing from my approach to Plato. In graduate school at the Graduate Faculty of the New School for Social Research, I learned to read Platonic dialogues in Greek and in English with my teacher, Stewart Umphrey. My interpretation of some of the dialogues discussed here was guided and influenced by his and motivated and inspired by my time reading them with him. I was also fortunate to attend classes on Plato and Aristotle taught at the Graduate Faculty by Seth Benardete when he was on the faculty at New York University. His interpretations of various Platonic dialogues, as well as of central Platonic concepts in ontology, influenced my ontological reading of Plato.

When I had just returned to reading twentieth-century continental European philosophy in the 1990s, Dana Hollander appeared in Reno as a gift and a guide to the field and to its institutions as well as its interpretive contexts and tendencies and their relevance to my own. My reading of Levinas, both in its content and in its impetus, is immeasurably influenced by her model. James D. Hatley's approach to Levinas, and to the issues that Levinas approaches and pushes us to approach, has been a comfort and a spur to me, as have our numerous conversations over the years. Thanks as well to Oona Eisenstadt, Martin Kavka, and Bettina Bergo for helpful discussions about Levinas and related topics in recent years. For institutional structure, intellectual community, and moral support, I am indebted to the members and leaders of the Levinas Research Seminar (LRS), the North American Levinas Society (NALS), and the Society for Continental Philosophy in a Jewish Context (CPJC). An early version of chapter 3 was read at LRS, and early versions of chapter 1 and chapter 7 at NALS. CPJC has been, and continues to be, an important and collegial institutional crossroads for me.

Thanks also to Silvia Benso for organizing the Levinas and the Ancients panel at the International Society for Philosophy and Literature meeting in Helsinki where I read an early version of section 1 of chapter 2, to Silvia Benso and Brian Schroeder for editing the volume, *Levinas and the Ancients,* in which early version of chapter 3 of this book appears, and to Antonio Calcagno for his interest in an earlier version of chapter 1 of this book (which he published in *Symposium: Canadian Journal of Continental Philosophy*). Thanks also to the many students with whom I have read and discussed Plato and Levinas including, recently, Matthew Abbott, whose masters thesis on Levinas I directed, Daniel Gebhardt and Shaun Grekor, with whom I read Plato's *Hippias Major,* and students in my recent classes on Plato and Levinas. Finally, thanks to what I am happy still to call *my department* at *my university,* the Department of Philosophy at the University of Nevada, Reno, for granting me the sabbatical during which I began work on this book and to the University of California, Los Angeles, and its Center for Jewish Studies where, sponsored by the center, I spent that productive and stimulating academic year.

In Reno, my work on this book has been supported by my department, by the College of Liberal Arts Scholarly and Creative Activities Grants Program and by the University of Nevada, Reno. Thanks to them for their overall support of my work, for the opportunity to read a version of chapter 3 at a Philosophy symposium, and, in addition, for editing support and travel support to various conferences where I presented papers on Levinas and Plato. My work has been supported as well by the owners, Paul Martin and Debbie Spieker-Martin, and all the baristas at Bibo Coffee Company, a locally owned Reno café where many parts of this book were written or revised. The fellowship and good coffee there—as well as the sense of being in a well-cared-for and humane environment—have been central to my academic life since Bibo first opened on Mt. Rose Street in 2003. Thanks also to the owners of the El Mono Motel in Lee Vining, California, on whose porch I have worked on this book at various times, with a glimpse of Mono Lake in the distance and easy and constant access both to their high-speed internet and to their café, Latte da Coffee.

Finally, thanks to the Nevada students, faculty, community members, legislators, and activists who fought to preserve public higher education, and social services, in our state against difficult odds. Without your activities, I might not have had the institutional context—or possibly the heart—to complete this book, the fruit of my work for many years on the topics it contains. Our joint activities continually buoyed my spirits and gave me hope, even when grounds for hope—if hope can have grounds—were not clear. This book is dedicated to you, to my colleagues named above, and to all those fighting against or suffering from the ravages of the globalized world's increasingly privatized economy. I hope the book addresses each of you, and that the thoughts it contains offer some measure of insight in these troubling and interesting times.

ABBREVIATIONS

Aristotle

De An.	*De Anima* (On the Soul) (Ross 1986)
Met.	*Metaphysics* (Jaeger 1978)
Phys.	*Physics* (Ross 1973)

Levinas

BV	*Beyond the Verse* (Mole 1994)/*L'au-delà du verset: Lectures et discours talmudiques* (1982)
EI	"Ethics of the Infinite" (1995)
GP	"God and Philosophy" (Bergo 1998)/"Dieu et la philosophie" (1986)
LF	"Love and Filiation" (1982)
LT	"Loving the Torah More Than God" (1990)/"Aimer la Thora plus que Dieu" (1993)
MS	"Meaning and Sense" (Lingis 1998)/"La signification et le sense" (1964)
OB	*Otherwise Than Being or Beyond Essence* (Lingis 1981)/*Autrement qu'être ou au-delà de l'essence* (1974)
OG	*Of God Who Comes to Mind* (1998)/*De Dieu qui vient à l'idée* (1998)
PI	"Philosophy and the Idea of the Infinite" (Lingis 1998)/"La philosophie et l'idée de l'infini" (1967)
SU	"Summary of *Totality and Infinity*" (Peperzak 1997)/"Résumé de *Totalité et Infini*" (1961)
TI	*Totality and Infinity: An Essay on Exteriority* (Lingis 1969)/ *Totalité et Infini: Essay sur l'extériorité* (1961)
ToO	*Toward the Other* (1994)/*Texte du Traite "Yoma" (85a–85b)* (1994)

Plato

Ap.	*Apology* (Burnet 1985)

Cr.	*Crito* (Burnet 1985)
Ep. 7	*Seventh Letter* (Burnet 1984)
Grg.	*Gorgias* (Burnet 1974)
Hipp. Maj.	*Hippias Major* (Burnet 1974)
Lys.	*Lysis* (Burnet 1974)
Meno	*Meno* (Burnet 1974)
Phdr.	*Phaedrus* (Burnet 1973)
Phb.	*Philebus* (Burnet 1973)
Prm.	*Parmenides* (Burnet 1973)
Rep.	*Republic* (Burnet 1972)
Sym.	*Symposium* (Burnet 1973)
Tht.	*Theaetetus* (Burnet 1985)

Thucydides

Hist.	*Histories* (Jones and Powell 1942)

Hebrew Bible

Deut.	Deuteronomy (JPS 1985)
Ex.	Exodus (JPS 1985)
Gen.	Genesis (JPS 1985)
Hos.	Hosea (Goldin 1983)
Isa.	Isaiah (JPS 1985)
Lam.	Lamentations (Kravitz, Olitzky 1993)
Mal.	Malachi (Kravitz, Olitzky 1993)
Mic.	Micah (JPS 1985)
Ps.	Psalms (JPS 1985)

Talmud

ARN	*Avot de Rabbi Natan* (Goldin 1983)
PA	*Pirkei Avot* (Kravitz, Olitzky 1993)

Midrash

Ex. R.	*Exodus Rabbah* (Lehrman 1983)
Mech.	*Mechilta de Rabbi Ishmael* (Lauterbach 2004)

ESSENTIAL VULNERABILITIES

Introduction

1.

Emmanuel Levinas sees Plato not as a philosopher of the other, but as a philosopher of freedom: "This primacy of the same was Socrates' teaching," Levinas says: "to receive nothing of the Other but what was in me, as though from all eternity I was in possession of what comes to me from the outside—to receive nothing, or to be free" (*TI* 43/13–14).[1] In what follows, I contest the idea that Plato is a philosopher of freedom for whom thought is a return to the self. Instead, Plato, like Levinas, is a philosopher of the other. More broadly, I maintain that Plato and Levinas are more similar than Levinas thinks because neither of them accepts the idea, often associated with early modernity, that human beings are fundamentally self-sufficient but instead thinks human beings are essentially vulnerable and essentially in relation to others.

The point of the book, however, is not simply to critique Levinas, but also to resituate his work and see what is most unique about it by carefully delineating how he and Plato are different. They are different because they conceive our essential vulnerabilities and forms of responsiveness differently. For Plato, when we are knocked out by beautiful others, we are knocked out by the beauty of what is, that is, by the vision of eternal form. We then respond to the beauty and form we have seen by acting in its light, and we relate to others by sharing that vision with them and by acting in the light of that vision in our relations to them. For Levinas, we are disrupted by the newness, foreignness, or singularity of the other. The other, for him, is new, not eternal. The other is foreign. The other is unknowable singularity. For Plato, what makes nonaggressive relations to the other possible is sharing in a common third through mutual beholding of what is. For Levinas, to the contrary, cognition is a source of violence because of its selectivity and inability to comprehend singularity. Whether contemplative or calculative, knowledge for Levinas cannot comprehend the new, the foreign, the singular.

Especially in his earlier writings, Levinas exposes his work by contrast to Plato. Some contrasts he draws are striking and helpful such as the one, just discussed, between beholding what is and respecting singularity, or the one between the eternal and the new. On the other hand, his view that Plato is a philosopher of freedom who thinks we receive nothing of the other but what is already in us involves, I maintain, an important misunderstanding of Plato's view of cognition or knowledge. The misunderstanding leads to a misleading contrast between their views that keeps us from seeing what is most unique in Levinas's own work. Plato does not think that "cognition is freedom." Instead, like Levinas, Plato thinks responsiveness is prior to freedom—but Plato construes knowledge itself as responsive while it is crucial that for Levinas knowledge is not responsive but active.

The book is divided into two parts referring to Levinas's two major works, *Totality and Infinity* (1961) and *Otherwise Than Being* (1974). Each chapter in the *Totality and Infinity* part includes an interpretation in some detail of one or more Platonic dialogues coupled with interpretation of relevant parts of *Totality and Infinity*. The first chapter, "Violence," proceeds by way of interpreting the theme of violence in the drama and argument of the first part of Plato's *Phaedrus*. In the chapter, I argue that both Plato and Levinas think we are essentially vulnerable and responsive, but they differ about what the vulnerability and responsiveness are like. For Plato, like the helmsman of the soul imagined as a chariot, when we human beings are knocked out by the beauty of an other, we are knocked out by the beauty of what is, that is, by the shining forth of eternal form. As a result of being knocked out, we cannot remain in ourselves. Instead, we act in the light of the beauty and form we have seen, and we relate to others not aggressively or selfishly but by sharing that vision with them and by acting in the light of that vision of beauty or goodness in our relations to them. For Levinas, in our everyday going on being, we are mastered, ruptured, and broken open by an other. The rupture results from the fact that the other is singular—not the individuation of a concept—and utterly new—absolute upsurge or absolute commencement—and therefore not assimilable to my self. In addition, though the rupture is disturbing or unsettling, it is peaceful: the mastery teaches us something, and the breaking open opens for us a new dimension. Moreover, because the other is singular and new, my relation to him or her is not need, since need according to Levinas fulfills a retrospective lack, but desire, since for him desire is accomplished in hospitality, directness, openness, and other forms of relation to what is singular. For Plato, then, we are knocked out by beauty and, as a result, endeavor to share it, while for Levinas, we are peacefully broken open by the singular other who is new and, as a result, experience desire for him or her and accomplish that desire in openness, directness, or hospitality. For Plato, nonviolent relations are accomplished through sharing a common third while for Levinas they are accomplished through types of relation to what can never be common. The topic of violence opens up one way of delineating the different types of responsive relatedness found in Plato and Levinas: one type takes place through mutual beholding of what is while the other is accomplished by bracketing all cognition and relating to the other as singular.

In chapter 2, "Freedom," I give a detailed interpretation of the drama and argument of Plato's *Meno,* arguing from it that Plato is not a philosopher of freedom but in fact a critic of the emphasis on freedom in Greek cultural life. I then go on to show, through detailed interpretation of the *Republic,* that Plato nonetheless has a concept of freedom—an unusual concept of freedom through response. Then, through analysis of *Totality and Infinity,* I show that Levinas also discusses two levels of freedom, including one he critiques, freedom as spontaneity or the ability to determine the other, and one he accepts, freedom as responsibility. Each, then, believes we are essentially in relation to an other, so in that sense not free, and that we are free only in an unusual sense of freedom as response to what is outside us. At the same time, I argue, the type of response they espouse is different, with Plato focusing on responsive knowledge of form including the form or idea of the good and Levinas focusing on noncognitive response to the singular other. The former frees us from being thwarted in all our activity while the latter frees us from the enchainment to self.

The third chapter, "Creation," delineates a distinction between the eternal and the new. Starting out with the fact that Socrates in the *Symposium* thinks love (*erōs*) is desire and desire a type of need, while Levinas, in *Totality and Infinity,* argues that desire is not a type of need, I argue that the two thinkers are closer together in their understanding of love and desire than it seems since Plato introduces need for the same reason that Levinas rejects it, namely, to highlight essential human vulnerability. I then go on to delineate how their views of love are nonetheless different since for Plato's Socrates essential human vulnerability is to the eternal while for Levinas it is to the new. The chapter includes detailed interpretation of the drama and argument of the *Symposium* and related parts of *Totality and Infinity.* It also includes discussion of the good beyond being in Plato supported by interpretations of the *Republic* and a new and detailed interpretation of Plato's dialogue on the beautiful, the *Hippias Major,* in which I argue that beauty, for Plato, is the appearance of form.

Chapter 4, "Knowledge," interpreting accounts of recollection found in the *Meno* and the *Phaedrus* and related images in the *Theaetetus,* again argues against a strong distinction Levinas draws, this time between Platonic maieutics and knowledge, on the one hand, and Levinas's teaching and revelation, on the other, and claims that they are more similar than Levinas thinks since each involves the learner's responsiveness or receptivity to what is outside herself. Nonetheless, the chapter argues that the two are significantly different since in maieutics and recollection I direct myself to something both transcendent and immanent, namely, form, but when I am taught by an other, in a Levinasian sense, I direct myself to what can never be immanent or comprehended, namely, the other who, as other, is absolutely foreign. The distinction between recollection in Plato and teaching for Levinas is between disclosure of what is hidden but indicated and revelation of what is absolutely foreign.

The *Otherwise Than Being* section of the book describes how Levinas, in his second major work, treats distinctions similar to those treated in *Totality and Infinity* but without reference to differences between Plato and Levinas. Chapter 5, "Time and the Self," begins by showing that something like the Plato/Levinas distinction recurs in *Otherwise Than Being* but as a metaphysical distinction between synchrony and diachrony rather than an intertextual distinction between Plato and Levinas and that the central metaphysical idea of *Totality and Infinity* also recurs in *Otherwise Than Being,* namely, that the self is essentially in relation while at the same time absolving itself of relation. In addition, I argue that for Levinas this metaphysical idea shows up in ethics, epistemology, religion, and, most centrally, the treatment of the self. The argument is accomplished through a discussion of the idea of sensibility (in both of Levinas's major works) including an interpretation and analysis of Levinas's use of the Yom Kippur morning *haftarah* portion on giving the bread from your mouth to the hungry (Isa. 58) as well as discussion of Levinas's portrayal of knowledge as active and selective and the resulting implication that, in all knowledge, part stands in for or is an image of whole and therefore conveys only part of the whole so that knowledge cannot be allowed to remain fixed lest truth be incomplete or one-sided.

Chapter 6, "Violence, Freedom, Creation, Knowledge," argues that Levinas's views on the topics named in the title remain the same in *Otherwise Than Being* and then goes on to argue that the central characteristic of knowledge distinguishing Plato and Levinas is knowledge as responsive for Plato and knowledge as fundamentally active and selective for Levinas. Because knowledge is fundamentally active according to Levinas, it is by itself fundamentally violent, even when it is a contemplative beholding of what is. Levinas deals with the issue of such violence by subscribing to what I want to call a principle of *epistemological humility* in the face of the problem of *epistemological idolatry,* that is, of a fixed saying of what is, which is a decision rather than simply a type of responsiveness.[2] Epistemological humility is realized through what Levinas in *Otherwise Than Being* calls *the reduction* (an idea closely related to Husserl's *epochē* and Derrida's *deconstruction*), the reduction of the said to the saying, that is, through a resaying—and resaying and resaying and resaying—a dizzying back and forth between positing and resaying of the said in order to avoid congealment.

The seventh and final chapter, "Glory and Shine," returns to comparison of Plato and Levinas and discusses their treatments of the accessible good—beauty for Plato and glory for Levinas. I show that each de-emphasizes the most accessible good due to our tendency to overidentify with it and, as a result, to overlook our deficiencies and our need to remedy them. The discussion of Levinas includes exegesis of *Otherwise Than Being* illuminated by comparisons to key passages in Jewish liturgy, Talmud, and Midrash. In it, I argue that Levinas's approach to glory and the holy has strong affinities to one traditional Jewish approach to them, and that this insight helps us think about how to interpret central themes in the discussion of the glory of the infinite and in his work as a whole. Some support for this claim is given through an interpretation of Levinas's later essay, "Loving the Torah More Than God." I argue, in addition, that the incomprehensibility of the singular other of whom we can only have a trace is echoed by Jewish notions of the holy, which is separate, and glory, which is immanent but because immanent must be articulated cautiously to avoid idolatry. I also argue against the idea that *Otherwise Than Being*'s austere emphasis on responsibility and gift implies that the more positive topics found in *Totality and Infinity,* such as love, desire, and marvel, have been superseded in the second work. Such topics are present but de-emphasized in each work, I maintain, though de-emphasized in different ways corresponding to the different rhetorical strategies each contains. My discussion of Plato shows that Socrates, when young, values beauty so highly that he overlooks his own deficiencies; learns later to care less about appearing beautiful if it stands in the way of self-improvement; but comes to value beauty once again, in the *Hippias Major,* when he learns that beauty is form or form's appearance. He learns, as a result, that beauty, as the most accessible human good and the source of grace and happiness in our lives, also can be dangerous, since our identification with it can lead us to overestimate ourselves. I also argue that, nonetheless, eros for the beautiful is not in fundamental conflict with passionate bodily eros for Socrates but, instead, begins with it. Eros for the beautiful, which results in beautiful action, is the final stage or development of what is intrinsic to bodily passion itself.

2.

My approach in this book is to utilize extended textual exegesis to show both Plato and Levinas as philosophers of the other and then go on to show how their philosophies of the other are the same and how they are different. To an extent, the texts, once interpreted and set side by side, speak for themselves. As a result, the focus of this book is not on analyzing Levinas's specific comments about his relation to Plato. Some discussion of those comments here, however, will set the stage for the exegesis and comparison to follow.

Levinas develops his own work in relation to Plato's in the 1930s and 1940s and extensively in his mid-century work—especially in *Totality and Infinity* (1961) and the one-page outline he wrote of *Totality and Infinity* when it was his thesis (1961), but also in other works such as "Philosophy and the Idea of the Infinite" (1957) and "Meaning and Sense" (1964). References to Plato decrease after mid-century.[3] In the references to Plato, Levinas vacillates on whether to identify his work and ideas with Plato's or to distinguish them. He distinguishes them most when he thinks that Plato in much of his work is a philosopher for whom thought and spirit more generally return to the self. He identifies them most when he identifies his own idea of the absolute or singular other with Socrates's idea of the good beyond being in the *Republic* or of the beautiful in the *Phaedrus.* We can put these two gestures together in the following way. For Levinas, Plato is a philosopher for whom thought and spirit more generally are a return to the self, though he is as well one among a few Western philosophers who sometimes catch sight of a beyond being that keeps philosophy from being such a return.

Levinas sees a return to the self in reason, knowledge, recollection, maieutics, philosophy, love, and desire as Plato understands them. For Socrates, according to Levinas, "sovereign reason knows only itself" and to know something is to remove its alterity from it: "To know amounts to grasping being out of nothing or reducing it to nothing, removing from it its alterity" (*TI* 43/14, 44/14). Knowing reduces being to nothing because knowing strips being of its alterity and reduces it to the self. Recollection, the Socratic way to knowledge, remains within the self and is contrasted with teaching as Levinas defines it: "The transitivity of teaching, and not the interiority of reminiscence, manifests being" (*TI* 101/74). Levinasian teaching conveys something that is outside the self and, for this reason, is truly transitive. Reminiscence, or recollection, to the contrary, is a simple return to the self. Teaching, thus, is preferable to maieutics, that is, to Socratic midwifery, because "teaching is a discourse in which the master can bring to the student what the student does not yet know. It does not operate as maieutics, but continues the placing in me of the idea of infinity" (*TI* 180/155). Maieutics brings out in me what I already contain. Levinasian teaching, to the contrary, brings me what I can never contain. Socratic philosophy relates to an other through the mediation of a third term found in the self: "The relation with the other is here accomplished only through a third term which I find in myself. The ideal of Socratic truth thus rests on the essential self-sufficiency of the same, its identification in ipseity, its egoism. Philosophy is an egology" (*TI* 44/14). To illuminate or know an other is to bring the other within the self. Socratic philosophy, as a result, is egology.

Similarly, Socratic love returns to the self according to Levinas. Socrates interprets love as a type of desire and desire as a type of need and, for Socrates, according to Levinas, "need is a void of the Soul; it proceeds from the subject" (*TI* 62/33). The alterity of what fills or feeds desire, according to Levinas, is "reabsorbed into my own identity" (*TI* 33/3). Here, too, Levinas distinguishes his views from Plato's. For Levinas, love is a type of desire and desire is for the absolutely other: "metaphysical desire tends toward *something else entirely,* toward the *absolutely other*" (*TI* 33/3). To the contrary, "love as analyzed by Plato does not coincide with what we have called Desire" since its first objective is not the other, the stranger, but immortality (*TI* 63/35). In addition, need for Plato is simple lack. "Need," Levinas says, "cannot be interpreted as a simple lack, despite the psychology of need given by Plato" (*TI* 114/87). Moreover, for Plato, the lack can be filled since need is the source of resource as described in the story detailed in the *Symposium* according to which Eros is the son of Need (*penia*) and Resource (*poros*)—that is, eros is need that spurs me to the satisfaction of need (*TI* 115/87). Desire, for Levinas, by its very nature can never be satisfied.

On the other hand, Levinas identifies his work with Plato's when he identifies his idea of the singular other—the other who, because singular, cannot be related to through qualities—with Plato's notion of the good or the beautiful as beyond being. Plato's philosophy is ontology and thus egology, but Plato sometimes catches sight of a beyond being. To the extent that Levinas sees Plato as a philosopher for whom the beyond being is important, he identifies his work with Plato's and considers himself a Platonist. For example, in the outline of *Totality and Infinity* Levinas publishes in 1961 in the *Annales de l'Université de Paris,* he concludes by describing *Totality and Infinity* as a "return to Platonism" ("Summary," 121/386).[4] What he finds important in Platonism, he says in the outline, is the idea of an absolute, that is, a principle that is absolved from history and culture. The first intelligible, he maintains, is the other revealed by the face rather than disclosed through qualities. The first signification, thus, since it is signification of the absolute other, emerges in morality and is independent of or absolved from history. To say that the other bared of all qualities is the first intelligible, he maintains, is "to affirm also the independence of ethics with regard to history" (SU 121/386).

Levinas makes a similar point in "Meaning and Sense" in 1964: "the contemporary philosophy of meaning is thus opposed to Plato at an essential point: the intelligible is not conceivable outside of the becoming which suggests it" (MS 83/30–31). Plato, to the contrary, believes that "the separateness of the intelligible world" means that "the world of meanings precedes language and culture, which express it" (MS 84/31).

Levinas associates this absolute first intelligible with the good beyond being of Plato's *Republic.* For example, in the section of *Totality and Infinity* on "Separation and Absoluteness," he says, "One of the ways of Greek metaphysics consisted in seeking a return to and the fusion with Unity. But Greek metaphysics conceived the Good as separate from the totality of essences, and in this way . . . it caught sight of a structure such that the totality could admit of a beyond" (*TI* 102/76). Greek philosophy totalizes, in other words but, with Plato's idea of the good beyond being, catches sight of something separate from or beyond the totality. In general, Levinas associates Plato's good beyond being with his own idea of the other as transcendent: "If the notions of totality and being are notions that cover one another, the notion of the transcendent places us beyond categories of being. We thus encounter, in our own way, the Platonic idea of the Good beyond Being. The transcendent is what can not be encompassed" (*TI* 293/269).

Levinas also associates his idea of the absolute other with the idea of the beautiful in Plato's *Phaedrus.* In that dialogue, Socrates claims that the greatest goods come to human beings through divine madness. The delirium is not irrational, according to Levinas. Instead, it is reason itself in its thinking of the ideas. The delirium has to do with "the presence in thought of an idea whose *ideatum* overflows the capacity of thought" (*TI* 49/20). Such madness is contrasted with "a thought that proceeds from him who 'has his own head to himself'" (*TI* 49/20, where the reference Levinas gives is to Plato's *Phaedrus* 244a). Possession by a god is not irrational but is experience of the noumenal and the new (*TI* 50/20). In other places, Levinas refers to such desire as non-nostalgic (PI 57/242). Regarding love, Levinas once again speaks of Plato as catching sight of the true view. For, when Plato's Socrates rejects Aristophanes's idea of love that brings us together with our ancient missing half, Levinas speculates that he has "caught sight" of love and philosophy as non-nostalgic: "Has not Plato, rejecting the myth of the androgynous being presented by Aristophanes, caught sight of the non-nostalgic character of Love and philosophy" (*TI* 63/34–35; compare PI 57/243).

As with Plato, so also with Western philosophy more generally for Levinas. Most often, he says, it is ontology: "Western philosophy has most often been an ontology: a reduction of the other to the same" (*TI* 43/13). However, there are exceptions—cases in which traces of the ethical break through (EI 190–91). In addition to Plato's idea of the good, Levinas also refers to Descartes's idea of the infinite as the relation between thought and an idea that thought cannot contain: "the 'I think' maintains with the Infinite it can nowise contain and from which it is separated a relation called 'idea of infinity'" (*TI* 48/19). Levinas also refers to Plotinus on the good (*OB* 95/121) and Aristotle on the agent intellect (*TI* 49/20) as exceptions.

In chapters that follow, I will indicate that desire that does not return to the self (homecoming) or to the past (nostalgia) need not be desire for the absolute or new but could be, and for Plato is, desire for the eternal. Similarly, I will question whether the image of divine madness in Plato's *Phaedrus* is of thought aiming at something singular or absolute that it cannot contain. I will also question Levinas's view that for Plato reason, knowledge, recollection, maieutics, philosophy, love, and desire all return to the self and will maintain instead that in each of these, for him, I am, in part, directed outside myself. Plato, in my view, is a philosopher of the other throughout his work. My point here is, simply, that Levinas is critical of Plato when he sees Plato as one for whom thought and spirit are a return to the self and that he identifies with Plato when he takes Plato to have the same notion of absolute otherness that Levinas has, namely, absolute otherness as an idea that thought cannot contain.

3.

A word about my approach to interpreting Plato and Levinas. Plato's dialogues are a combination of argument and action (*logos* and *ergon*). The teachings of the dialogues—what we might venture to call Plato's teachings or Plato's views—are found in both. Argument must be understood in relation to action and action in relation to argument.

For example, at one point in the *Meno*, a dialogue I will discuss in more detail in chapter 2, Socrates argues that true opinion is as good as knowledge in practice and that, therefore, the prior conclusion they reached that virtue is knowledge is incorrect (*Meno* 97b9–10). Reading the argument he gives on behalf of true opinion by itself might lead the reader to the conclusion that Socrates no longer believes that virtue is knowledge. However, after Socrates gives that argument, Meno is affected and begins to wonder. He wonders why knowledge is valued more highly than true opinion (*Meno* 97c11–d3). After he does so, Socrates brings into the discussion the statues of the great sculptor Daedalus, which are thought to be so lifelike that they run away if they are not chained down, and uses them as an analogy for true opinions since true opinions, according to Socrates, run away from a human being's soul if they are not chained down by reasoning about cause (*Meno* 97d4–98a4). The imaginative interlude indicates that their earlier conclusion that virtue is knowledge in fact has not changed since knowledge is more secure than true opinion. Meno has changed, though. He stops simply repeating what he has heard and instead expresses himself. Even more, he expresses wonder. Wonder involves awareness of one's own lack (if you wonder, then you do not know). Socrates has created the conditions for Meno to wonder and, as a result, actually think instead of simply absorbing someone else's views. Moreover, he has given Meno a reason for valuing knowledge over opinion, namely, that knowledge is more secure. Arguments in Plato, the example shows, need to be interpreted in their dramatic context.

Drama also is intrinsically important in the dialogues. The whole drama of Meno ordering Socrates around in argument and refusing to think is part of the dialogue's teaching on its topic, virtue. The drama illuminates the opening question of the dialogue, namely, is virtue teachable and, more generally, how is virtue acquired. If virtue is knowledge, then the drama itself is an example bearing on the dialogue's topic since it is the drama of a particular search for knowledge. Virtue is as difficult to teach as it is difficult for Socrates to get Meno really to inquire about what virtue is. The dialogue, in other words, performs an answer to the question whether virtue is teachable. Because it does so, it functions as well as an apology or defense of Socrates on the charge of corrupting the young. Though Meno is known for his viciousness after the dramatic date of the dialogue, the dialogue does not show Socrates as culpable but as trying to lead Meno in a better direction and failing due to Meno's own strong tendencies.

I see Plato's Socrates—the Socrates created by Plato in the dialogues—as having the skills of a good teacher, if *teacher* is the right term, given that Socrates, in the *Apology*, says he is not one. As a good teacher, or at least someone very much like a good teacher, Socrates speaks differently to different types of people. Doing so is a principle Socrates himself enunciates in the *Phaedrus* where he laments writing on the grounds that it speaks to every person in the same way instead of speaking differently to people who have different soul-types (*Phdr.* 271c10–d2). Socrates is well aware of different soul-types—of different personalities or characters, we might say—and addresses what he says differently to different people. The reader needs to keep this in mind in interpreting Socrates's claims and arguments.

For example, in the *Crito*, at one point Socrates imagines that the laws come in and speak to Crito. They tell him that they are his mother and father who bore him and raised him. Therefore, they claim, he should treat them well in return (*Cr.* 50a6–51c4). Why does Socrates personify the laws in this way? The answer lies in recognizing Crito's age and what it tells us about his soul-type or personality. Readers, in my experience, often think Crito is young. Instead, he is about Socrates's age and from the same deme (*Ap.* 33d9–e1). What his age indicates about Crito is that his difficulty in understanding Socrates does not result from youth and inexperience but likely from an ingrained tendency only to see things a certain way. Specifically, he cannot comprehend any obligation other than an obligation to *philoi* (family or friends) such as Socrates, his contemporary and fellow demesman. Once Socrates sees Crito's ingrained tendency, he realizes that he can only make his point about obligation to the city and its laws through personification. Crito understands obligation to his *philoi*—it is because Socrates is a friend that Crito comes to steal him out of prison—so Socrates makes the laws into two of Crito's most important *philoi,* his mother and father. In a number of Plato's dialogues, a crucial moment in the dialogue is a dramatic moment such as this one in which Socrates can connect the topic of the dialogue's argument to something about which the interlocutor cares deeply. In the *Crito,* it is family. In the *Meno,* it is whether there is anything such as virtue and, if so, how to get it.

Another aspect of Socrates as a good teacher is that he makes one point at a time. A teacher knows that, generally, students can absorb only one or two or a few new ideas at once. As a result, what may look like Socrates's whole argument on a topic may in fact just be part of one. For example, book 1 of the *Republic* appears to be a complete argument on justice. In fact, it could pass for one complete shorter Platonic dialogue on a "what is it" question where the question is, specifically, what is justice—but in the end it takes nine more books for the topic to be explored in somewhat complete fashion. Socrates is ready to conclude discussion at the end of book 1, but he is pulled back into the argument by Glaucon (*Rep.* 2.357a1–b2). He also might have transitioned at the beginning of book 5 right into discussion of the decline of regimes, but he is forced by Polemarchus and Adeimantus to continue (*Rep.* 5.449a1–b9). If Socrates had gone on to discuss the decline of regimes at that point, we would not have seen some of the most important images in the Platonic corpus, the images of the sun, the divided line, and the cave. Moreover, we would not have seen that the tripartite account of the soul and of virtue was not Socrates's final account of the soul and of virtue but only an account of the partial development of a soul and of the political or conventional virtue that accompanies such partial development.

Similarly, Socrates is ready to stop after he gives his first speech on eros in the *Phaedrus* but is compelled by Phaedrus and Socrates's daimon to stay and give a second (*Phdr.* 241d2–243e3). There are a number of reasons why Socrates might want to stop at that point. Perhaps he simply does not want to make the effort to give an account of the highest or, as we might put it, most abstract levels of ontology. Or, knowing Phaedrus's soul-type, perhaps Socrates does not think Phaedrus is, either dispositionally or intellectually, up to a discussion of higher-order ontology. In addition, Socrates presumably is aware of the erotic possibilities of the discussion. Alone with Phaedrus on a hot summer day, the challenge for Socrates is to discuss erotic passion without exploiting beautiful Phaedrus. The possibilities of a sexual encounter are evident. We know from other dialogues that Socrates tends to avoid such encounters: from the *Symposium,* for example, where Alcibiades describes Socrates as having spurned beautiful Alcibiades's sexual advances even in bed and, for another example, the *Charmides* in which Socrates is aroused at Charmides's naked bodily beauty and calls on a poet and a discussion of the question what is moderation (*sōphrosynē*) to calm himself down.

What the above examples indicate is the importance for us of contextualizing even relatively complete parts of Plato's dialogues lest we miss Plato's points. It would be mistaken to think, due to the interlude on true opinion in the *Meno,* that Socrates has abandoned his earlier view that virtue is knowledge or, because of the parts of the soul account of virtue in the *Republic,* that Plato has abandoned the view that virtue is knowledge. Similarly, in my view, it would be inappropriate to critique Plato on virtue on the grounds that the argument that virtue is knowledge in the *Meno* does not state what type of knowledge virtue is. The argument is not deficient but incomplete. The type of knowledge is spelled out in the *Republic* where we learn that virtue is knowledge of all time and all being including the brightest part of being, the idea of the good, as I will discuss in chapter 2. Once someone has that knowledge—knowledge that results from an extensive education—not only will they know the good, but also they will love the good and do what is good. In the *Meno,* unlike the *Republic* and *Phaedrus,* Socrates does not give the full ontological account that would explain what kind of knowledge is needed for one to be virtuous in the full sense.[5]

In the *Phaedrus* and *Republic,* we see that Socrates also defers, or provides an alternative for, direct discussion of higher-order metaphysics by utilizing beautiful images, images to be discussed further in chapters 1, 6, and 7. In the *Phaedrus,* Socrates gives an image of the soul as a winged chariot and recollection as the ascent of the chariot to a place beyond the heavens where the form of beauty is imaged as sitting on a beautiful throne. The image is unforgettable. In the *Republic,* the form of the good is imaged as an illuminating sun and learning (and dare we say recollection?) as the ascent out of a dark cave. In the *Meno,* the image of recollection is one of remembering what the soul learned in a prior life (as we will see in chapter 2). In the *Theaetetus,* recollection is imaged as having birds in a bird cage and then taking them out (as we will see in chapter 4).

Images such as these fulfill a pedagogical function in the dialogues. They make the abstract metaphysics under discussion easier to comprehend and harder to forget. They are not, however, to be taken literally. In both the *Meno* and the *Phaedrus,* for example, Socrates gives two accounts of recollection, first one through an image, and then one that is more literal. In the *Meno,* Socrates's more literal account of recollection is that it is securing true opinions through causal reasoning (or, we might say, reasoning about why) (*Meno* 98a3–4). He indicates that the second is the more literal version of the first when he says, about the second, "as we agreed previously" (*Meno* 98a4–5). The two are one because the second is the literal version of the first. Similarly, in the *Phaedrus,* Socrates first gives an image of recollection—as the ascent of a chariot to the place beyond the heavens—and then a more literal definition of recollection as understanding what is said according to form, moving from multiple perceptions to what is gathered into one by reasoning (*logismōi*) (*Phdr.* 249b6–c4).

Socrates's use of images is another example of good teaching. People have different inclinations for and types of comprehension, and good teaching involves recognizing these and approaching different people differently. Socrates does not hide the more literal accounts, though. Instead, he states them clearly. However, the images are so powerful that they remain, indelibly, in our memories, while the literal accounts and long arguments resist such easy assimilation. This is another reason for the use of images—though here the reason is as much Plato's reason as that of the Platonic Socrates—or, if not his reason, lest we commit the intentional fallacy, at least the effect of his choice. Plato utilizes images so striking and beautiful that virtually no one who reads the dialogues can forget them. They function as devices for remembering and taking in basic claims and arguments, thus aiding both those who are adept at arguments more literally conveyed as well as those who are not. The images bring the teachings of the dialogues home.

Where does that leave us on how to interpret the dialogues as a whole? Following what has been said so far, it is important that each dialogue be interpreted on its own terms since, for one reason, different interlocutors in each dialogue will necessitate different dialogical approaches. Still, as indicated above, one dialogue may need another for completion—not for completion of the dialogue as a literary product since, in my view, each of Plato's dialogues, as a well-composed whole, is in that sense complete. Nonetheless, dialogues may treat only one aspect of a Platonic-Socratic truth, thus making it necessary to read the different dialogues together. What one dialogue hints at or discusses only on one level, another dialogue may take further. Plato's teachings, thus, are not only found in a whole dialogue under consideration, rather than simply in one part or interlocutor in that dialogue, but also are found in the dialogues as a whole. Plato's views are not found in Socrates's mouth, but in the dialogues, and not just in one or two dialogues, but in the dialogues as a whole, including all the speakers' speeches as well as the drama of the dialogues.

This, however, does not mean that Plato's views or teachings—that is, the teachings of the dialogues—do not often coincide with things that Socrates says. Young Socrates introduces forms in the *Parmenides.* Forms or ideas are an important part of the ontological teachings of Plato. He puts them in Socrates's mouth though we know that it is Plato, rather than Socrates, who invented or discovered them (Aristotle, *Met.* 1.6 987b1–10). Even though on good literary grounds we cannot simply assume Socrates as the mouthpiece for Plato, since sometimes it is the interlocutors who contribute to our understanding, nonetheless, often it is the Platonic Socrates, suitably interpreted, who articulates the views of Plato in the dialogues. For example, we learn a lot about Socrates himself from interlocutors such as Parmenides and Zeno in the *Parmenides,* Meno in the *Meno,* and Alcibiades in the *Symposium.* Moreover, we learn a lot about Plato's views on the different dialogues' topics from the drama of each dialogue, whether the particular drama is one that involves Socrates or simply involves one of the interlocutors—about virtue from Meno's resistance to inquiry, about the beautiful from Hippias's distaste for publicly admitting his own deficiency, about spiritedness (*thymos*) from Polemarchus's readiness to come to the defense of Cephalus, and so on. On the other hand, ontological ideas Socrates discusses, such as the forms—including mathematical forms, qualitative forms, and evaluative forms (the levels found on the divided line in the *Republic*)—are ontological inventions or discoveries we can safely say are Platonic teachings. That ontology and its levels are reflected as well in the discussion Parmenides and Socrates have of what things there are forms of in the *Parmenides* where Socrates, when first introducing the notion of forms, is more certain of the type I will call transcategorials, such as the one, the beautiful, and the good, than he is of a categorial form such as human being (*Prm.* 130b3–d9). Also, whatever other interpretive issues there may be for Plato's Seventh Letter, forms that correspond to definitions are mentioned in it, specifically, "circle itself" (Ep. 7 342c2–3), and Socrates says we can know such forms when they come to light, like a spark, all of a sudden (Ep. 7 341c7–8). The reference to light calls to mind the shining light referred to in the *Republic* and the *Phaedrus*. As both of those dialogues indicate, there is no discursive knowledge of forms. They are understood instead through *nous* or immediate intellectual insight.

A word, now, about my approach to reading Levinas. Levinas interpretation is much more recent than Plato interpretation, of course. Moreover, issues about how to interpret Levinas's work are ongoing ones in which only a little at this stage has been worked out to the point of consensus. Because of these factors, I will work through the major Levinas interpretive issue that affects this book in the book itself, not in the introduction. Some remarks here, however, will point to what is to come later.

Of the two major works, Levinas's main exposition of his work by relation to Plato is found in *Totality and Infinity*. As a result, in the comparisons of Plato and Levinas in part 1 of this book, my focus on Levinas is on his views in *Totality and Infinity*. The question of the relation between *Totality and Infinity* and *Otherwise Than Being* is a live one with the answer still much-discussed and debated by Levinas interpreters and, given the recent date of composition of each work, likely to continue for some time.

An answer that I do not accept is that the basic metaphysics of the first of the two works is rejected in the second. If it were, given that much of the most important material on Levinas and Plato is in the earlier work, that material might be merely of historical interest and much of the central exposition of this book largely unnecessary. In part 2 of this book, then—specifically in chapters 5 and 6—I argue that Levinas's fundamental metaphysics remains the same in his two major works.

4.

Finally, what about other interpretations of the relation between Plato and Levinas? At this point, not much has been written on the topic. Major accounts are those by Adriaan Peperzak, Francisco Gonzales, Sarah Allen, and Tanja Staehler.

Adriaan Peperzak's "The Platonism of Emmanuel Levinas" (1997) brings our attention to Levinas's 1961 summary of *Totality and Infinity*, Peperzak's translation of which is appended to the article. In addition, the article focuses on the Platonism Levinas avows in the summary and also introduces the reader to basic similarities and differences between Levinas's thought and Plato's.

The most important similarity Peperzak describes is the idea of an absolute. Other similarities he mentions are important to note here but of less importance: the use of Plato's distinction, found in the *Sophist*, between the same and the other in Levinas's idea of reduction of the other to the same ("Platonism of Emmanuel Levinas," 114–15); the *Phaedo*'s contrast between bodily life and the life of the soul, which Peperzak sees as clearly retrieved in the contrast Levinas makes between ego and ethics; the use of *kath' hauto,* a Platonic term describing a form as pure or without instantiation (116–17). Peperzak points out that we cannot take the *Phaedo* connection very far because Levinas does not describe the two lives that interest him in terms of a body-soul distinction as Plato does nor can we take the *kath' hauto* comparison to go very far since for Plato it is essences that can be known or intuited that are *kath' hauto* not the unknowable other as it is for Levinas. In these two cases, the use of Plato is more the use of a Platonic motif than something substantive. Similarly, though the same/other distinction in Levinas comes from Plato's *Sophist,* the substantive Platonic contribution of the concept is not too great. In the *Sophist,* the same/other distinction is contrasted with the being/nonbeing distinction and that is crucial for Levinas—namely, that there is something other than being that is not simply nonbeing. However, the *Sophist*'s distinction merely gives Levinas room to articulate his own way of thinking of that. The idea of a singularity that is beyond essence or otherwise than being is Levinas's idea, not Plato's.

Regarding the differences Peperzak describes, each of them needs further treatment, in my view. Levinas does not always articulate the most important distinctions between his work and Plato's. Peperzak rightly indicates a central difference Levinas points out on love or eros, namely, whether desire is a species of need as Socrates and Diotima suggest or not as Levinas claims: "at least one radical difference separates Levinas from Diotima and Socrates: desire is not a need; it cannot be satisfied; it does not circle back to some lack of mine" (115). Platonic need, according to Levinas, aims at completion or satisfaction and returns to the self while desire, he maintains, does not. In chapter 1, however, I argue that it is not the desire/need distinction that is crucial to distinguishing Plato and Levinas on eros since Levinas rejects need for the same reason that Plato has Socrates accept it, namely, in order to stress human vulnerability. The more important distinction, I argue, is about the object of love: for Socrates, the object of love is the eternal, while for Levinas it is the new.

Peperzak also points to Levinas's critique of Platonic maieutics as a return to the self (117) and Levinas's substitution of teaching, as he understands it, for maieutics. In chapter 2, I will argue against Levinas that maieutics is not a return to the self for Plato. Instead, the object of learning is both immanent and transcendent for Plato, since the object of learning is form for him while, to the contrary, it is the absolutely transcendent for Levinas since, according to him, only the other can teach us. These distinctions lead to another important one, between what is hidden but can be disclosed for Plato and the foreign that can never be comprehended for Levinas.

Against Levinas, Peperzak asserts that Levinas's idea of the good is not the same as Plato's. Peperzak's discussion of his assertion is brief, though, due to the length of the article in which it occurs (118–19). I agree that the two are different and, in chapter 3, work out my own extended idea of the difference, in part by giving an extended interpretation of the good and the beautiful for Plato. As Peperzak says, the good for Levinas is "the Good of human proximity" (118). But what is the good for Plato? I shall answer that question in some detail.

The most important similarity between Plato and Levinas according to Peperzak is their shared notion of an absolute that is absolved from history and culture (discussed in section 2 of this introduction). Peperzak emphasizes such an absolute in order to bring out Levinas's "Platonism" as a response to and critique of various philosophical and intellectual tendencies of his time that would reduce human beings to parts of a whole from which they derive their being or meaning (113–14).

Levinas's critique of then contemporary "anti-Platonists" is more of a focus for Peperzak in his article than for me in this book. Levinas, as I interpret him, is a transitional figure between modern and postmodern thought. The reason for this lies in his basic metaphysics of the self, an idea I delineate and discuss in detail in the chapters to follow. For Levinas, the self is essentially in relation while, at the same time, it absolves itself from relation (*TI* 110/82). Postmodern thought has affinity with Levinas's idea that the self is relational or essentially outside itself since postmodern thought also has a critique of the sovereign self. Modern thought has affinity with Levinas's idea that the self absolves itself of all relation since such a view gives some freedom or autonomy to the self. To the extent that Peperzak, in order to bring out the idea of Levinas as a critic of the major movements of his time, emphasizes Levinas's claim that both human beings and the good are absolute, he overstates the importance of human absoluteness for Levinas, in my view, and understates the importance of essential relationality for him.

In "Levinas Questioning Plato on Eros and Maieutics" (2008), Francisco J. Gonzales, like Peperzak, discusses basic similarities and differences between Plato and Levinas: Levinas's acceptance of Plato's ideas of the transcendent good and of the same and the other (40–42), his critique of Plato's view of eros as an egoistic need understood as lack that requires satisfaction, and his criticism of maieutics as a return to the self that, as such, denies exteriority (46–50). He also mentions in passing, but does not elaborate on, the idea that there are different objects of eros for Plato and Levinas: "What Levinas opposes to Socratic eros, in short, is a ravishment beyond all project, a movement that does not uncover what already exists as hidden, but that instead moves toward what does not yet exist and has no quiddity" (49). In chapter 3, I will discuss the difference of objects in detail and maintain that the object of love for Plato is the eternal while for Levinas it is the new.

Gonzales's main point, however, is that the fundamental difference between Plato and Levinas is participation in Plato and separation in Levinas. For Levinas, Gonzales says, the soul is fundamentally separate, that is, self-sufficient or atheist. The soul must be absolutely separate if the other is to be absolute in its transcendence (53). For Plato, to the contrary, the same is essentially a transcending toward the other. Gonzales complicates his critique by arguing that Levinas's view involves an unbridgeable dichotomy—a "dichotomy between absolute interiority and absolute exteriority"—that Plato's view of the soul does not contain (56).

Like Peperzak, however, Gonzales understresses essential relationality in Levinas. For Levinas, there is a relation between the absolved self and the absolutely other even though the relation is not participation. Making the central difference between the two philosophers one between separation (Levinas) and participation (Plato) occludes that fact. In my view, the distinction would better be articulated as one between two fundamental types of relation to the other, one that is a participation relation and one that is not. Levinas describes the latter relation in different ways, for example, as respect, desire, openness, directness. If we characterize the fundamental difference between the two philosophers as the difference between participation for Plato and, say, respect for Levinas, we have a more fruitful distinction from which to begin our thinking. For, put that way, we have two different alternatives both of which have appeal rather than two alternatives of which we must choose one: one alternative suggests important relations based on sharing; the other suggests important relations based on respect for what cannot be shared.

Similarly, Tanja Staehler, in "Getting Under the Skin: Platonic Myths in Levinas" (2008) and in *Plato and Levinas: The Ambiguous Out-Side of Ethics* (2010), does not see the relation between the self and the other in Levinas as a dichotomy. The self for Levinas is absolute in that it can separate itself from other and be self-sufficient, she maintains. But, once the self encounters an other, such closure is put in question—specifically, its ethical nature is put in question. "We can hide in our invisibility, in the interiority of the ego. We can do so—but we cannot be right as we do so," she states in discussion of Levinas's use of the Platonic myth of the ring of Gyges ("Getting Under the Skin," 67). Like Gonzales, she points out that I can only relate to an other as other if I have separated. Without the separation and concomitant self-sufficiency, my relation to the other is based on need. Unlike Gonzales, however, she claims that my ability to separate is a retreating from participation and not an original separation that is followed by participation: "this encounter [with the other] conditions my enjoyment, since such egoistic happiness depends on the fact that I am retreating, no longer participating" ("Getting Under the Skin," 68). In the same vein, I would point to Levinas's idea of a postponement. Referring to a thinking being, Levinas says, "Life permits it an as-for-me, a leave of absence, a postponement, which precisely is interiority" (*TI* 55/26). Gonzales's distinction, then, might better be redone in another way—not between participation and separation but between participation and postponement.

My general approach to Plato and Levinas shares a lot with Staehler's, then. However, she accepts the idea that the reason the good is beyond being for Plato is that the good is outside and disruptive of any totality: "the Good," she says, "ruptures and breaks open the totality of beings; this is the true meaning of '*epekeina tēs ousias*'" (*Ambiguous Out-Side,* 120). In chapter 3, I give a different interpretation of the good for Plato. According to my interpretation, the good and the beautiful are aspects of ontology that have to do with the relation between forms and things, specifically, with the fact that forms are in one sense immanent in things and in another sense transcend them. I argue that Plato identifies the good with that immanence and the beautiful with that transcendence. The good and beautiful, on my account, do not rupture being but, instead, are central to it.

In a different vein, in *The Philosophical Sense of Transcendence: Levinas and Plato on Loving Beyond Being* (2009), Sarah Allen gives a God-centered account of Levinas according to which transcendence "comes to us from God" (5) who, for Levinas according to her, is a "source of order that gives direction and place to the various voices that constitute philosophical thinking" (315). Levinas's God is similar to the good in Plato for Allen, then, because each is a source of order though God is different from the good according to her since the good is not personal and not a creator. As an other, though, God for Levinas is not so much a source of order for us as a source of rupture, I maintain.[6] Thus, Levinas's God would be different from Plato's good in that way as well. How could God be a source of order for us given that we cannot cognize him?

For Staehler, then, Plato's good is, like Levinas's other, a source of rupture in being, while for Allen, Levinas's God is, like Plato's good, a source of being's order. Instead of either of these two approaches, I want really to preserve two alternatives, alternatives I will describe in different ways in what follows, for example, as the difference between form and singularity, sharing and respect, knowledge and openness, the hidden and the foreign, or the eternal and the new.

For Levinas, then, multiplicity of persons is the condition for the fullness of truth, and multiple standpoints are not a departure from truth but lead to truth's expansion: "It is as if the multiplicity of persons . . . were the condition for the plenitude of 'absolute truth'; as if every person, through his uniqueness, were the guarantee of the revelation of a unique aspect of truth, and some of its points would never have been revealed if some people had been absent from mankind" (*BV* 133/163). Levinas's writing, replete with references and allusions to a multiplicity of other philosophers, reflects his view of truth. As a result, it can be expanded through interpretations that open up differently situated approaches that his comments on and claims about different thinkers invite. This book endeavors to accept the invitation found in Levinas's engagement with Plato. Many interpreters of Levinas are minimally familiar with Plato or Greek philosophy as a whole while many philosophers and theorists who focus on Plato and ancient Greek thought do not work on Levinas. *Essential Vulnerabilities* aims to bring these two groups together since Levinas, as portrayed in it, is of interest to Plato scholars and Plato, as I describe him in it, is of interest to Levinas scholars, in each case due to the book's stress on essential vulnerabilities, a topic of interest to both Plato scholars and Levinas scholars in their development of critiques of early modern views of the self. By opening up overlapping strains of interpretation of Plato and Levinas, the book aims to affect to some extent the trajectory of both fields and of how scholars in them situate their own views in relation to others. More broadly and humanely, though, the book, by reflecting on Plato and Levinas, is intended to open up for broader reflection two importantly contrasting ways in which the self is essentially vulnerable and responsive to others.

PART I

Totality and Infinity

CHAPTER 1

Violence

In one direction, relationships point to violence. For what does the presence of an other hold out for me? Will the other harm me, destroy me, subsume me, overwhelm me? Or will the other help me flourish, help me develop or grow, let me be, let me be me? Plato, in the *Phaedrus,* and Levinas, in *Totality and Infinity,* are concerned with this issue.[1] But their treatment of it strikingly differs. For Socrates in the *Phaedrus,* reason makes possible a contrast between love and assaultive *hybris.* For Levinas, in *Totality and Infinity,* we must go beyond reason to avoid violence. Why are their views on violence so different? Answers revolve around their different treatments of being, desire, and cognition. For Plato, being is transcendent and immanent, thus shareable, and desire is cognitively intentional, as such the source of our ability to share with one another the shareable aspects of being. Since desire, for him, is for shareable being, my relation to an other need not be a violent, zero-sum game. For Levinas, being is transcendent, not immanent—it includes a multiplicity of separate and singular entities that cannot be cognized or comprehended—and desire is noncognitive openness that makes pacific relations to singular others possible. Since desire, for him, is a noncognitive relation to an utterly transcendent other—to an other who, as transcendent, can neither be subsumed by me nor a threat to me—my relations to him or her need not be violent.

The similarities in Plato and Levinas's views on violence are equally striking. Each thinker is concerned about ordinary, concrete violence, such as rape for Plato and war for Levinas. Each focuses on essential human vulnerability—described by Plato as being wounded, knocked out, and falling on your back and by Levinas as being hollowed out and wounded or tenderized—and thinks such vulnerability is key to overcoming concrete violence. Each, in other words, adduces a figurative type of violence as the solution to the problem of ordinary or concrete violence.[2] In fact, for each of them, delineating this figurative violence and distinguishing it from violence in a more ordinary sense is a major task or goal. For Plato, this figurative violence is described metaphorically as being wounded, knocked out, and falling on your back, in descriptions that suggest both being overcome and letting something in. Levinas uses similar terms, such as *wounded, hollowed out,* or *tenderized,* and, in addition, calls the figurative violence *essential violence* since, in allowing yourself to be vulnerable to it, your going on being *what you are* is interrupted or violated. Each thinker counsels such openness, vulnerability, or wound, even though it is frighteningly similar to our vulnerability to rape or to the violence of war, in part because such openness promises great human goods to those who can overcome their fear of it.[3] If we allow ourselves to be vulnerable or wounded in this figurative sense, they suggest, we will experience not violence but beauty for Plato, not violence but a new dimension or a teaching for Levinas. Each thinker, then, rejects the ideal of utter human self-sufficiency and instead favors responsiveness in part since each believes that, through opening ourselves to what is external to us, we achieve great human goods. Finally and centrally, each, in addition, sees responsiveness as leading to or being constitutive of service—Levinas in *Totality and Infinity* speaks of being affected by and also having a fecund relation to the other, and Plato in the *Phaedrus* of being moved by and also serving or being a slave to the other.

These similarities in Plato and Levinas's views are even more striking for us because Levinas himself does not see them. He sees Plato not as a philosopher of the other, but a philosopher of freedom: "This primacy of the same was Socrates' teaching," Levinas says, "to receive nothing of the Other but what was in me, as though from all eternity I was in possession of what comes to me from the outside—to receive nothing, or to be free" (*TI* 43/13–14). Levinas here mistakenly supposes that Socrates teaches us that thinking and knowing are a return to the self rather than vulnerability to what is outside us. The image of being knocked out and falling on your back suggests otherwise, as we will see in what follows.

In this chapter, I shall describe both Plato and Levinas as philosophers of the other, and delineate their similarities and differences on violence that I have outlined above. In doing so, I will open up for broader reflection two importantly contrasting ways in which the self is essentially responsive to—as well as vulnerable to violence from—the other. The chapter also will suggest a new way of situating Levinas in the history of philosophy, not, as he himself suggests, as one of the few in the history of philosophy who has a philosophy of the other but, instead, as one of a number of twentieth-century philosophers who turn to premodern thinkers for aid in critiquing early modern thought on a variety of topics including whether the self is essentially closed or instead vulnerable, open and responsive to what is outside it. As Heidegger—as well as some next-generation thinkers such as Arendt and Strauss—turns to the pre-Socratics, Plato, and Aristotle, so Levinas turns to Hebrew thought. This way of situating Levinas leaves us not with the task of considering the implications and legacy of Levinas as one of the few philosophers of the other in the history of philosophy, but with the task of sorting out the twentieth-century philosophic legacies of two similar and also very different premodern philosophies of the other, a task that in one rather traditional frame could be seen as part of deciding on, or synthesizing, the twentieth-century legacies of Athens and Jerusalem.[4] This chapter carries out part of that task.[5]

1.

The *Phaedrus* includes a reference to rape near the beginning—when Phaedrus points out their proximity to the site of Boreas's mythical rape of Oreithyia, daughter of the king of Athens (*Phdr.* 229b4–5)—and ends with Phaedrus repeating the Greek proverb "the things of friends are in common" (279c6–7). In this way, the dialogue is framed by two directions in which relationships point: in one direction toward the possibility of violence or a zero-sum game; in the other direction toward mutuality. The setting reflects these possibilities. Socrates and Phaedrus walk alone together, outside the city, by the river Ilissus, in the warmth of the noonday sun. They talk as they walk. At a certain point, Socrates lies down, and they continue talking. What will happen between them? Who will get what from whom? Will one take advantage of the other?

Violence plays a role in other dramatic aspects of the dialogue as well. When Socrates tells Phaedrus that he does not think Lysias's speech is good, Phaedrus playfully threatens to force Socrates to speak: "We two are alone in solitude, I am stronger and younger, and from all these things, 'understand what I say to you' and do not wish to speak as a consequence of violence rather than willingly" (236c8–d3). Socrates gives his first speech and is ready to leave by crossing the river when Phaedrus encourages him to speak further. Socrates then charges Phaedrus with being the cause of a speech being made and Phaedrus responds by saying, "You do not exactly announce a war!" (242b6). Phaedrus moves from pointing out the site of a mythical rape, to playfully threatening force against Socrates, to recognizing that war and speech (sharing a speech) are opposites, to, at the end, declaring that loving relationships involve a common third. What is suggested is that violence is a zero-sum game in which one benefits to the detriment of another and that its opposite is a situation in which two share in a common third with the paradigmatic case being two people, such as Socrates and Phaedrus, sharing in a speech.

At the beginning of the dialogue, Phaedrus comes to Socrates with a speech in praise of nonlovers that he is intrigued by and wants to recite. Socrates's central criticism of the speech, written by Lysias, is that its main presuppositions about love (*erōs*) and about the springs of human action are false. The speech, Socrates maintains, presupposes that love is the irrational desire for bodily pleasures and that there are two sole sources of human action (237d6–7)—an innate desire for pleasures and acquired opinion that aims at what is best. Sometimes desire and opinion have the same goal, but sometimes they do not (237d7–e1). For desire and rational opinion have no intimate connection. Desire is not shaped by reason but is irrational and has its own natural goal while opinion has no intimate connection with desire and, when rational, comprehends what is good or just. When desire and opinion do not have the same object, one can control or master the other, and then the one in control is the source of our action. Moderation (*sōphrosynē*), a virtue, is one type of mastery or control, specifically, control by rational opinion that guides us toward what is best. *Hybris,* a vice, is the other kind, rule by irrational desire that drags us toward pleasures.[6] There are a number of types of *hybris* or mastery of desire over reason (logos) including one that has to do with the pleasures of food, called *gluttony,* one that has to do with the pleasures of drink, and eros or love, which has to do with the pleasures of bodily beauty, that is, with sex. In love, the desire for sex masters opinion that has an impulse toward what is right (238b7–c4). With these presuppositions in mind, Socrates says, Lysias concludes that since love is a type of *hybris,* it is better to have a relationship with a nonlover than a lover since the nonlover will control his desires and aim at what is good.

Socrates does not accept Lysias's account for he does not accept the idea of human self-sufficiency or control on which it rests. In his own speech on love, the palinode, Socrates strikingly associates love with lack of control and being outside yourself. He associates love with being moved, with being enthused (that is, with having a god within), being enslaved, with awe (254b8), humility (254e7) and, generally, madness (*mania*). But he declares that "the greatest good things come to us by way of madness when, that is, it is given by the divine" (244a6–8) and that love is one example of such divine madness. The helmsman or governor of the soul, who is identified with reason (specifically, with *nous*), falls on his back at the sight of the beloved and then loves him and serves him. He is knocked out and no longer in the things of himself (250a6–7).

Given that Socrates is a rationalist, we might have thought that the picture of sober relationships drawn by Lysias would appeal to him. For, since European modernity, many philosophers have associated rationalism with control or mastery. Descartes, for example, associates his rationalism with mastery and possession of nature rather than with responsiveness to it. His method is a method of conducting reason, not of being conducted by it or by something else to it, and, for him, what we know best are ideas that are in the mind rather than mind being fundamentally in relation to something outside itself. Cartesian reason is autonomous, and the Cartesian self is closed, not transcendent. Cartesian philosophy announces the self-sufficiency of the self and of reason.

Socrates's view of love reflects a different view of reason and the self. For him, a certain type of madness or being out of your mind is preferable to sober moderation. Eros, according to Socrates, is not simply the desire for the pleasures associated with beautiful bodies but a type of divine madness; it pulls you out of your self (ecstasy) and draws you up (transcendence). Moreover, though eros is madness, it is not irrational. Instead, in eros, two lovers together cognize beauty. They cognize what really is. The ecstatic madness of eros leads lovers to the most important kind of rationality, a responsive rationality that is a simple beholding of what is.

To illustrate this, Socrates compares our soul to a chariot with a team of winged horses, representing spirited and erotic passions, and a winged charioteer, representing reason (*nous*).[7] The beautiful and good horse is a lover of honor but with moderation and shame, comrade of genuine reputation,[8] driven by commands and speech alone. The bad horse, snub-nosed like Socrates, is a comrade of *hybris* and boasting, deaf and barely yielding to whip and goads. When we see beauty in the world, we discern its likeness to the eternal beauty we saw before we were born. We are drawn up to something outside ourselves. We want to fly upward and see that beauty, the very form of beauty. When the lover sees a beautiful youth, the hybristic and boastful erotic horse jumps on the youth and, carried along by violence, pulls them all forward to mention the pleasures of sexual gratification. At the same time, the honor-loving spirited horse, since he loves moderation and shame and cares about true reputation, due to shame refrains from going forward and pulls them all back. They struggle again and again, until the snub-nosed erotic horse wins out and leads them to the boyfriend whose face flashes like lightning. The charioteer, seeing the bright boy, remembers beauty itself and, in fear and awe, falls on his back (254b7–8). He is knocked out and no longer in the things of himself (250a6–7).[9] His fall compels him to pull back on the reins and restrain the horses. He restrains the unruly horses again and again, until the charioteer wins out and the erotic horse is humbled and follows the charioteer's forethought (*pronoia*). Then the soul of the lover follows the beloved with shame and fear and serves the beloved's needs. He even serves like a slave to him. The youth, seeing the service, is knocked out, and experiences love in return. The two share in the vision of the beautiful that flows between them. In the best love, their wings grow, and they both ascend to the beautiful itself through the activity of philosophizing together (253c7–257b6).

Socrates's palinode requires interpretation. The ascent to the hyperouranian place is recollection where recollection is spelled out by Socrates in the dialogue as understanding what is said according to form, moving from multiple perceptions to what is gathered into one by reasoning (*logismōi*) (249b6–c4). Recollection, in other words, is, roughly, movement from perception to the conception or idea implicit in it. When the lover sees the lovely youth, his reaction is not just to the boy's body but also to the boy's beauty, which shines through him or, more mundanely, beauty of which the beautiful youth is a visible example or instance. As recollection is movement from perception to the conception or idea implicit in it so, Socrates indicates, love is not an entirely bodily experience, but cognitively intentional. I love and desire the beauty that is in and beyond the boy and his body. Love and desire are not simply brute response, in other words, but are cognitively intentional. They are response to the beauty I perceive in the boy.

In intimate relations, then, violence is one possibility, nonviolence another. Violence results from uncontrolled desire, specifically from uncontrolled desire for the pleasures associated with bodily beauty. Such desire overcomes any rational opinion about what is good and results in using the other for self-satisfaction at the other's expense. The dialogue's frame suggests rape as a paradigm case of this. One type of nonviolence results from Lysian virtue understood as the tense control of reason, which aims at what is good, over desire, which has a different object. Such control, though, is unstable, given the lack of connection between desire and reason. Socrates describes another, more stable and complete type of nonviolence, one that comes through an astonishing mutuality in love, contrary to the normative pattern between lovers and youths in Athens. Socrates says the boy feels love in return but calls it friendship, since he does not comprehend it. Both feel intense love because of the form of beauty that flows between them (255c4–d6).[10] For Socrates, then, the two come together over a common third, the form of beauty, which they both behold. In love, two come together over something beautiful and good that can be shared. Since a form is both in and beyond one who knows it, it can be shared by another who knows it as well. This is one of Socrates's great discoveries, and the core to his solution of the problem of violence in relationships. Since being is fundamentally shareable, nonviolence is possible. The soul need not be a closed and masterful Cartesian self but, in knowledge and in love, can be and is open and vulnerable. Vulnerable to the boy's beauty, the soul opens to the very idea of that beauty and shares it, nonviolently, with the boy.

Socrates's account of love points to his notion of being. Being, for him, is fundamentally ecstatic or transcendent. Things are and are not what they are since their real being is the form in which they participate but with which they do not fully coincide. The very being of things transcends them. The transcendence is not utter transcendence, though, since things do share in the forms. But it is transcendence nonetheless, since things get their being from the forms. Human beings are ecstatic and transcendent, too, in two ways. First, like all beings, their being, their form, transcends them. Second, since knowledge is of the forms, human knowing is ecstatic and transcendent. It is of something outside human beings. Knowing is, fundamentally for him, being together with something outside yourself—not of something only as outside yourself, though, since knowing is recalling something, or bringing out the conception that is implicit in a perception you already have. Eros, too, since it is fundamentally a rational or cognitive process, is transcendent. But, like knowing, it also is of something within, something you possess, a god within, a directedness you already have. Being, then, is ambiguous. As Socrates says in the *Republic*, the things around us tumble about between being and nonbeing (5.479d3–5). Things are and are not what they are. Knowledge and eros are and are not for something outside. And it is this structure that makes nonviolent intimate relationships possible between human beings. For to be outside yourself is not to lose yourself but to enrich yourself, and mutual enrichment or growth through mutual beholding of what is—through mutual participation in the forms—is possible.

Socrates resolves the issue of violence in relationships, then, through understanding desire as fundamentally cognitive or intentional and as both transcendent and immanent, where what is in you is also outside you and can be shared by another. When I am in love with an other, something is in me but it is also outside me and in and outside the other as well. Being is fundamentally shareable.

2.

But according to Levinas on the first page of *Totality and Infinity*, "being reveals itself as war"—even more, war is "the very patency, or the truth, of the real" (*TI* 21/9). Being is war because of *conatus,* the fundamental and self-interested drive of beings to persist in their being above all else, a drive that leaves human beings fundamentally threatened by or allergic to others. Nonetheless, peace is possible. For peace, Levinas states in the book's final chapter, is "the unity of plurality" (*TI* 306/283), and plurality ruptures being. Like the *Phaedrus,* then, *Totality and Infinity* is framed by two directions in which relations to others point: in one direction, toward violence, in another, toward the peace of plurality, difference, or alterity. Moreover, as with Plato in the *Phaedrus,* so Levinas in *Totality and Infinity* focuses on figurative violence—on an interruptive vulnerability that nonetheless is peaceful—as the resolution of the problem of violence in the more ordinary sense. There is a rupture in being, he says (*TI* 35/5, 278/255), an "ontological scission" (*TI* 305/282).[11] The rupture produces plurality without harm to the constituents of the plurality: "The fundamental fact of the ontological scission into same and other is a non-allergic relation of the same with the other" (*TI* 305/282).[12] There is a resistance in being (*TI* 44/14, 197/171), a contestation (*TI* 171/145), a mastery (*TI* 171/146), a breaking of the ceiling or a breaking open of a closed circle (*TI* 171/146), an opposition (*TI* 197/171). But it is a peaceful one: "pacific opposition" (*TI* 197/171), nonviolent resistance (*TI* 197/171), nonhostile opposition (*TI* 171/146), mastery that does not conquer but teaches (*TI* 171/146), a breaking open that opens a new dimension (*TI* 197/172). The other is something or someone new (*TI* 219/194), absolute upsurge (*TI* 89/62), absolute commencement (*TI* 272/250). A peaceful master who breaks totality open expansively not oppositionally.

Since the other is new and ruptures being, my peaceful relation to him or her is not need but desire. For need aims at fulfillment of what already is rather than aiming at or intending something other or new (*TI* 34/4). Desire is the nonallergic relation with the other. Apperception of desire, as a result, is the aim of the book: "The effort of this book is directed toward apperceiving in discourse a non-allergic relation with alterity, toward apperceiving Desire" (*TI* 47/18). Desire is connected to love or eros and fecundity, where love, for Levinas, is for what absolutely is not yet (*TI* 264/242) and fecundity is a relation to an other that is not a power over possibles (*TI* 267/245). Put differently, desire, eros, and fecundity are, according to Levinas, for the transcendent—the absolutely transcendent, not found even in potential in anything whatsoever that already exists (*TI* 35/5).[13]

Like Socrates in the *Phaedrus,* then, Levinas attacks the problem of violence by reconceiving desire. For him, though, the important distinction is not between desires that are and are not cognitively intentional but between need, which is ontological, and desire, which is metaphysical. What distinguishes desire and need is transcendence. Need is for completion, satisfaction, or fulfillment and thus essentially refers back to the self. Desire is for what is absolutely other, for what is something else entirely, where *absolutely* and *entirely* indicate that the other is not found at all in the one who desires, not even in potential. Desire is not completed but deepened by what it desires: metaphysical desire "desires beyond everything that can simply complete it" (*TI* 34/4).[14] In desire, the remoteness of the other is not overcome but preserved (*TI* 34/4).

Since desire is for something not relatively but absolutely other, desire is not knowledge. Knowledge is a relation to an other through the mediation of a third term already given. As a result, knowledge cannot comprehend the absolutely other. Knowledge is associated with ontology, or theory as comprehension of beings, and is contrasted with metaphysics, or theory as respect for exteriority. Ontology promotes freedom since the reduction of what is other to the same through a neutral third term prevents alienation by the other and preserves my self-sufficient and thus spontaneous activity.[15] Metaphysics is concerned not with freedom but with critique since the presence of an unassimilable other, not reducible to my thoughts or to anything whatsoever that I already have, calls my spontaneity into question. Knowledge, the reduction of the other to the same, finds only what is already in itself, rests on the self-sufficiency of the same, and thus is an egology, a return to the self (*TI* 42–44/12–14). Levinas, like Socrates, then, solves the problem of violence through resort to transcendence but, unlike Socrates, resorts to an utter transcendence, with no trace of immanence, found in a fundamentally noncognitive relation to an other. For Levinas, peace in relationships comes from our openness to or respect for an other with whom we are in relation but whom we can never contain or comprehend.

Socrates resolves the issue of violence in relationships by reconceiving desire as cognitively intentional and being as fundamentally shareable. Desire, for him, can comprehend and desire what is good or beautiful, and what is good or beautiful in the most important sense, since it is transcendent and immanent, can be shared. The best relationships are those in which desire for the other is consummated through sharing the shareable aspects of being. Levinas's approach is to conceive desire as noncognitively intentional. One main goal of *Totality and Infinity* is to describe a type of intentionality that is not knowledge. That type of intentionality, according to Levinas, enables us to reach beyond being, which is war, toward the absolutely other and, by doing so, to establish the peace of plurality. It is an intentionality of a wholly different type (*TI* 23/xii), an intentionality of transcendence (*TI* 49/20), a signification without a context, a vision without an image (*TI* 23/xii). It is not representation (*TI* 27/xvi), knowledge (*TI* 64/36), categorization (*TI* 69/41), disclosure (*TI* 64/36, 74/47), thought of an object (*TI* 49/20), or consciousness in the ordinary sense (*TI* 274/252). As Heidegger argues that our relation to unknowable death is central to our being in the world, so Levinas makes our directedness to the unknowable other the central movement of spirit, central as a result to desire and eros.

Neither knowledge nor power, eros is sociality or multiplicity. Knowledge reduces sociality: "Consciousness appears as the very type of existing in which the multiple *is* and yet, in *synthesis, is no more,* in which, consequently, transcendence, a simple relation, is less than being. The object is converted into an event of the subject" (*TI* 274/252). Eros, for Levinas, is not fusion but plurality: "Sexuality is in us neither knowledge nor power, but the very plurality of our existing" (*TI* 277/254). In eros, the "I springs forth without returning" (*TI* 271/249). Eros takes place beyond war with an other and his or her freedom for "the amorous subjectivity is transubstantiation itself" (*TI* 271/249). In eros, being is produced as multiple or, even more, as infinite. For the child is new—a rupture in being, a commencement (*TI* 278/255). The child produced through eros and fecundity is also erotic and fecund and thus productive of another, and another, and so on. Fecundity engenders fecundity (*TI* 269/247).[16] Moreover, the child produced is free. The relation to the child in fecundity is creation ex nihilo, and "Creation *ex nihilo* breaks with system, posits a being outside of every system, that is, there where its freedom is possible" (*TI* 104–5/78). As a result, "Being is here produced not as the definitiveness of a totality but as an incessant recommencement, and consequently as infinite" (*TI* 270/248).

Finally, though eros and fecundity are transcendent, they are not ecstatic (*TI* 269/247).[17] Love produces plurality, not unity. When I love, I am not outside myself nor do I lose myself. Even more, the I is effectuated by its relation to an other. Fraternity constitutes ipseity (*TI* 279–280/257). It is for this reason that Levinas calls peace the *unity* of plurality (*TI* 306/283). The ipseity or unicity of each is preserved. Given the nonheroic nature of eros, including the fact that in eros I lose my subject position, it may seem strange that, according to Levinas, I do not lose but gain my self in love. But this is one of Levinas's fundamental ideas. Through losing my position as a subject, I become my self. The self is not static. It does not remain the same. Instead, the self is the being whose existence consists in recovering or identifying itself through all that happens to it (*TI* 36/6). I sojourn in the world but remain at home with myself (*TI* 37/7), beings "remain at their post but communicate among themselves" (*TI* 48/19), each of us has a "universal identity in which the heterogeneous can be embraced" (*TI* 36/6).[18] In desire and love, for Levinas, I go toward the other while retaining my self. The other as such, then, is not threatening for Levinas—though, of course, specific others may in fact be threatening—since my relations to others are in part constitutive of my self.

Levinas writes at a deep metaphysical level. What does he mean more freely? In desire, for Levinas, I intend the other while putting my own interests, needs, concerns, cares out of play. In that sense, I am hollowed out or excavated by the other rather than completed by him or her (*TI* 34/4). In addition, I intend the other apart from any preconceptions I have of him or her, any evaluations, any standpoints, any categories. Levinas calls this type of response to the other a response to the other simply as other, as absolutely other or absolute alterity, as singular. When I desire in this way, rather than being diminished, I am increased. I receive a teaching, Levinas says (*TI* 197/171), the other opens a new dimension (*TI* 197/172), the other speaks to me (*TI* 198/172). In addition, when I desire in this way, though I put my own cares and interests out of play, I do not lose my self. I remain at a distance (*TI* 34/4, 179/154), but this remaining at a distance from the other is the very process in which my self is developed. The self comes into existence in a process of responding to an other. The self comes about through a process of recovering my self through all my intentions of or responses to the other. As a result, I can both retain my self and relate to the other as more than an extension of me.

To intend the other while putting my interests and preconceptions out of play is not to do something but is to be affected by someone (*TI* 197/171). When I lose my mastery, Levinas says, I am moved or, better, tenderized (*TI* 270/248). Love arises in the passivity of a wound (*TI* 277/254). Love is an open responsiveness that, though responsive rather than active, is productive. Through it, the other comes to be. Levinas calls the productive or generative quality of desire and love *fecundity* (*TI* 267–69/244–47). I stand back and give the other space to be, moreover, to be whatever and whoever he or she will be. The concrete case of fecundity is desire leading to the birth of a child—a new individual, a singular being, of no genus. Fecundity extends beyond this and is the quality of my desire and love for any other person. Through open response to an other, I enable the other to be and facilitate his or her future projects. My relation to my self can also be fecund. Through not conceptualizing but simply responding to my self, I give my self space to be, to be me, to be some me I am going to be.

Though the goal is peace, not war, the figurative language in which it is discussed is the language of violence—of excavation, rupture, wound, resistance, breaking a circle open, tenderization. The violent language plays a role in the account of peace. For the breaking open opens a new dimension rather than being destructive. This type of rupture is not ordinary but "essential violence": "What, in action, breaks forth as essential violence (*essentielle violence*) is the surplus of being over the thought that claims to contain it, the marvel of the idea of infinity" (*TI* 27/xv).[19] I cannot contain the other in thought—but the inability points to surplus, not to destruction or diminution. Essential violence, unlike ordinary violence, is a marvel. It disrupts my essence—my going on being *what I am*—by supplementing it rather than harming or annihilating it. Essential violence is a breaking open that does not destroy or diminish but opens a new dimension. The other peacefully opens me up.

We have seen this type of violent figure of speech before, in Plato. The helmsman of the soul feels fear and becomes a slave. The youth, in response, is knocked out. Feeling fear, becoming a slave, being knocked out—all suggest vulnerability to the other. It is Socrates's job to describe a beneficial, rather than harmful, vulnerability, a vulnerability that is not a violation of limits, a vulnerability that enables one to develop, grow, or flourish. Phaedrus fears the other. Socrates teaches him that there are others to whom one may be vulnerable without fear. What the helmsman feels is not fear in the ordinary sense. Hence, when Plato says the helmsman feels fear and awe, he means *fear, that is, awe.* Similarly, the lover's service to the beloved may feel like slavery to one unaccustomed to vulnerability, but it is not. For it is a mutually beneficial service, rather than the harmful service to a master that is slavery in the ordinary sense. We are witness to Socrates's ontological expansion of vocabulary.

Similarly, Levinas uses the language of violence—of *essential violence*—to describe a vulnerability that is not a violation but a type of increase. Commerce with "the alterity of infinity does not offend (*blesse*) like an opinion," he says; "it does not limit a mind in a way inadmissible to a philosopher" (*TI* 171/146). Why not? Because "limitation is produced only within a totality, whereas the relation with the Other breaks the ceiling of the totality. It is fundamentally pacific" (*TI* 171/146). The contrast to our relation to the absolutely other is our relation with others as conceived by those who see us as arbitrary, spontaneous, pure freedoms who as a result are necessarily in conflict one with another. "The other is not opposed to me as a freedom other than, but similar to my own, and consequently hostile to my own. The Other is not another freedom as arbitrary as my own, in which case it would traverse the infinity that separates me from him and enter under the same concept" (*TI* 171/146). The other breaks me open—peacefully. I am not just an arbitrary freedom for whom the encounter with any other freedom, any other person, is essentially threatening.[20] The other is not essentially a threat but is instead an addition. Levinas goes on to say about the other, "His alterity is manifested in a mastery that does not conquer, but teaches. Teaching is not a species of a genus called domination, a hegemony at work within a totality, but is the presence of infinity breaking the closed circle of totality" (*TI* 171/146). The other teaches me, where teaching is giving me more than I already contain. Commerce with the other, then, does not hurt you, harm you, destroy you.

Essential violence is clearly distinct from violence in the ordinary sense, as awe is different from fear. I learn from the other's teaching without shock: "The idea of infinity, the overflowing of finite thought by its content, effectuates the relation of thought with what exceeds its capacity, with what at each moment it learns without suffering shock" (*TI* 197/171). The relation with the other absolutely other "is maintained without violence, in peace with this absolute alterity. The 'resistance' of the other does not do violence to me, does not act negatively" (*TI* 197/171). The other resists me. I cannot grasp the other. There is "total resistance to the grasp" (*TI* 197/172). But the resistance occurs "only by the opening of a new dimension" (*TI* 197/172).

Finally, as with Socrates, so also with Levinas, not only his conception of desire, but also his conception of being is key to his solution to the problem of violence. Being, in *Totality and Infinity,* is plural.[21] Outside any conceptual scheme, any totality, lies the other. The other is singular where singularity is different than particularity. For a particular is always a particular of a certain genus. A singular has no genus: "The unicity of the I does not merely consist in being found in one sample only, but in existing without having a genus, without being the individuation of a concept. The ipseity of the I consists in remaining outside the distinction between the individual and the general" (*TI* 117–18/90). What makes the other is not a set of properties that distinguish it but its refusal of properties: "the refusal of the concept is not only one of the aspects of its being, but its whole content" (*TI* 118/90).

For Levinas, too, then, the issue of violence in relationships is resolved by reconceiving desire and being. Desire for him is noncognitive intentionality, noncognitive vulnerability to an other who is beyond any conceptual scheme or totality, in which we are resisted but not violated, mastered but not conquered, broken open expansively and not oppositionally. Desire, in addition, is fecund or generative rather than threatening. Through open responsiveness, desire makes others, and their future projects, possible. Finally, desire is transcendent but not, in Levinas's sense, ecstatic. When I desire, I move toward an other without losing myself. As a result, desire's transcendence is nonviolent. Desire points to plurality or multiplicity, to the peaceful coexistence of a multiplicity of singular beings.

3.

Though Plato argues that reason is the source of nonviolence and Levinas that we must go beyond reason to overcome violence, we can see now that the two thinkers' views on violence and the other are not completely different but share a common core: each, in his treatment of violence, stresses vulnerability and responsiveness to the other and rejects the idea of fundamental human self-sufficiency. As we have seen, a personified reason, according to Socrates, falls on its back when it sees the beautiful youth. The image is a dramatic, lovely, and philosophically important one. The helmsman of the soul, *nous,* sees the boy, remembers the form of beauty and, in fear and awe, falls on his back. He is knocked out and no longer in the things of himself (*Phdr.* 250a6–7). Reason, then, is not turned in on itself and in control but affected by the other outside itself. Being affected in this way causes reason, and eventually the reason-infused whole soul, to follow the beloved in awe and to serve the beloved's needs. Even eros in the end is affected by the youth and, once affected, along with the rest of the soul, follows and serves him.

The language used to describe eros is violent but is used to convey something that is not, literally, violent. Love need not be assault, Socrates teaches the beautiful and justifiably nervous Phaedrus. Socrates's lesson is not just for Phaedrus, but for any Athenians still influenced by a decayed heroic ideal. Love always disrupts you, Socrates suggests. It knocks you out. It takes you outside yourself. But the disruption is welcome. It stimulates you to grow and puts you in touch with something good. As Socrates puts it, it causes your wings to grow and draws you up to the form of beauty.

Levinas's term for the disruption we experience in love, and in all direct relations to others, is *essential violence,* which, as we have seen, is not violence in an ordinary sense but rupture that gives me something I do not already have. When Levinas speaks of a breaking open that opens a new dimension, or of a mastery that does not conquer but teaches, he, like Plato, is referring to an initially shocking but ultimately welcome or desirable vulnerability to an other. I learn from the other "without suffering shock," Levinas says. What I gain from the rupture called *essential violence* is a surplus, a marvel: "What, in action, breaks forth as essential violence is the surplus of being over the thought that claims to contain it, the marvel of the idea of infinity" (*TI* 27/xv).

Moreover, for Levinas, the self is not harmed but effectuated by its vulnerability to an other. Fraternity constitutes ipseity, as we have seen (*TI* 279–80/257); I become my self by being affected by the other; the existence of the self *consists* in recovering itself—or, better, in identifying itself—through all that happens to it (*TI* 36/6); I sojourn in the world but remain at home with myself (*TI* 37/7); each of us has a "universal identity in which the heterogeneous can be embraced" (*TI* 36/6). Each of these statements is a formulation of Levinas's central metaphysical idea, of a self that is essentially in relation while, at the same time, absolves itself from those relations (*TI* 110/82).

With Plato and Levinas, then, we have not a philosopher of freedom and a philosopher of the other, but two philosophers of the other. Each considers human beings to be essentially, shockingly, and marvelously open, vulnerable, and responsive rather than closed, self-sufficient, and self-involved. Each finds the solution to the problem of violence in that openness to an other. At the same time, the type of responsive relatedness described by each is different: one type is cognitive and takes place through mutual beholding of what is, while the other is accomplished by bracketing cognition of what is and relating to the other as singular.

Do philosophies of the other fall into two fundamental kinds on the model of the two kinds that Plato and Levinas delineate for us? The ideas developed in this chapter leave that an open and lively question to be pursued. At the very least, the chapter leaves us with grounds for disagreeing with Levinas's characterization of himself as one of very few in the history of philosophy who have a philosophy of the other. Instead, our inquiry in the chapter suggests we might best characterize Levinas as one in a group of twentieth-century philosophers who find rich resources in premodern thought for critiquing early modern ideas of the self as closed rather than open, vulnerable, and responsive to the other, with Levinas turning to a fundamental kind of resource he describes as Hebrew and Heidegger and his students turning to a fundamental kind we, if we follow Levinas, could call Greek.[22]

CHAPTER 2

Freedom

1.

As we have seen, when Levinas, in *Totality and Infinity,* asserts that Plato is not a philosopher of the other, he focuses his critique on the concept of freedom. Speaking of Socrates's views, he says, "This primacy of the same was Socrates's teaching: to receive nothing of the Other but what was in me, as though from all eternity I was in possession of what comes to me from the outside—to receive nothing, or to be free." Still speaking of Socrates's views, Levinas goes on to amplify and delineate his critique by claiming that Socrates identifies cognition and freedom: "Freedom does not resemble the capricious spontaneity of free will; its ultimate meaning lies in this permanence in the same, which is reason. Cognition is the deployment of this identity; it is freedom" (*TI* 43/13–14).

Levinas tends to speak of the history of Western philosophy as though it had one chapter—the chapter about freedom according to which the other is a threat and cognition is freedom. Speaking of the relation with absolute otherness, he says, "it does not limit a mind in a way inadmissible to a philosopher" (*TI* 171/146) as though all philosophy were coextensive with the philosophy of freedom—except for a few rare cases in which traces of the ethical are visible "breaking through" the ontological but not quite breaking through all the way ("Ethics of the Infinite," 190–91). Similarly, Levinas praises Aristotle's conception of agent intellect for being a receptivity of something external, something that comes "in by the gates" (*TI* 49/20, 51/22), as if it were not the case that even sense perception is a type of receptivity (*to dektikon*) according to Aristotle (*De An.* 424a17–19). For Aristotle, cognition is not freedom but receptivity.

Freedom is not a central concept in Plato's work. There is no dialogue on freedom. Freedom is not on Plato's list of virtues. In the *Gorgias,* it is Gorgias and Callicles who espouse freedom as an ideal and Socrates who refutes them.[1] When Callicles defines virtue and happiness as luxury, uncontrol, and freedom, Socrates claims against him that an orderly life is better than an uncontrolled one (492c3–493c7). Freedom appears at the beginning of the *Lysis* where Socrates argues against the view that we are happy when we are free to do whatever we want with respect to something rather than when we are wise about the thing, using as example a boy rather than a knowledgeable charioteer driving a chariot (208e4–c2, 210a9–c4). In the *Republic,* greed for freedom in democracies leads to neglect of law and decline into tyranny (562a4–b12). In the *Laws,* the Athenian stranger claims freedom in the city must be supplemented by concern for wisdom and criticizes the Athenians for allowing unlimited freedom (698a5–701e8). Plato's views, then, have more in common with Levinas's than Levinas supposes. Both value responsiveness over freedom, heteronomy over autonomy.

Levinas, for example, questions the "undiscussed value of spontaneity" (*TI* 83/55) and the centrality of freedom understood by him as "the determination of the other by the same" (*TI* 85/57). His whole work is devoted to providing an alternative to viewing the other as a threat ("Ethics of the Infinite," 182). "The Other," Levinas says in *Totality and Infinity,* "is not opposed to me as a freedom other than, but similar to my own, and consequently hostile to my own" (*TI* 171/146). Instead, as we have seen, Levinas seeks a nonoppositional relation to the other: "The effort of this book is directed toward apperceiving in discourse a non-allergic relation with alterity, toward apperceiving Desire" (*TI* 47/18). In desire, as we have seen, I am opposed (*TI* 197/171), mastered (*TI* 171/146), or broken open (*TI* 171/146) by the other, but the opposition is a "pacific opposition" (*TI* 197/171), the mastery a "mastery that does not conquer but teaches" (*TI* 171/146), the breaking open a breaking open that opens "a new dimension" (*TI* 197/171). We can summarize, then, that the other is not a threat to my freedom but is a peaceful master who breaks totality open expansively not oppositionally. Justice, too, for Levinas is not "reconciling my freedom with the freedom of the others" (*TI* 83/55) but "consists in recognizing in the other my master" (*TI* 72/44). Justice is the "face to face approach" (*TI* 71/43), the most direct approach to an other there is. The "work of justice" is "the uprightness of the face to face" and "nothing is more direct than the face to face, which is straightforwardness itself (*la droiture même*)" (*TI* 78/51).

Levinas's attack on Plato as a philosopher of freedom who believes that I receive nothing from the other that was not already in me perhaps finds its source most centrally in the *Meno.* However, in the *Meno,* it is not Socrates but Meno who is characterized as seeking freedom—in fact, as letting his desire for freedom get in the way of his ability to recollect or think for himself. Moreover, the dialogue is replete with references to limitation, some of them functioning as similes for virtue. Overall, the dialogue can be seen as a critique of the emphasis on freedom common in Greek cultural life rather than as an exaltation of it. To have virtue, for Socrates, is to be limited in a certain way—specifically, in a good way. It is not to be free.

Readers of the *Meno* wonder about the role of the geometrical demonstration Socrates conducts with a slave, one of Meno's entourage, a geometrical proof used as a demonstration of Socrates's idea of recollection, the view that the soul knew all things before we were born and, as a result, all learning is simply recollection of something the soul knew before. The demonstration seems inconclusive, at best, if not ludicrous, with Socrates asking the slave leading questions to help him solve a difficult geometrical problem the solution to which rests on knowledge about irrational magnitudes. The slave does not contribute much to the solution he reaches since he only solves the problem after Socrates shows him where to draw the figure on which the solution depends. Though there is some truth to Socrates's belief that he is demonstrating the truth of recollection through his interchange with the slave,[2] what is more obvious is that the demonstration is a big joke. Socrates uses it to draw a picture of Meno as a slave. Earlier in the dialogue, Meno makes an image of Socrates as an ugly numbfish, with bulging eyes and a flat nose, who paralyzes anyone who comes into contact with him. Socrates says he will not take Meno up on the challenge to make a return image of him, a verbal game of mutual insult common at the time, and goes on instead with the topic of their discussion, namely, the question of what is virtue. Later, though, after Meno has himself paralyzed inquiry entirely by raising a question about the very possibility of inquiry in the well-known Meno problem, Socrates does draw an image of Meno in return. It is Meno as no better than a slave—no better, or even worse, since his ignorance does not spur him on to inquiring further. Socrates's goal in using a slave as an image of Meno is to shame Meno into inquiring further, that is, to shame him into recollecting, a goal Socrates never achieves, except briefly later in the dialogue.[3]

In the protracted and funny slave demonstration, Socrates gets revenge on Meno by doing what he said he would not do, making an image of him in return, an image of Meno as a slave. It is Meno, not as Levinas thinks, Socrates, who prides himself on his freedom. At one point in the dialogue, Socrates says that Meno, being spoiled, orders Socrates around in the discussion like a tyrant would (76b4–c2). Later, after the dialogue's long digression on recollection, Socrates again points out that Meno wants to rule him and adds that Meno does not want even to be ruled by himself since he wants to be free: "you do not even try to rule yourself, so that you may be free, but you try to and do rule me" (86d6–7). Meno is a rich, handsome, spoiled youth who prides himself on being free—on being in control, on being the boss.

The geometrical demonstration is interrupted by asides in which Socrates speaks to Meno and, clearly, compares Meno to the slave. At one point, when the slave declares he does not know what the double square is, Socrates says, "At first he did not know what the base of the eight-foot square was just as even now he does not yet know, but then he believed at least that he knew, and answered confidently like a knower, and he did not think himself at a loss. But now he does think himself at a loss, and as he does not know, so he does not believe he knows" (84a4–b1). A few lines later, Socrates says, "Indeed, we have probably accomplished something useful, as it seems, for discovering how things stand. For now, since he does not know, he would pleasantly inquire while then he believed he could easily and often make fine speeches before many people about the double square and said that it must have a base of double length" (84b9–c2). This refers back to what Meno said when he was at a loss about the definition of virtue, "I do not have an answer to give you. Yet, on a thousand occasions, I have made very many speeches before many people about virtue, and made them very well, as at least it seemed to me, but now I cannot even say at all what it is" (80b1–4). Socrates goes on to say that being numbed, a reference back to Meno's assertion that he has been numbed by Socrates, is a benefit to the slave, since now he will begin to inquire. Socrates's point, to Meno, is that he is no better than an ignorant slave. Socrates at least is ruled by himself. It is Meno, then, not Socrates who wants to be free and would be ashamed to be the opposite of free, namely, a slave.

Earlier in the dialogue, shape is used as a simile for virtue. Shape is defined as the sole thing that always follows color (75b10–11) and then as the limit of a solid (76a6–7). About the first definition, Socrates says, "I would be satisfied if you defined virtue to me in this way" (75b11–c1). In the *Meno,* the examples themselves echo the freedom/slavery subtheme of the dialogue, suggesting that virtue would not be freedom, but would be a form of limitation or of following (or, alternately, that if virtue is a type of freedom it is the type that results from observing limitation, like the freedom a chariot driver has when he limits what he does in accord with the observed conditions of the road).[4] If the teaching of the dialogue is that virtue is knowledge or wisdom, and I think it is, then the point would be that virtue is being limited by or following the forms. Socrates, referring to the two definitions of shape as one, says he likes the (one) answer regarding shape better than a later answer he gives regarding color (76e6–7). Virtue is a form of being limited by or following something—specifically, we can imagine, it is being limited by or following, the forms.[5]

Socrates's argument in the *Meno* that virtue is knowledge is preceded by another major argument, namely, that no one desires anything bad (77b2–78a8). Meno, at one point, tries out a definition of virtue as desire for fine things and the ability to get them. Socrates divides the proposed definition into two parts and changes *fine* to *good,* leaving for their consideration the claim that virtue is the desire for good things.[6] He then argues that no one desires anything bad, at least as end not means, since no one desires to be miserable or unhappy. Socrates's argument that virtue is knowledge is that there is nothing good that knowledge does not comprehend. External goods such as health, strength, beauty, and wealth (a proverbial list) are only good if used correctly by good qualities of the soul such as moderation, justice, courage, intelligence, or quick thought (*eumathia*), magnificence (*megaloprepeia*), and these qualities of the soul are only good if they are knowledge or wisdom. What is called courage, for example, if it is not wisdom, is not good but instead is recklessness. Since virtue is good and there is nothing good that is not knowledge or wisdom, virtue, then, must be knowledge or wisdom.

This is a simple and powerful argument. There is no desire for anything bad, thus ruling out the possibility that there are desires or impulses that run counter to the simple model of positive for positive, negative for negative: positive feelings for positive things (love for beauty, for example) and negative feelings for negative things (for example, fear for danger). This rules out the existence of will, since will is an impulse that breaks the model—we can will something unpleasant, or have a weak will when we cannot make ourselves will what is unpleasant. There is no concept of will in the *Meno* and, I maintain, in all of Plato. But, without a concept of will, how does action take place? Simply put, we are compelled to do what we perceive to be good. That is why Socrates can claim that virtue is knowledge. All our desires are for what we take to be good. The only thing that is missing for us to do what is good, then, is knowledge of what good is. We do not need, in addition, a faculty that pushes us toward it, the will, since the desire is already present. As Chrysippus, the Stoic, later points out, the Academic view of action theory is simply that when something appears to us in a certain way, namely, as good, action follows without any other function of soul taking place. Chrysippus, to the contrary, adds a third: between perception and action lies *synkatathesis,* sometimes translated as *assent,* and properly seen as a forerunner of or in the same family with the idea of will.[7]

If all this is correct, then Socrates's view of human motivation does not rest on the idea of freedom or of autonomy. Instead, something outside me limits me and governs me, namely, I would argue, the forms. When I see the form of the good or, more specifically, when I see something or someone as good, I am compelled to move toward it, toward him or her. I always follow them, just as shape always follows color. They are a limitation on my action, on what I can and will do. Socrates's views are not as different from Levinas's as Levinas thinks.

We saw in the preceding chapter that, in *Totality and Infinity,* Levinas describes my relation to the other—the absolute other—as one in which I am not agent but instead am moved by the other (*TI* 270/248), my spontaneity or freedom is called into question by the other (*TI* 42–44/12–14), I lose my subject position (*TI* 270/248) and am wounded by the other (*TI* 277/254), resisted (*TI* 44/14, 197/171, 197/172), mastered (*TI* 171/146), and so forth.[8] This relationship to the other is, as mentioned in the preceding chapter, a noncognitive intentionality in which I put all my preconceptions and interests out of play in an intentionality that is not full-blown Husserlian intentionality but what Levinas calls "an intentionality of a wholly different type" (*TI* 23/xii) or an "'intentionality' of transcendence" (*TI* 49/20). Describing this type of intentionality is the very goal of *Totality and Infinity* according to Levinas: "But it is a 'vision' without image, bereft of the synoptic and totalizing objectifying virtues of vision, a relation or an intentionality of a wholly different type—which this work seeks precisely to describe" (*TI* 23/xii).[9]

The intentionality Socrates utilizes, as we have seen, is not Levinas's noncognitive intentionality but is cognitive—a seeing *this* as *that* as Socrates indicates by comparing knowledge to imagination in the divided line section of the *Republic.* Still, the lack of agency he describes is strikingly similar to that described by Levinas. In the *Phaedrus,* as we saw in the preceding chapter, Socrates describes the helmsman of the soul as being moved, knocked out, outside himself,[10] enslaved, and falling on his back in response to the sight of a youth. Then the soul is drawn upward to the place beyond the heavens where the forms dwell. Since the helmsman of the soul is identified with *nous,*[11] we can say less poetically that reason does not act but is acted upon by the form, specifically, by the youth as visible instantiation of the form.

The process of going from the beautiful youth up to the form of beauty is, for Socrates, an example of recollection. Recollection, in the *Phaedrus,* is described in two ways, one poetic and in need of interpretation (Socrates says he is saying what the soul is *like* not what it is), one more literal. The poetic interpretation is that recollection is an ascent of the chariot of the soul to a place beyond the heavens. The literal interpretation is that recollection is the movement from perception to idea implicit in it. In the *Phaedrus,* then, as in the *Republic,* Socratic intentionality is a seeing *this* as *that.* The poetic interpretation is helpful, though, because it makes clear that the form is not in the soul but outside it. The helmsman is portrayed as outside himself and ascending to the place of the forms—outside and ascending since *outside* suggests other and *ascent* suggests value. The issue in the *Phaedrus* is whether relations to others can be valuable.

Someone could object, though, that these examples are from the *Phaedrus* not the *Meno,* and take Levinas's position that, in the *Phaedrus,* Socrates is changing his position and beginning to glimpse Levinas's position, though perhaps not fully. The point of the *Meno* on action, though, is the same as that of the *Phaedrus,* namely, that I am moved by the form, or by instantiations of it. Once I know what is good, I have no choice but to do what is good. I am not free. I am compelled. I am moved by what is good.

On the other hand, in the *Meno,* Socrates says that the forms are in my soul. This, again, would be problematic for Levinas since if the forms are already in my soul, to be moved by them is not to be moved by something other or new but by myself. Remember, Levinas charges that the primacy of the same is Socrates's teaching: "to receive nothing of the Other but what was in me" (*TI* 43/13–14). But are the forms really in the soul for Socrates, even in the *Meno*? In the *Meno,* as in the *Phaedrus,* there are two accounts of recollection, one poetic, one literal. Interpreters often miss the second one. Socrates says that recollection is tying down true opinions by *aitias logismōi,* reasoning about cause (98a). What exactly he means by *aitias logismōi* is not made clear, but it might mean reasoning about the *why,* that is, why an opinion is true, or, alternately, it might mean reasoning about the most important causes for Plato, namely, the ideas. In either case, there is no sense here that what you know is something you have always known. Instead, what you know but have forgotten is spelled out either as what you can reason to from your true opinion about why the opinion is true or the form implicit in your true opinion that causes it to be true. The latter definition of recollection is a close variation of Socrates's clearer definition of recollection in the *Phaedrus* as moving from perception to the idea or concept implicit in it. What it means, then, in the *Meno* to say poetically that what you seek is something you already know is that what you seek is implicit in or connected to what you already know and simply needs to be made explicit or discovered by following out the connections.[12] At the very least, we could point out that to say that learning is remembering what the soul knew but forgot is not clearly saying that what I seek is in the soul, but saying that it is and is not in the soul, since I knew it, but forgot it: *in the soul* suggesting that what I seek is connected to or implicit in what I already know; *not in the soul* suggesting that what I seek is not determined by me but determines me—it limits, governs, and compels me, as we have seen. If I, the same, am determined by the other that I seek, then I am not free since, as we have seen, freedom for Levinas is the determination of the other by the same (*TI* 85/57).

Contrary to Levinas's belief, then, Socrates does not have a philosophy of freedom. He does not understand cognition as freedom. Instead, cognition, and virtue, are types of response to the external or other, as the ethical is for Levinas. We are, according to Plato, moved by the idea of the good or the beautiful—or, more specifically, by an other who is beautiful or good—as we are moved by the singular other according to Levinas.

2.

But the picture is not that simple. In a complex and often understated way, Plato *is* a proponent of freedom—a complex type of freedom that results from wisdom. What reader of the *Republic* can forget the image of the one who, bound in a cave, frees himself from the bonds—bonds of convention—and ascends to the ideas? Central to the *Republic,* the image is in addition a paradigm of a certain way of thinking about what philosophy is. Freedom is not a negligible idea for Plato, then. Philosophy *is* associated with freedom for him, as Levinas maintains—specifically with the type of human freedom we have when we are wise. Moreover, wisdom, as we have seen, is a type of responsiveness for Plato. For Plato, then, human beings possess freedom, but freedom of a complex sort. We are free, paradoxically, when we are in response.

Levinas, too, gives freedom a significant role in his thought even though initially he is freedom's critic. Merely espousing some kind of freedom, then, cannot be a mark of distinction between the two thinkers. For Levinas in *Totality and Infinity,* an arbitrary freedom first emerges on the atheist stage when I resist the totality to become a psychism or self. It is this accomplishment of the self and of freedom that makes will possible. On the sociality stage, however—beyond arbitrary freedom—lies a different type of freedom, namely, responsibility as freedom. The other calls my arbitrary freedom into question (*TI* 43/13). The other's presence arouses me to responsibility or goodness and so promotes and founds my freedom. Responsibility to the other, then, is not a restriction on freedom but founds it. For Levinas, too, then, human beings have a complex type of freedom that paradoxically is found in response.

Levinas is wrong, then, when he attacks Plato as a philosopher of freedom and suggests that he himself is not one. To the contrary, each thinker discusses a type of arbitrary freedom: freedom as doing whatever you desire for Plato; freedom as resistance to the totality for Levinas. Each rejects arbitrary freedom and puts in its stead a fundamental responsiveness: knowledge or wisdom (understood as responsive) for Plato; responsibility to the other for Levinas. Each finds true freedom—a complex type of freedom—there, in that very responsiveness, as I will show in what follows.

Socrates, the gadfly, is a critic of Athens, the city that prides itself on its freedom. In perhaps the best-known image in the *Republic,* an image of human beings in their education and lack of it, he portrays human beings bound in a cave. He tells Glaucon that they are like us, indicating that the image is universal and does not exempt democratic Athens (nor, we might add, does it exempt us). Instead, human beings in general are in bonds, compelled as a result to perceive the images cast on the wall of their cave as true. What they think are true are simply the shadows of artifacts held up by hidden but important others (*Rep.* 7.515c1–2).

The presence of the others in the image indicates that we are seeing in it human beings in different stages of the education that leads up to and culminates in philosophy. There are those in bonds, being educated. There are those standing behind a wall that is placed above and behind those being educated. The people behind the wall hold up artifacts, of human beings and other animals. The artifacts, due to a fire above and behind them all, cast shadows on the wall of the cave that those in bonds can see. Since the bonds prevent them from looking behind themselves, they take the shadows they see to be what is true.

What they think are true are shadows of artifacts held up by others. Since artifacts are human-made and the image is about education, knowledge, and philosophy, we can assume that the artifacts are opinions or views. In our early education, what we think are true are simply reflections of the views of others—authoritative others who make sure that their views are influential in our milieu, that their artifacts cast shadows placed so that we will see them from our limited position in our particular cave. We do not know it, then, but our opinions are reflections of the opinions of others—others who, with good or bad intentions (the image does not say, so they could be either), wish for our views to reflect or be based on theirs. In a Spartan cave, for example, we would see a man with military prowess as one with the highest virtue. In an Athenian cave, we would see a man who speaks well in the assembly as possessing it. We would see the person that way because of the particular artifact of a human being that is held up in the cave in which we live. Our perceptions of a human being, and of other things, are shaped by the dominant views in our city, in our cave. If we lived in a Homeric cave—that is, if we lived in a Homeric milieu—we would see a short and ugly man as negligible, such as Thersites, the only short, ugly man in the *Iliad* or *Odyssey* whom, appropriately, Odysseus beats up. In a Platonic cave, we would see one short, ugly man as a new type of hero—Socrates, of the prominent eyes and flat nose.

The *as* structure is important. One sees the warrior as virtuous. Another sees the statesman as virtuous. Such perception is based on a conception—based on an idea, to speak more platonically. In the cave, we assume that idea—in this case, an idea of what virtue (*aretē*) is. Without making explicit and investigating that idea, we simply apply it. If virtue is associated with virility (*aretē* with *ar-* meaning maleness, as in Ares, the god of war), we perceive the warrior to be virtuous, and not the statesman or philosopher. What we think is real—the warrior really is the height of virtue, for example—is simply the reflection of authoritative views in our milieu, in this example, in our Homeric cave.

Of course, not everyone remains bound. Some are behind the wall projecting images for us to see. And there is one or more who, by nature, are forced to go up (7.515c4–8). They break the bonds—the bonds of convention. Why call them bonds of convention? In the *Republic* the leaders of the city put forward opinions meant to shape the citizens' opinions, as we see in the discussion of virtue that accompanies the account of the tripartite soul. Virtue, in that discussion, is based on those views—meant to have the force of convention—not on knowledge, and it is the job of the rulers to promote those conventional views. What the citizens think are real are reflections of conventional views, just as what the prisoners think are real are reflections of artifacts—unless they break their bonds.

To break the bonds and become free, then, is to break the bonds of convention. But there are two stages to achieving freedom. The first stage is turning around and seeing that the views I think are mine are instead reflections of the authoritative views of others in our cave. The second stage—a stage not reached by very many according to Socrates—is ascending out of the cave and checking whether those views accord with reality. Outside the cave are human beings, the moon, the stars, the sun, sunlight, and so on. These represent ideas as we know from the fact that the sun is one of them, and the sun, for Socrates in the *Republic,* represents the idea of the good. What really is good? What really is virtue? What is a human being? By answering these questions, we could decide who is right about the paradigm of virtue: Is it the warrior? The statesman? The philosopher? All this depends on what a human being is, what virtue is, what it is to be good. In other words, we decide whom we should honor as most virtuous by seeing the forms that are alluded to when we answer "what is it" questions—when we answer them for ourselves rather than simply taking and applying the answers others have provided us.

Socrates does not use the word *freedom* in this passage, however. Moreover, the passage is about imprisonment, not about slavery, Socrates's most common opposite for freedom. Still, he does talk about one who breaks the bonds, bonds I have argued are the bonds of custom or convention. The image as a whole, then, is still an image of liberation or freedom—freedom from an imprisonment even more powerful in one sense because those who suffer from it do not realize that they do and why. In addition, the freedom portrayed is a complex kind. We are not exhorted in this image, as in Rousseau, to reject custom and follow our own mind: "Today . . . one follows custom, never one's own genius."[13] This image is not Emerson exhorting us to reject the newspaper that constructs reality for us and instead trust ourselves: "Trust thyself: every heart vibrates to that iron string."[14] Rather, for Socrates, we turn from custom not to ourselves but to the ideas. They should shape and determine how we perceive things. We lose our bonds and are free, then, according to Socrates when what we think and do is in response to what is, that is, to the ideas including the idea of the good. Without perceiving and following the ideas—that is, without understanding things and persons in terms of the forms they instantiate and basing our actions on such understanding—we are not completely free. Some presumably make it only to the first level of freedom, the stage of seeing that the views they hold are not actually their own. Only a few work out their own views in a philosophic way, going all the way up to the forms and to the first among the forms—the brightest part of being—the idea of the good (*tou ontos to phanotaton,* 7.518c9). What results is a complex type of freedom as Socrates's description of the one who frees himself indicates. He is described as being compelled by nature to go up. He is forced, in other words, to be free. This is Socrates's way of indicating the complexity of freedom as he understands it. We are most free when, paradoxically, we are in response—specifically, in response to what is.

Moreover, it is these people, according to Socrates in the *Republic,* who ought to rule in a city, who ought to come back down into the cave and project their philosophically supported views to influence others, some of whom will simply be shaped by those views, others of whom will themselves actually reflect philosophically on those views. Freedom eventually means service to others for Socrates as it does for Levinas. For Levinas, freedom is found in responsibility, which is a type of response to *autrui,* the other person. For Socrates in the *Republic,* freedom results in political service since the philosopher becomes a philosopher-king. This is not the only kind of service Socrates describes in the Platonic corpus, however, since he also describes service in the *Phaedrus.* In that dialogue, as we saw in chapter 1, service results from seeing the form of the beautiful and is a more personal kind. It is service to one's beloved—erotic not political service we could say.

It is not only in the *Meno,* then, but also in the *Republic* that Socrates stresses following and being limited by the forms. The best city will be one that is based on them—particularly on the form of the good and on justice—and the best human beings will be those who know and follow them. Moreover, and crucial for the argument of this chapter, it is when we are, in this way, responsive to the ideas that we are free.

If Plato's Socrates believes in human freedom, though, why is he so quiet in espousing it? Why is his defense of freedom so understated? As mentioned before, there is no dialogue on freedom; freedom does not appear on any list of virtues; and generally it is the interlocutors who appear to espouse freedom as an ideal and Socrates who refutes them. A plausible answer is that the ethos of freedom in Athens is so dominant that, rhetorically speaking, Socrates must emphasize the response aspect of complex freedom rather than the freedom aspect if his point is to be effective and heard. Socrates wants freedom-enchanted Athenians to see the responsiveness that is necessary—more specifically for him, the wisdom that is necessary—if they are to have any real freedom. Moreover, he does, in an understated way, espouse freedom. As we have seen, in the *Meno* Socrates playfully and pointedly images Meno as more of a slave than the actual slave who participates in the geometrical demonstration. The slave is politically enslaved while Meno, though politically free, is enslaved in his soul. Meno believes what Gorgias believes, as a number of opening passages are meant to suggest (71c8–d2). Socrates's suggestion is that Meno will only truly be free if he recollects—breaks the Gorgianic bonds—and attains wisdom. When Socrates says, as previously quoted, "you do not even try to rule yourself, so that you may be free" (86d6–7), there is an ambiguity that points to two different types of freedom. The passage suggests, on the one hand, that Meno does not try to rule or control himself because he wants to be free (that is, "you want to be free by not ruling yourself"). The other suggestion is that if Meno did rule himself, then he would in fact be free ("you do not do what would make you free, namely, rule yourself"). The latter suggests, once again, a complex type of freedom, namely, freedom attained through self-rule or self-control. Self-rule, for Socrates, is another way of describing the freedom that comes from responding to what is, that is, to the forms or to things and persons in terms of the forms that make them what they are. Freedom results from the type of response to what is that is knowledge or wisdom. Such freedom can also be called self-rule or self-control.

Socrates mentions self-rule in response to an assertion of unlimited freedom also in the *Gorgias.* When Callicles says that justice is for the rulers to have more than the ruled, Socrates asks him if he means that rulers should have more than themselves. Don't you think it is necessary, Socrates goes on, for each person to be his own ruler? Or do you think that each person must rule only other people and not also himself? He goes on to explain, to an uncomprehending Callicles, that what he means is nothing complicated but simply moderation and control (*Grg.* 491c6–e1). Callicles's response to Socrates's suggestion of self-control indicates the job he has in persuading his cohorts of any kind of limitation. "How can a human being be happy," Callicles asks, "if he is a slave to anything at all?" (*Grg.* 491e5–6). The ethos of freedom is so strong that there is an aversion to any kind of control, even self-control, even the freedom of self-guidance by wisdom or idea. The identification of happiness with freedom is not simply the view of a few unsavory characters such as Callicles. Instead, that identification is a central component of the Athenian ethos. Consider, for example, the association of happiness with freedom in Pericles's funeral oration as described by Thucydides: "happiness is freedom" (*Hist.* 2.43.12–13).[15]

The same connection between happiness and freedom is mentioned by Socrates in his discussion with Lysis, in the dialogue on friendship, of Lysis's relation to his parents. Freedom is identified in the discussion with doing whatever you desire or wish. First, Socrates and Lysis agree that Lysis's parents want him to be happy. Socrates then asks Lysis whether it is possible for a human being to be happy "if he is a slave and not able to do everything he desires" (*Lys.* 207e1–2). Lysis agrees that it is not. Socrates goes on more explicitly to make the connection between freedom and wisdom that is indicated more imagistically in the description of the cave in the *Republic.*

He does so by arguing that one who does what he desires does not necessarily do what he wishes. He points out that Lysis's parents do not actually allow him to do whatever he wishes but prevent him from doing many things—driving a chariot in a contest, ruling over a mule team, touching and using the parts of a loom, or even ruling over himself. In each case, it is not Lysis but one who is knowledgeable or wise who does what he wishes: the charioteer (a hireling), the muleteer (a slave), his mother (a woman), his attendant and teachers (slaves). On the other hand, they do allow Lysis to do whatever he wishes with regard to letters (reading or writing them in whatever order he wishes) and in regard to a lyre (loosening, tightening, plucking, or striking its strings as he wishes). The reason for allowing him to do what he desires in these cases, Lysis maintains in response to a question from Socrates, is that Lysis knows (*epistamai*) letters and the lyre. It is not, Socrates points out, because of Lysis's status—as young not old, or a freeman not a slave. The slaves, hireling, and woman are more free regarding the things about which they are knowledgeable than free, male Lysis is. Even the son of the Great King, though eventually he will rule all of Asia, Socrates points out, would not be allowed to do whatever he wishes—to throw things in a meat sauce that is cooking or to take care of his own eyes if they were diseased.

It is not some conventional status, in other words, but lack of knowledge that leads parents to prevent their child from doing whatever he wishes in certain circumstances. Even more, according to Socrates making his culminating point, if we are wise about things, we will do whatever we wish in regard to them, we will be free with regard to them, they will be ours, and we will benefit from them: "With regard to the things in which we become wise (*phronimoi*), everyone—Greeks as well as barbarians and both men and women—will entrust them to us, we will do in regard to these things whatever we wish, and no one will voluntarily impede us. Instead, we ourselves shall be free (*eleutheroi*) with regard to them and rulers over others, and these things will be ours, for we shall profit from them" (*Lys.* 210a9–b6). On the other hand, if we lack intelligence (*nous*) about things, we will in fact be subject to others regarding them, and, because they do not benefit us, they will not be our property: "But regarding those things in which we do not acquire intelligence (*nous*), no one will entrust us to do what seems best to us concerning them, but everyone will impede us as much as they are able—not only aliens but also our father and mother and whatever may be more closely akin than they are. And we ourselves shall be subject to others in regard to those things, and they will be alien to us, for we will not profit from them" (*Lys.* 210b6–c4). Socrates's crucial point about freedom in this passage is that we are free if we know or are wise about the things to which we relate. If we are not wise about them, we do not do with them what we wish. In addition, Socrates appears in the passage to be suggesting that the reason we are free regarding things we know is that things we know profit us. If we are knowledgeable charioteers, for example, we will attain the end we had in driving.

That Socrates believes that the reason we are free regarding things we know is that things we know profit us is borne out in the *Gorgias*. There Socrates explains the claim that people who do what seems best to them do not necessarily do what they wish and that they do what they wish if they have wisdom. Socrates argues with Polus that we do not wish for what we do each time or for what seems best to us but we wish for the end at which our action and opinion aim. For example, when we take medicine, what we wish for is not the drinking of the medicine itself but the aim of that unpleasant action, namely, health; when merchants or traders go to sea, they do not wish for the dangers and discomforts of the long sea voyage itself but the aim of their voyage, namely, wealth; and so on for all actions, we wish not for the action itself but for the end at which it aims. Similarly in the case of the rhetor whom Polus says can put someone to death, banish someone, or take someone's property as he wishes, Socrates maintains that he does these negative things because he believes he is achieving some good for himself by doing so. We choose all such bad things as well as neutral things such as sitting, walking, running, sailing, or, in a different vein, stones and wood, for the sake of something good. When we do bad or neutral things believing they benefit us when in fact they harm us, we do not do what we wish even though we do what we desire. The rhetor whose beliefs about what benefits him are false, Socrates implies, does not do what he wishes—even though he does what seems best to him, even though he kills, banishes, and takes property with impunity.

The argument brings out the meaning of Socrates's claim, to Lysis, that freedom results from wisdom. It is not simply that we are free of parental or societal impediment when we are wise. For, why are those impediments lifted? Why do not Lysis's parents allow him to drive a chariot? Because what would seem best to him when he is driving will not be what actually is good since he lacks the relevant knowledge. When we lack wisdom, we do not actually do what we wish even though we do what seems best to us. The dialogue invites us to consider this in relation to each of the examples Socrates has given. If Lysis does not know how to drive a chariot, he will crash rather than racing forward with speed and accuracy. If he does not know how to rule a mule team, he will have resistant rather than cooperative mules and will stall. If he does not know how to use a loom, he will tangle rather than weaving the wool. If he does not know how to rule his own life, he will be exposed to harmful rather than beneficial things and people and will learn slowly if at all. Since he does not understand these things, the chariot, mules, and loom themselves will prevent him from doing what he wishes (to race forward, to weave, etc.). You are not doing what you wish when you crash a chariot in a race, stall a mule team, or tangle a loom. The parents' constraint of Lysis, then, reflects a more primary constraint that, if unimpeded, he would experience from the things themselves as a result of his lack of wisdom. Without wisdom, then, he is not free because he does not do what he really wishes. Without wisdom, Lysis is more of a slave than a hireling, a conventional slave, or a woman for he in fact does not do what he wishes.

Freedom for Socrates, then, results from wisdom (*epistēmē, phronēsis, nous*). The *Lysis* and *Gorgias* square with and elucidate the suggestion in the *Re-*

public's image of the cave that we are free when we are wise where wisdom is identified with knowledge of ideas, especially knowledge of the idea of the good. As in the *Lysis* and *Gorgias,* so the centrality of the idea of the good in the cave image suggests that we are not free when we simply do what we desire unless what we desire in fact is good. We must break the chains of convention and learn what really is good. The *Lysis, Gorgias,* and the cave image in the *Republic* all suggest that Socrates is a proponent of a complex form of freedom, freedom as response, specifically, the type of response Socrates calls wisdom or knowledge of what is good.

Later parts of the *Republic,* too, bear out this suggestion since in them Socrates maintains that the tyrant is a slave—specifically, a slave to his desires. This claim is part of Socrates's general defense of an argument on behalf of justice, specifically of the argument that justice is happier than injustice. Once again, Socrates identifies happiness and unhappiness with freedom and slavery. The tyrant, because he is a slave—a slave to his desires—is not happy.

The claim is not immediately persuasive because *slave to* is in need of justification. Why not say, simply, that the tyrant is in accord with or follows his desires? Why the pejorative term? In addition, since the one who is fond of wisdom, that is, the philosopher, is the contrast term to the tyrant, why not say that the philosopher, too, is a slave—a slave to ideas—and hence unfree and unhappy?

A simple answer is that, for Socrates in the *Republic,* the tyrant is a slave because the best part of his soul is enslaved by the worst part and the worst part is master of the best. Such a soul, according to Socrates, is slave not free and will least do what it wishes. When the soul is forcibly pulled by desire, the soul will be full of confusion and regret (9.577d1–e3). Such a soul is not guided by reason (it is full of confusion) and, as a result, experiences bad things that it has reason to regret. It is alright to be directed by, even enslaved by, wisdom since wisdom, unlike confusion, leads toward what is good.

The *Republic* has much more to say on the topic, though. How free are we? Who is free? How? One way to think about these questions is to look at the two, even three, accounts of the soul in the *Republic* as well as the two, even three, accounts of the virtues. The first account of the soul is the well-known tripartite soul in book 4 accompanied by the first account of the virtues. Readers often overlook Socrates's clear statement that there is something deficient about the first account. Socrates says, for example, that another, longer road is required to get the finest look at the soul and the virtues and that the statements made in the first account of them are lacking in precision (*Rep.* 6.504b1–7). The longer road takes Socrates and his interlocutors up to the ideas, all the way up to first and brightest among them, the idea of the good.

There is, Socrates says then, a turning around of the soul from becoming to being and the brightest part of being, the good. After asserting this, he says, "Therefore, the other so-called virtues of the soul probably are somewhat close to those of the body—for they really are not present at first but later are produced by habits and practices—while the virtue of exercising wisdom is something more divine than anything, as it seems" (*Rep.* 7.518d9–e3). True virtue, then, is not virtue as understood in the book 4 account of the parts of the soul. Instead, virtue in its strongest sense is wisdom.

In the myth of Er in book 10, Socrates underscores that there are two levels of virtue. He says there of the one who practiced virtue by habit without philosophy in his life that in the afterlife he will choose for his next life the greatest tyranny (through folly and gluttony and without considering clearly) (10.619b7–9, 619c6–d1). When there is no constraint from the regime, the one who has the type of virtue described in book 4 will do what he or she really desires. The point about superficial, constraint-induced virtue is made another time in the discussion of the soul that in sleep is not constrained in its dreams either by shame (spiritedness) or wisdom (calculation) and dares to do all the things it would not do in life: have sex with a mother or anyone else at all, human being, god, or beast; commit every type of foul murder; eat every type of food (9.571b2–d4). Once again, when societal constraints are off, the soul's underlying tendencies come out, indicating the superficiality of the virtues so understood.

Socrates argues for the tripartite soul in book 4 based on the law of contradiction. Since the same thing cannot both desire and be averse to the same thing, there must be two parts of the soul, the calculative part and the desiring part, one that, for example, desires drink and the other, the calculative part, that draws it back from drink. There is a third part, too, the spirited part, since, as the example of Leontius suggests, often something else draws us back. Leontius desired to see corpses but was disgusted by them at the same time and says to his eyes: "Look, unhappy ones, take your fill of the beautiful sight" (*Rep.* 4.440a2–3). Desire and spiritedness are not partners. They conflict, indicating two nonrational parts of the soul.

Book 4 virtues are based on these parts—calculation, spiritedness, desire. In justice, each part of the soul does what belongs to it—the calculating part rules, the spirited part obeys or is an ally, and these two are set over desire (4.441d12–e6). In courage, the spirited part preserves, through pains and pleasures, what has been proclaimed in speeches about what is fearful and what is not (4.442b11–c3). In wisdom, the ruling part possesses the knowledge of what is beneficial for each part and for the whole composed of the community of the parts (4.442c5–8). In moderation, the ruling part and the ruled parts are of the same opinion that the calculating part ought to rule and do not make faction against it (4.442c10–d1). We can see that the person who has these virtues will be somewhat freer than one who does not—so long, at any rate, as the ruling part really does know what is beneficial for each part of the city and for the city as a whole. For desires and wisdom will be in accord so that what he or she desires and what he or she wishes will not be in conflict. But the good opinions the soul has are liable to "run away from the soul," to use a phrase from the *Meno,* since the book 4 virtuous person does not have knowledge but has true opinions ingrained in him or her through hearing music containing salutary speeches and engaging in salutary gymnastic habits and practices. The afterlife story and dream account suggest that that education is not ingrained in us like the grain that grows naturally in wood. It is more superficial, liable to dissipate. One who has book 4 virtue does what he wishes—but, in the strongest sense, is it what *he* wishes? Or is it what the city wishes?

There are other difficulties as well with the book 4 account. For example, have the parts of the soul been delineated in the best possible way? Socrates calls the rational part *calculative.* We would expect him to call it wisdom (*phronēsis*), knowledge (*epistēmē*), or insight (*nous*). Calculation (*logistikē*), for Socrates, is only the first stage of higher education (*Rep.* 7.521c1–528e2). It precedes and does not include knowledge of the good. Perhaps calculation would be useful for strategizing how to achieve what is good, but not for knowing what in fact is good, a necessary component in any strong account of Socratic virtue.

In addition, gone in this account is Socrates's often stated view that we all desire what is good so that all we need to ensure that we will do what is good is to know what the good is. Instead, in book 4, each desire has its own proper and descriptive, not evaluative, object—thirst is for drink, for example, and thirst of a particular kind for drink of a particular kind (4.439a1–b2): "Therefore the soul of the one who is thirsty, to the extent that it thirsts, wishes for nothing other than to drink, and stretches out for this and is impelled by this" (4.439a9–10). Thirst is for drink, as Socrates self-consciously goes some length in this account to maintain, and not, as we would expect him to say, for good drink. So long as desire is understood in this way, it has its own object and will sometimes be out of sync with the good objects reason would prescribe. There is need for an account of the soul in which reason and desire are not so separate that reason could go one way and desire another and virtue be achieved only through some kind of constraint or inculcation. Virtue understood in this way is second-order virtue of the soul, close in its nature to virtues of the body. It is habitual virtue, not virtue in the strong sense. It is something superficial added on top, not something already there that later is shaped and developed.

For all these reasons, it is not surprising, though often overlooked, that Socrates gives a better account of virtue, virtue as wisdom, as we have seen. It is developed through the entire higher education Socrates describes, starting with calculation but culminating in dialectic that includes knowledge of the ideas including the idea of the good. This virtue, "the virtue of exercising wisdom," is "something more divine" than book 4 virtues (*Rep.* 7.518e2–3). Not many people will achieve it, but those who do will have all the virtues described in book 4 in a stronger way.

What is this higher-level virtue of the soul like for Socrates? As we have seen, the soul can be turned around from becoming to being and to the brightest part of being, namely, the good. Once it is, we are virtuous. Those who are turned toward being's brightest part are those who love wisdom, that is, philosophers. Philosophers, like lovers of all kinds, love everything related to what they love, in their case wisdom. They love every type of learning and delight in and are insatiable about it. They care for everything related to wisdom, especially truth and what is rather than what seems or convention. They have an insatiable love for it so that they do not care about the pleasures of the body. They are moderate and do not care about money, since what it makes possible are pleasures about which they do not care. They contemplate what is eternal—all time and all being—and, out of the resulting magnificence, do not take human life to be anything great. As a result, they do not fear death. This is virtue of the soul: to know the good and, because knowing it, love it and love it so much that other objects of desire have little or no appeal and the fears ordinarily in need of spirited control have little or no impact. For Socrates, to know the good is to love it and to love it is to do it since nothing else in comparison has any considerable motivational appeal.

The difference between this type of virtue, virtue in the strong sense, and habitual virtue is that, in virtue in the strong sense, what reason knows and what desire desires are the same, namely, the good. Desire's object is not a descriptive but an evaluative one and, as a result, can be, and in the case of wisdom is, the same object reason would counsel. Reason and desire are not completely separate but united in their object. Reason is not calculation but wisdom and so is capable by itself of guiding toward what is good. There is no need for rule over spiritedness and desire. There is no need for preservation in spiritedness of a salutary view of death. Instead, desire of this kind can be allowed full activity. When such desire is active, money, death, and pleasures of the body all have negligible impact. With virtue of this kind, we can be truly free for our desires are shaped by our very own reason—by wisdom, in fact—so that when we do what we desire, we in fact do what *we* wish. This second account of the soul and virtue—the soul that knows and desires the good and in so doing has virtue—corrects the first and resolves the problem of freedom.

In book 9, there is a third account of virtue and the soul. In the third account, the soul has three parts, as in the first, but they are described differently—desire as money-loving and gain-loving, spiritedness as victory-loving and honor-loving and reason not as calculation but as learning-loving and wisdom-loving or philosophic (9.581a3–b10). The soul, so described, is also imaged as a complex beast composed of a human being (also considered divine), a lion, and a many-headed beast composed of tame and savage heads in a ring. All three of these animals are found inside a human being (9.588d10–e1) with the result that a human being is described in total as a human being with a many-headed beast, a lion, and a human being inside.

This third account of the soul is better than the first, though not as good as the second. It is the account of the soul that has been informed by the good, not just by convention, but only informed by the good to a certain extent. In the account, calculation is replaced by learning and wisdom—so that the soul has, or at least can strive for, knowledge of what is good. It gives each part of the soul its own characteristic two desires in which, in the case of desire and spiritedness, the first of the two is more specific and descriptive—like desire as described in the dialogue's first account of the soul—while the second is more general and evaluative; and, in the case of reason, each avoids separating wisdom and desire. As a result of each of these, the third account gives wisdom more influence over desire. In addition, the account provides an answer to the question, what justifies Socrates in using the pejorative term *a slave to* when arguing that the tyrant is unhappy because he is a slave to his desires. Why for Socrates is the tyrant, who follows his passions, a slave while the philosopher, who loves or follows wisdom, is free? The answer is found in the fact that Socrates identifies the wisdom-loving part of soul with the human being and maintains that it is better for us to be ruled by the human being than by the beast within (9.588c7–590d6). Socrates, then, has a hierarchy of human passions and desires, those that are human and those that are not—that is, we may say, those that are our own and those that are not. In following those that are not his own, he does not do what *he* wishes even though he does what he desires or what seems best to him. The philosopher, to the contrary, is not slave but free, for in doing what he desires or what seems best to him, he in fact does what *he* wishes.[16]

The philosopher, then, is free because in doing what he desires he does what he wishes. He does what he *wishes* because his desires are shaped by wisdom, which is knowledge of what is good, that is, of what is best for him. He does what *he* wishes because his passions and desires are his own: they are not shaped by others whose views he unreflectingly accepts, as in the image of the cave, but they are shaped by him since they are shaped by his wisdom and wisdom is the human being within.

In *Totality and Infinity,* Levinas, too, is a proponent of a complex type of freedom that results from response. For him, there are two types of freedom, an arbitrary freedom that emerges when I resist the totality to become a psychism or self and a justified freedom that results when, aroused by the presence of an other who calls my arbitrary freedom in question, I respond to him or her. The former is fundamentally atheistic or all about the self. The latter is fundamentally social, fundamentally in relation to an other. In that type of freedom, the presence of the other, for Levinas, does not restrict but founds my freedom. I am free when I respond to the other.

Levinas describes three stages of human development. Freedom is found in the second and third stages. In the first, the *il y a* stage, I am immersed in the totality, immersed in what is or would be external to me, not clearly distinct from it. The self, for Levinas, is not there from the beginning. It is not a given. Instead, it is an event—specifically, an event of resistance: I resist the totality to produce a self, a psychism, an interiority. Referring to the one who resists in this way as *the Same,* Levinas says, "The separation of the Same is produced in the form of an inner life [*une vie intérieure*], a psychism. The psychism constitutes an event in being" (*TI* 54/24). Psychism and thought, for Levinas, do not merely reflect what is. This is crucial for our discussion of differences between Plato and Levinas. Instead, from the beginning for Levinas, our inner life is active: "The original role of the psychism does not, in fact, consist in only *reflecting* being; it is already a *way of being,* resistance to the totality" (*TI* 54/24). Thought or psychism opens a new dimension: "Thought or the psychism opens the dimension this *way* requires. The dimension of the psychism opens under the force of the resistance a being opposes to its totalization; it is the feat of radical separation" (*TI* 54/24). Far from being a mere given, the self or psychism is an accomplishment, a feat of radical separation—and with radical separation, I am in the second stage of development, the atheist stage.

Atheism, for Levinas, is separation—"separation so complete that the separated being maintains itself in existence all by itself without participating in the Being from which it is separated" (*TI* 58/29). The psychism or soul, "being an accomplishment of separation, is naturally atheist" (*TI* 58/29). On the atheist stage, I resist integration and relation. In that sense, I am free. I am not immersed in the totality of what is, but separate from it. Using spatial language to refer to my original immersion, Levinas says, "by virtue of the psychism the being that is in a *site* remains free with regard to that site; posited in a site in which it maintains itself, it is that which comes thereto from elsewhere" (*TI* 54/25). It is an absence or postponement: "The being that thinks at first seems to present itself, to a gaze that conceives it, as integrated into a whole [*un tout*]. In reality it is so integrated only once it is dead. Life permits it an as-for-me, a leave of absence, a postponement, which precisely is interiority" (*TI* 55/26). If development stopped at the atheist stage for Levinas, he would not be a philosopher of the other.

For Levinas, interiority or psychism is the condition of freedom. Interiority is contrasted with history since history is a realm of causality. As a historical being, I am part of a whole, controlled by its forces, effected by its causes. On the atheist stage, there is a "refusal to be purely and simply integrated into history" (*TI* 57/28). Human beings, according to Levinas, possess "a *secrecy* that interrupts the continuity of historical time" (*TI* 58/29). Historical objectivity does not exhaust the real. There is, in addition, interiority and its intentions. Human beings have an inner or psychic life that is "a dimension in being, a dimension of non-essence" that "does not exhibit itself in history" (*TI* 57/28). Psychism—my resistance to the totality—makes free will possible: "We name 'will' a being conditioned in such a way that without being *causa sui* it is first with respect to its cause. The psychism is the possibility for such a being" (*TI* 59/30). The "free will is necessity relaxed and postponed" according to Levinas. It is "détente or distension" (*TI* 224/200). Psychism makes freedom possible, then, since psychism—my resistance to the totality—is the condition for free will.

Separation or psychism is accomplished through enjoyment (*jouissance*). Essential to enjoyment is nourishment, the transmutation of the other into the same: "an energy that is other, recognized as other . . . becomes, in enjoyment, my own energy, my strength, me" (*TI* 111/83). In enjoyment, in other words, what is other becomes me—and this is so whether what is other is air, light, spectacles, work, ideas, sleep, handling a hammer or machine. I "live from" these things. They nourish me, like "good soup" (*TI* 110/82). "These contents," Levinas says, "are lived: they feed life" (*TI* 111/ 83).

One might conclude from this that in enjoyment we are not free but dependent since I live from contents. However, we are not dependent or "enslaved," according to Levinas, because we enjoy contents. In enjoyment, we depend on contents but then embrace and master them: "enjoyment is the ultimate consciousness of all the contents that fill my life—it embraces them" (*TI* 111/83). "*Living from* . . . is the dependency that turns into sovereignty, into happiness—essentially egoist" (*TI* 114/87). What I enjoy becomes me.

The me, the ego, the psychism is reasserted in enjoyment: the psychism "dwells in what is not itself, but it acquires its own identity by this dwelling in 'the other'" (*TI* 115/88). Enjoyment, according to Levinas, is "the very pulsation of the I" (*TI* 113/85). The I expands to take in contents and contracts to make them itself. In enjoyment we see Levinas's central metaphysical idea, of the I that connects to what is other while at the same time remaining itself.

What is this, however, but freedom? According to Levinas, "freedom denotes the mode of remaining the same in the midst of the other" (*TI* 45/16). "Such is the definition of freedom," Levinas says, "to maintain oneself against the other, despite every relation with the other to ensure the autarchy of an I [*moi*]" (*TI* 46/16). Separation is freedom, then, since separation is accomplished in enjoyment and enjoyment is taking in contents but remaining distinct from them. In enjoying contents, I make them my own. I transmute the other into the same. Such "imperialism of the same is the whole essence of freedom" (*TI* 87/59).

How, concretely, do I maintain myself as a self (a psychism, an ego) while living from what is not myself? That is, how do I, concretely, maintain my freedom? I do so in a home. A home both protects me from what is outside and enables me to connect to and utilize it. In a home, I withdraw from the elements in which I have been immersed—elements that are indefinite (*apeiron*) and thus threatening—and recollect myself. Interiority, in other words, is accomplished in a home. The home breaks "the plenum of the element" (*TI* 156/130), and it does so without isolating me. The dwelling remains open to the element from which it separates. It is both removal and connection (*TI* 156/131). The window concretely makes the ambiguity of removal and connection possible.

Enjoyment is sensibility. It is prior to consciousness and comprehension: "'anterior' to the crystallization of consciousness, I and non-I, into subject and object" (*TI* 188/162). Its function is not objectification, not even a "fumbling objectification [*objectivation qui se cherche*]" (*TI* 187/161), but a "transcendental function" (*TI* 188/163). Enjoyment is "by essence satisfied" (*TI* 187/161). It is an "immediate relation" (*TI* 158/131). In it, sensibility is "steeped in the element" (*TI* 158/131) and "'possesses' without taking" (*TI* 158/131).

Enjoyment can, however, move into objectification with vision or the gaze: "objectification operates in the gaze in a privileged way" (*TI* 188/163). Vision and representation move into grasp, specifically, into touch and labor: "The connection between vision and touch, between representation and labor, remains essential. Vision moves into grasp" (*TI* 191/165). Unlike enjoyment, vision is not transcendental but is horizonal or perspectival: "Vision opens upon a perspective, upon a horizon, and describes a traversable distance, invites the hand to movement and to contact, and ensures them" (*TI* 191/165). Concretely, when I look through the window of a home, I am not immersed in elements but gain some distance on them so that I can grasp the elemental and labor (*TI* 158/131). The laboring hand that grasps, Levinas says, "takes and comprehends" (*prend et comprend*) (*TI* 161/135). The hand that comprehends "is mastery, domination, disposition," and these "do not belong to the order of sensibility" (*TI* 161/135). In grasping or comprehending, the hand postpones the future through possessing, storing, protecting, and so on: "Possession masters, suspends, postpones the unforeseeable future of the element—its independence, its being" (*TI* 158/132). Labor "in its possessive grasp suspends the independence of the elements" (*TI* 158/132). The suspension is comprehension or ontology: "in this suspension possession comprehends the being of the existent" (*TI* 158/132). "The thing evinces this hold or comprehension—this ontology" (*TI* 158/132). The postponement or separation takes place in the body, which is "the very regime in which separation holds sway" (*TI* 163/137). But there, as with enjoyment, there is an ambiguity in the mastery of freedom: "*To be a body* is on the one hand *to stand* [*se tenir*], to be master of oneself, and, on the other hand, to stand on the earth, to be in the *other*, and thus to be encumbered by one's body" (*TI* 164/138). The ambiguity is simultaneously one "of sovereignty and of submission" (*TI* 164/138). This simultaneous ambiguity is consciousness: "The ambiguity of the body is consciousness" (*TI* 165/139). Comprehension and consciousness, then, evince a higher degree of freedom on the atheist stage. Enjoyment is the ambiguity of independence through dependence on another. Comprehension or consciousness is the increased freedom of postponement and comprehension which ambiguously takes place within suffering.

The freedom found within consciousness, comprehension, and ontology delineates clearly the second stage of development according to Levinas as well as taking us into the central concepts of *Totality and Infinity*. The first stage is the stage of the *il y a* or immersion in the totality, in which there is no clear distinction between I and not-I. The second stage is the stage of atheism or interiority, in which there is objectification and ontology. Ontology, as Levinas says in a crucial passage, is the intelligence of beings, which promotes freedom by reducing the other to the same. Intelligence is "the logos of being—that is, a way of approaching the known being such that its alterity with regard to the knowing being vanishes. The process of cognition is at this stage identified with the freedom of the knowing being encountering nothing which, other with respect to it, could limit it" (*TI* 42/12). "Ontology, which reduces the other to the same, promotes freedom—the freedom that is the identification of the same, not allowing itself to be alienated by the other" (*TI*

42/13). Ontology, then, postpones being that affects it, objectifies being and reduces it to the same. Consciousness is not mere reflection or reception but is, from the very first, active and resistant. The resistance takes place through enjoyment, postponement, objectification, and reduction of the other to the same. What I enjoy becomes me (my contents, my contentment). What I comprehend is brought into my horizon (my perspective). This, for Levinas, is freedom on the atheist stage. It takes place first through enjoyment and then through comprehension, intelligence, or knowledge. Knowledge is the height of this type of freedom: "If freedom denotes the mode of remaining the same in the midst of the other, knowledge, where an existent is given by interposition of impersonal Being, contains the ultimate sense of freedom" (*TI* 45/16).

But there is a way of relating besides knowledge and a level of development beyond interiority, namely, the social stage on which I accept that there is something—someone—other than me, separate from me, radically exterior to me. Hence the subtitle of the book, *An Essay on Exteriority*. By sociality, Levinas means relating to an other without assuming the other to myself, that is, without either enjoying the other, and thus transmuting the other into my contents, or knowing the other by bringing the other into my own horizon. On the social stage, I do not reduce the other to the same but welcome the other, where welcoming is not sensibility or comprehension but a different type of response. With sociality, I cease ontologizing. I do not see the other as an object. Instead, sociality is metaphysics: "Metaphysics, transcendence, the welcoming of the other by the same, of the Other by me" (*TI* 43/13). Metaphysics is transcendental not atheistic. It welcomes the other rather than being all about the self. It is exteriority not interiority or immersion. With sociality, metaphysics, transcendence, exteriority, we attain a new level of freedom, a grounded or founded freedom not an arbitrary one. It is because Levinas believes there is a metaphysical stage that he can be a philosopher of the other.

Metaphysics "is concretely produced as the calling into question of the same by the other" (*TI* 43/13). What is called into question, more specifically, is my freedom. Ontology, we have seen, reduces the other to the same and promotes freedom. Metaphysics "calls into question the freedom of the exercise of ontology" (*TI* 43/13). Metaphysics is critique: "critique does not reduce the other to the same as does ontology, but calls into question the exercise of the same" (*TI* 43/13). The calling into question cannot occur within the free self turned in on itself. Instead, the other brings it about: "A calling into question of the same—which cannot occur within the egoist spontaneity of the same—is brought about by the other" (*TI* 43/13).

Reason is the manifestation of arbitrary freedom since, as Levinas regularly maintains, thought and reason know themselves: "That reason in the last analysis would be the manifestation of a freedom, neutralizing the other and encompassing him, can come as no surprise once it was laid down that sovereign reason knows only itself" (*TI* 43/14). The manner in which this arbitrary freedom of the interiority stage takes place is through understanding the other by way of a concept or a theme, through understanding the other as an object. I reduce the other to the same, and in so doing produce my arbitrary freedom "by interposition of a middle and neutral term that ensures the intelligence of being" (*TI* 43/13).

But I am not successful. Something—someone—is beyond me. The other cannot be captured in my concept, but escapes it. This is not surprising to us as readers, since we know that, according to Levinas, the other, like ourselves, is a self by resisting the totality, that is, by resisting concepts (*TI* 118/90). Knowledge, then, does not by itself attain its own goal of letting the other appear without it being affected by the process of knowing: "Knowledge or theory designates first a relation with being such that the knowing being lets the known being manifest itself while respecting its alterity and without marking it in any way whatever by this cognitive relation" (*TI* 42/12). Another relation is required to achieve the goal of relating to being or the other without affecting or marking it. Sometimes Levinas calls the relation *respect:* metaphysics, he says, is "respect for exteriority" (*TI* 43/13). Often he calls it *desire* or *metaphysical desire,* that is, the type of desire that does not stem from need: "The metaphysical desire tends toward *something else entirely,* toward the *absolutely other*" (*TI* 33/3). "Metaphysics or transcendence is recognized in the work of the intellect that aspires after exteriority, that is, Desire" (*TI* 82/54). Sometimes he calls it transcendence: "the transcendence of the relation does not cut the bonds a relation implies, yet . . . these bonds do not unite the same and the other into a Whole" (*TI* 48/19). Sometimes he refers to it as *openness:* the transcendent "is openness preeminently" (*TI* 193/167).[17] More generally, he calls it *response.* Speaking of the other who puts my freedom in question by overflowing me, Levinas says, "I do not struggle with a faceless god, but I respond to his expression, his revelation" (*TI* 197/171).

My freedom is put in question not by an experience that shows my powers to be weak but by an experience that shows a certain type of power to be completely lacking, namely, the power to transmute the other into myself: "Over him, I am not able to be able [*je ne peux pouvoir*]" (*TI* 39/9).[18] I cannot integrate the other, I cannot reduce the other, for the other, like me, is resistance to totality, to concept, to history. The other, in other words, is singular and cannot be conceptualized. Levinas speaks of "singularities, irreducible to the concepts they constitute in communicating their world" (*TI* 252/230) or to any other generic classification we might wish to use: "The unicity of the I does not merely consist in being found in one sample only, but in existing without having a genus, without being the individuation of a concept" (*TI* 117–18/90).

The other resists me by a resistance that does not weaken me or do violence to me but instead is an amplification, an opening: "The 'resistance' of the other does not do violence to me, does not act negatively" (*TI* 197/171). The other, being without determination, is infinite and "the infinite presupposes the finite, which it amplifies infinitely" (*TI* 197/170). "The relation with the Other breaks the ceiling of the totality. It is fundamentally pacific" (*TI* 171/146). The other is other than me, more than me, higher than me: "The Other—the absolutely other—paralyzes possession, which he contests by his epiphany in the face. The other can contest my possession only because he approaches me not from the outside but from above" (*TI* 171/145). He, or she, overflows me: "The presence of a being not entering into, but overflowing, the sphere of the same determines its 'status' as infinite" (*TI* 195/169–70). The other is not an arbitrary freedom, hostile to my arbitrary freedom, aiming to integrate me. Instead, the other gives me something—a teaching—and opens me up: "The Other is not another freedom as arbitrary as my own, in which case it would traverse the infinity that separates me from him and enter under the same concept. His alterity is manifested in a mastery that does not conquer, but teaches. Teaching is not a species of a genus called domination, a hegemony at work within a totality, but is the presence of infinity breaking the closed circle of totality" (*TI* 171/146).

The responsive rather than subsumptive relation to the other takes place in language—not in *speaking about* but in its *speaking to* or interpellation. When I address someone directly, I respect their singularity: my effort "to reach the other is realized in the relationship with the Other that is cast in the relation of language, where the essential is the interpellation, the vocative. The other is maintained and confirmed in his heterogeneity as soon as one calls upon him" (*TI* 69/41). In *speaking to* him, I am not reducing him to a category but instead "he is 'respected.' The invoked is not what I comprehend: *he is not under a category.* He is the one to whom I speak—he has only a reference to himself; he has no quiddity" (*TI* 69/41).

My freedom, then, is put in question but not in the way Sartre would suggest. For Sartre, the other sees me and, thus, I am not free but object, which leads to conflict: "The essence of the relations between consciousnesses is not the *Mitsein* [being with]; it is conflict" (*Being and Nothingness,* 555). Instead, for Levinas, my freedom, understood as the ability to determine whatever is other than I am, is put in question by something that I cannot determine, the other who escapes determination. I cannot determine the other. Instead, I can only respond to her, open myself up to him. I can only receive the other who, unique to my categories and classes, is a gift.

What, then, happens to my freedom? On the interiority stage, it is arbitrary. On the sociality stage, it is put in question. I respond to the other who is beyond me. Does this mean that I am not free? Even more, the questioning of my freedom is put into play by the other. Does this mean that I am determined by him or her? Instead, for Levinas, as for Plato, it is in the response to the other that mature freedom lies. Levinas says that my encounter with the other founds, grounds, or invests my freedom. In this way, it is no longer arbitrary.

To say that the other founds freedom is to raise the question whether the foundation of the self is in the self. Levinas rejects the view that it is, common since the Enlightenment. Instead, it is "the other who founds," and by asserting this Levinas separates himself "from a whole philosophical tradition that sought the foundation of the self in the self, outside of heteronomous opinions" (*TI* 88/60). For Levinas, there is for me a dependence on an other that nonetheless allows me to retain my independence. This is another version of Levinas's central metaphysical idea, of the self that connects while retaining itself, that relates while remaining across from the other, of beings in relation that absolve themselves from the relation. This is, on the deepest level, what the self is like according to Levinas: I am a self *by* relating to another while remaining myself. The self *is* the process of relating to other while retaining identity. "The I [*le moi*]," Levinas says, "is identical in its very alterations." It is "universal identity in which the heterogenous can be embraced" (*TI* 36/6). He says, "The I [*le moi*] is not a being that always remains the same, but is the being whose existing consists in identifying itself, in recovering its identity throughout all that happens to it" (*TI* 36/6). Though I relate to the world, the world does not absorb me. Using temporal language to explain what in fact is fundamental ontology, or metaphysics as he calls it, he identifies the relation of the I to the world as a sojourn, that is, a temporary stay. "The world, foreign and hostile, should, in good logic, alter the I [*le moi*]. But the true and primordial relation between them, and that in which the I [*le moi*] is revealed precisely as preeminently the same, is produced as a sojourn in the world" (*TI* 37/7). My relation to the world is a stay, a visit, because I relate to the world, a temporary stay because I remain myself in the relation. Using spatial language, Levinas speaks of sojourning but also of staying at home with oneself [*chez soi*]: "The way of the I against the 'other' of the world consists in *sojourning*, in *identifying oneself* by existing here *at home with oneself* [*chez soi*]" (*TI* 37/7). The I, *le moi,* is produced by remaining oneself while relating to other.

Freedom has a similar dialectic. We experience, Levinas says, "a dependence upon an exteriority without this dependence absorbing the dependent being, held in invisible meshes. This dependence, consequently, *at the same time* maintains independence" (*TI* 88/61). Freedom of this sort takes place only in relation, only in response to another (as the self is produced only in relation, only in response to the other). The relation of dependence that maintains independence is, specifically, the face to face relation (*TI* 88/61). The face to face relation, in which I relate to the other as other and the other relates to me, takes place in language (*TI* 39/9). Language is "a relation in which the terms *absolve* themselves from the relation, remain absolute within the relation" (*TI* 64/35–36).

The dialectic of the self and of freedom are interconnected for Levinas. "The 'at home' ['*chez soi*'] is not a container but a site where *I can,* where, dependent on a reality that is other, I am, despite this dependence, or thanks to it, free" (*TI* 37/7).[19] Just as despite my relation to the world, I remain my self, so despite my dependence on the world, I remain free. Similarly, just as owing to my relation to the world, I remain my self, so owing to my dependence on the world, I remain free.

So, in my relation to the other, my dependence on the other, my response to the other, I become myself and I am free. What, though, about the other? Does the other remain free? Since the other is like me, the answer ought to be, and is, *yes.* "He escapes my grasp by an essential dimension," Levinas says. "He is not wholly in my site" (*TI* 37/7). The other, "despite the relationship with the same, remains transcendent to the same" (*TI* 39/9).

For Levinas, then, I am free in dependence, free in response to the world and, most of all, to the other. The other, whose presence leads to the critique of my freedom, founds my freedom. On the unfounded, atheist stage, it is all about me, not about an other. But is it, really? No, I only take it to be so. In enjoyment, I forget what it is that I enjoy. In comprehension, I forget the things comprehended (and the other perspectives and horizons in which I can see them). Instead, enjoyment is *of* something—something indefinite that goes beyond me. Comprehension, too, is of something—in the case of a personal other, of something infinite that transcends me. It is in relating to those others that I am me.

Both Plato and Levinas, then, believe that I am free when I am in relation to an other outside myself. Each, in other words, believes in complex freedom. Nonetheless, their views on freedom are different since for Plato we are free when we respond to the other by knowing the forms the other instantiates, assumes, or is, while for Levinas we are free when we respond to the other as a singular other that, as such, has no form. For Plato, when I behold others as what they are, my ways of responding to them are not thwarted. For Levinas, when I respond to the other as singular, I break up the enchainment to my self that sovereign reason produces and maintains (since "sovereign reason knows only itself," *TI* 43/14). For each, freedom in the strong sense is not achieved by turning within but by allowing oneself to be vulnerable to and affected by the other outside the self. At the same time, their approaches to essential human vulnerabilities are as different as the responsive knowledge of form is from the noncognitive response to the singular other.

3.

But the difference has to be traced further. Why do Plato and Levinas differ in this way? What is the source of the difference? One answer to that question is that their views of what knowledge is are so different. As stated before, for Plato knowledge is vulnerability and response, portrayed as falling on your back and then loving and serving the other in the *Phaedrus,* and as being moved to action in the *Meno.* For Levinas, to the contrary, knowledge is active from the very beginning. The very development of the psychism is an active resistance of what is. Thought, too, is active rather than a mere reflection: "to know," Levinas says, "is not simply to record, but always to comprehend" (*TI* 82/54).

In this distinction, Plato and Levinas stand in for (some) ancients and (some) moderns, respectively. Aristotle, too, understands knowledge as receptivity, specifically, receptivity of form, and many starting in the Renaissance but going on into the Enlightenment and beyond maintain that knowledge is active. For Vico, knowledge is a form of making. Bacon, in a rape metaphor, portrays knowing as forcing nature to give up her secrets. Descartes describes knowledge as mastery and possession of nature. And for Husserl, so influential on Levinas, there is no consciousness without meaning or, put differently, thought is fundamentally noematic. Levinas, in his approach to the other, draws the consequences of modern views of knowledge for our relationships to the other. It is the very activity of knowledge as understood by many thinkers since the Enlightenment that implies knowledge is not freedom. The activity of knowledge implies that in knowing we are chained to the self. As we have seen, "sovereign reason knows only itself" (*TI* 43/14). Knowing, for Levinas, is horizonal, and the horizon is always *my* horizon. Only in relating to the other in a relationship other—or otherwise—than knowing do I break the chains that bind me to myself. Levinas draws in detail the consequences for our relationships to others of his view that knowledge is active. Not knowing, but going before knowing, or beyond knowing, is what is needed in those relationships—before knowing, to what makes knowing possible, the other; beyond knowing, past any forms or determinations.

I will discuss creation, a third key concept in *Totality and Infinity,* in chapter 3, and look further at Plato's and Levinas's views on knowledge in chapters 4, 5, and 6. In chapter 4, I will compare and contrast maieutics and knowledge for Plato with teaching and revelation for Levinas. In chapter 5, I will discuss Levinas's idea that knowledge is active and selective so that, in it, part stands in for whole and therefore conveys only part of the whole, and so must not be allowed to remain fixed lest truth be incomplete or one-sided. In chapter 6, I will discuss Levinas's idea of *the reduction,* a process of reducing the said to the saying or whole back to part. Through the reduction, according to Levinas, we avoid the idolatry of taking what is incomplete to be complete, perspective to be the thing itself, or ideology to be truth.

CHAPTER 3

Creation

For Socrates, in the *Symposium,* eros is a type of desire, and desire is a type of need. For Levinas, in *Totality and Infinity,* desire is contrasted with need. Are their views of desire, then, completely different? No, I will argue in this chapter, they are not as different as they seem since Socrates invokes need for the same reason Levinas rejects it: in order to highlight human vulnerability to the other—for Socrates, to reject a decayed masculine ideal of self-sufficiency, for Levinas, to eliminate the return to the self predominant in Western philosophy. How, then, do their views of desire differ? After all, as Levinas rightly points out, Socrates rejects Aristophanes's view that love reunites a split being, a view Levinas appropriately takes to imply that love is a return to the self (*TI* 254/232).[1] Why, then, does Levinas nonetheless charge Socrates with an egoist understanding of love (*TI* 63/35)? One answer, I will argue, is found in the centrality, for Levinas, of a concept of creation (*TI* 63/35, 104/78, 292–94/268–70), a concept that, as Levinas claims, is lacking in Plato who, in the *Timaeus,* substitutes instead the demiurgic informing of matter (*TI* 63/35).[2] Love and desire, for Levinas, are accomplished in fecund production, for example, the fecund production of a child who, though the father's issue, is nonetheless absolutely other than the father—a creation ex nihilo, a true other (*TI* 63/35). The created other is, according to Levinas, absolute upsurge (*TI* 89/62) where the absoluteness of the upsurge indicates that the other's coming to be is not the informing of matter or the development of potential, but the coming to be of something entirely new. Love, Levinas says, aims at the other, the stranger and not, as Socrates would have it, immortality (*TI* 63/35).[3]

Levinas is not consistent, however, in contrasting his view of desire with Socrates's. For though Levinas contrasts his creation ex nihilo or absolute upsurge with the informing of matter in the *Timaeus,* he also associates desire both with his absolute other and with Socrates's good beyond being (*TI* 292/268; *Rep.* 6.509b6–10). For Socrates, the beautiful is a closely related transcategorial to the good beyond being, and the beautiful and the good are the ultimate objects of love. If Socratic transcategorials are the same as Levinas's good beyond being, then the Socratic and Levinasian views of desire do not really differ and Levinas's critique of Socrates on love and desire collapses. If instead Levinas and Socrates have different ways of thinking of the good beyond being, as I will maintain, desire is different for them as well: for Socrates, desire is responsiveness to the forms of persons or things while for Levinas instead desire is an open responsiveness, a responsiveness to the singular beyond or before form.[4] On my interpretation, then, though each philosopher highlights fundamental human vulnerability and responsiveness to the other, creation ex nihilo—absolute upsurge—distinguishes their views of love and desire.

In this chapter, I will show that Socrates invokes the concept of need for the same reason Levinas rejects it, namely, to highlight human vulnerability to the other (section 1); that their concepts of desire are, nonetheless, different owing to the presence or absence of a concept of creation ex nihilo (section 2); and that Levinas's good beyond being is not the same as Socrates's so that the outlined difference in their concepts of desire due to creation remains and points to two fundamental types of human vulnerability to the other (section 3).

1.

References to human vulnerability are legion in the *Symposium*, beginning with the dramatic date of the drinking party itself: 416 B.C.E., the year that Agathon put on his first tragedy. The dramatic background, as a result, is the Peloponnesian War during which a self-confident Athens overextended itself and fell. Even more, Socrates claims for himself a teacher who is a woman, Diotima, and, as a woman, hardly a symbol of heroic self-sufficiency, not to mention the fact that she identifies eros with pregnancy, a paradigm of being taken over by another.[5] Diotima is from Mantineia, too, where in 418 B.C.E. the Athenians overestimated themselves and were defeated by the Spartans. And she teaches Socrates that love is not all-good or all-beautiful but in between, a peculiar combination of ability and vulnerability, power and need, *poros* and *penia*—a lot like Socrates himself, a powerful, magnetic figure sought out by the young for his wisdom though the only wisdom he claims is awareness of ignorance, and a lot like philosophy, too, which is not wisdom, according to Socrates, but the loving pursuit of it based on awareness of its lack. According to Diotima, "love is a philosopher" (204b4).

The critique of the male model of heroic self-sufficiency begins earlier in the dialogue in the frame dialogue between Apollodorus and his companion. The companion wonders about Apollodorus's nickname, *the soft,* given how savage Apollodorus is in his attacks on those who spend their time in pursuits other than philosophy (*Sym.* 173c2–d3). Apollodorus is a comic image of Socrates, comic because he goes too far both in his savagery and, as his nickname suggests, his softness.[6] The dramatic foreshadowing continues when Aristodemus and Socrates, in the next frame dialogue, are on their way to the party according to Socrates "to corrupt the proverb 'to a good man's feast the good go uninvited'" (174b3–c4). The superficial corruption is the pun on Agathon's name, which means *good*—as if the proverb were to say "to Goodman's feast the good go uninvited"—while the deeper corruption is a disagreement with the claim that the good go to the good, the beautiful to the beautiful. Instead, the soft or vulnerable, such as Menelaus, *the soft warrior,* go to the good, such as Agamemnon (174c5–d1). Clearly, the heroic model is under attack in this dialogue.

Soon, too, those present in the central dialogue, the dialogue that takes place at the symposium itself, are divided into those who are capable and those who are incapable—again foreshadowing the ability/vulnerability theme of the dialogue, though in this case, ability and vulnerability regarding drink, with Aristophanes, Pausanias, and Agathon on the side of those who are capable; Eryximachus, Aristodemus, and Phaedrus on the side of those who are incapable; and Socrates, not surprisingly, in the middle since he can go either way. The capacity to drink large quantities of wine is associated with madness and incapacity with soberness, leaving Socrates in the middle associated with what we might call sober madness. Socrates can drink or not. He is able and vulnerable, sober and mad, in his mind and out of it. It sounds like the son of Poros and Penia is Socrates and not, as Diotima claims later in the dialogue, Eros. That's not surprising, though, since not only does Diotima describe eros as a philosopher, but Socrates identifies himself with eros when he says that the only subject he knows is "*ta erōtika,*" love matters or erotic things (177d6–e3). The *Symposium* is another dialogue in which Socrates is identified with a more than human figure—with Achilles in the *Apology,* for example, with Heracles in the *Republic,* and here in the *Symposium* with Eros.

Before considering the central dialogue's series of speeches about love, what in general were the issues about the love in classical Athens? Homosexuality was not the issue, nor was the age of those involved in homosexual love (since youths had relationships with men at about the same age that girls were married). Instead, what was at issue was aggression (*hybris*) and insatiability.[7] That Plato was concerned about the former is clear from the dramatic framing of the *Phaedrus*'s discussions of love in the context of the mythical rape of Oreithyia by Boreas (*Phdr.* 229b4–5). Insatiability comes up in the

Gorgias when Socrates caricatures Callicles's view of the hedonistic good life as being like the life of the *charadrios,* a mythical bird that constantly eats and immediately excretes (*Grg.* 494b6–7). In the background of the *Symposium,* then, as in the background of the *Phaedrus,* is the Greek male concern with the idea of control—represented in Greek iconography by the heroic small penis.[8] It is a concern with not overstepping the boundaries of others, as in rape, and with not allowing others—other things, such as food, drink, or sex, or other people—to overstep one's own. Here again Socrates is a peculiar, and striking, middle figure. Aware of the problem of aggression, he nonetheless is comfortable with the idea that, in love, we're out of our minds. In fact, according to Socrates, the greatest good things come to human beings by way of madness if that madness is divine (*Phdr.* 244a6–8). So there is divine and human, all-too-human, madness and moderation, the divine represented by love, philosophy, or Socrates and the human, all-too-human, by the comic figure of Apollodorus as well as various less savory figures such as Callicles, who pictures the good life as constant inflow, or Lysias, who, in the *Phaedrus,* would seduce Phaedrus for sex through a lie about love, namely, that he is not in love with Phaedrus and that nonlove is better anyway since it is moderate, not mad.

At the drinking party, Phaedrus, a sober speaker, makes love, a great god, something useful. Great benefits would be derived from having a city or army composed of lovers and their youths since before their boyfriends lovers would be inspired toward virtue by shame and love of honor and would even die for their boyfriends' sake. There is nothing better for a youth, Phaedrus maintains, than a "good lover" (*Sym.* 178c3–5). But Phaedrus's language is the language of heroism, all about avoiding shame and being motivated by love of honor to do great deeds. He neglects love as vulnerability or a source of incompetence. In quoting Hesiod's description of Eros, Phaedrus leaves out the description of Eros as the limb-loosener who weakens the mind in the breasts of human beings and gods (178b5–7).[9] For Phaedrus, love is all about seriousness, virtue, and boldness and not at all about being soft or vulnerable. His example of vulnerability is Orpheus who, soft and lacking the boldness to die for the woman he loves, dies at the hands of women (179d2–e1).

Pausanias, a mad speaker and Agathon's lover, is less sanguine about love. He does not think all of it is good and describes better and worse types, Uranian (heavenly) and Pandemian (popular). Uranian lovers are manly. They love only youths—stronger youths who have mind—and love them only after their mind has begun to form. Pandemian lovers, to the contrary, love both women and mindless youths. They care only about the sex act itself and, unlike Uranian lovers, leave the youths they have sex with rather than loving for life (180c3–182a6). There is a queasiness in Pausanias's feelings about love that is evident even when he argues for what he takes to be the better type of it. In attending to their youths, Pausanias maintains, lovers "are willing to perform slavish acts not even a slave would perform"—acts that would be seen as flattery and unfree if done to attain wealth, office, or power—and beloveds, too, are voluntarily slavish when they have sex with their lovers, though they are justified in engaging in those slavish acts if the acts are for the sake of virtue (183a2–c2). Pausanias's association of love with slavery echoes tyrannical Meno's refusal, in the *Meno,* to be governed even by the forms of things when he is thinking, as discussed in chapter 2. In the *Phaedrus,* Pausanian willing slavery foreshadows Socratic eros later in the dialogue as ability and vulnerability, power and need, *poros* and *penia* but differs since Pausanian love has an extrinsic aim—sex for the lover and virtue for the beloved. For Socrates instead, love's vulnerability is for its own sake since it is vulnerability to the good or the beautiful itself—the good or beautiful the youth instantiates. For Socrates, service is not something shameful endured because it is for the sake of something else that is good. Instead, the service itself is something good.

Eryximachus, one of the sober speakers, is a doctor. An orderly technician, he's puzzled by Heraclitus's view that opposites are unified. If they are unified, they cannot be opposites. If things differ, they cannot agree. That, he says, would be "quite absurd" (*pollē alogia*) (187a6–8). But is he right? Love relationships suggest the opposite since often it is because two people differ that they are agreeable to one another. It seems it is the very tension—their very vulnerability to the other—that they crave. In addition, separation often brings us together. "Absence makes the heart grow fonder," as we proverbially say. Perhaps then Heraclitus is right to say, presumably about all of reality, that "being brought apart (differing), it is brought together with itself (agrees); there is a back-stretched connection, as in the bow and lyre."[10] Perhaps, as Heraclitus suggests, unity, at least for human beings, requires a certain tension and vulnerability, requires something brought apart that is brought together, as the unity of a bow results from the fact that, at one and the same time, the string pulls in and the bow pulls out.

Not so for sober Eryximachus whose idea of eros is of a great and wonderful god, found not just in love relationships but in all things, an all-powerful source of happiness. For Eryximachus—Phaedrus's lover—all sciences are erotic sciences, and the better eros is an orderly eros that makes hostile elements come to love one another (186b2–188d3). Love, in other words, is harmony of elements that previously differed not of elements that currently do (187a8–c2). It is unity with no difference, tension, or vulnerability, whether in relationships or in medicine, music, astronomy, or other areas (186b2–188d3).

The drama of the dialogue suggests a different view of love. Eryximachus's speech is preceded by Aristophanes's hiccups (185c4–e5). Their rhythmical quality mimics the sex act and reminds us that human beings willingly engender its tension. Eryximachus's suggestion that, to cure the hiccups, Aristophanes should tickle his nose and induce sneezing mimics the sex act, too, as well as all activities in which we induce tension in order to resolve it. Love, the dialogue suggests at this point, is not an orderly unity without tension and difference. Instead, in love we intentionally make ourselves vulnerable and tense in order to enjoy the tension's resolution.

For Aristophanes, whose well-known speech follows, human beings are, to the contrary, a paradigm of vulnerability to the other. Previously, we were circle people, terrible in our strength and power, who thought great thoughts and tested the gods (190b5–6). We had two heads and necks, four arms, four legs, two sets of genitals, and we moved by rolling around with great force. Now, we are sick and need healing because the gods, frightened of our power and *hybris,* sliced us in half (190d6–7). Love draws our archaic nature back together and tries to make us one out of two. What lovers desire is to be fused together into one. Love, then, is the desire and pursuit of wholeness (192d2–193a1). For Aristophanes, eros is not a sign that human beings are manly, powerful, and invulnerable, as the first three speakers suggest, but a sign that human beings are wounded and need healing. His comic speech critiques the heroic ideal, which stresses human ability and downplays human need. It makes fun of manly pretensions and points to what we lack. Eros is a sign that we are missing part of ourselves, part of what it is to be complete, to be fulfilled, to be whole.

The fact that there are more speeches about love at this climactic point suggests some aspect of the critique of the heroic ideal of self-sufficiency may remain to be discussed. Agathon, the tragic playwright, provides the need for continuing the critique when, in his speech, he praises eros as most beautiful and best—beautiful because young, tender, and graceful; best because possessed of all the virtues. Eros is just, not violent, since people willingly serve it; moderate because stronger than all other desires and pleasures; courageous because Aphrodite defeated Ares; wise because eros makes every person a poet, creates all living beings, and brings renown to the varied craftsmen it teaches (195a5–197b9). Eros, Agathon says, is of beauty. There's nothing ugly about it. And eros is the cause of peace, intimacy, goodwill, and more. Eros, in other words, is all-good.

Agathon's vacuous tragic speech gets the most applause presumably because it is a tour de force, beautiful in poetic form. In content, it is similar to the part of Phaedrus's speech that makes eros fundamentally good. Socrates refutes Agathon in short order using wisdom he received from his female teacher, Diotima. Love, Socrates argues, is a species of desire, and desire a species of lack or need. If love is of what is beautiful, then love lacks what is beautiful and is not itself beautiful. Since beautiful things are good and love lacks beautiful things, love lacks what is good as well (200a2–e6). Socrates has learned well his lesson from Diotima—whom, presumably, he made up—that love involves vulnerability, lack, or need. As a young man, he, like Agathon, thought love was beautiful and good. Instead, love is not a god but a *daimon,* the son of Poros (resource) and Penia (need) (203c5–6). Human beings are not utter vulnerability, as Aristophanic comedy suggests, nor are they complete ability, as Agathon's tragic poetry maintains. Instead, Socratic philosophy teaches, human beings are in between—as is awareness of ignorance. Ignorance makes us needy; awareness is the resource for overcoming our need. In Socratic eros, awareness of need becomes the resource to overcome it. In addition, eros is not a desire for wholeness. It is not a desire for one's lost other half but for what is good. Socrates agrees with Aristophanes that eros is a sign of need or lack. But he disagrees that what is needed or lacking is a part of oneself. For Socrates, eros does not return to the self.

It does not return to the self even though, as Socrates learned from Diotima, eros is desire for immortality (207a3–4). For immortality according to her is found most of all in form as she suggests in remarking on the fact that a body remains even though all its material parts—hair, flesh, bones, and blood—pass away (207d4–e1). Similarly, the pregnant lover reproduces eternal form, for example, in a child who reproduces human form or, for another, in speeches about what makes a man good, speeches he shares with a youth he educates that are reflective of the beautiful itself—the form of the beautiful, which is eternal (208e1–209c7). Love begins as a desire to have what is good forever (206a11–12). Since that is not literally possible, love becomes the desire to generate and reproduce in someone beautiful (206e5). As such, it is a desire for immortality (207a3–4). Love is not, then, a desire for one's missing half but is a vulnerability or need that results in generation and reproduction, realization and sharing, of eternal form. We begin by loving beautiful bodies, then beautiful souls, then beautiful practices, laws, and knowledge, and then beauty itself, the form of the beautiful—beauty in all its universality and of every type—and, as a result of our love, we generate and reproduce it. Socrates introduces need, then, to highlight human vulnerability and critique the heroic ideal of masculine self-sufficiency dominant in his time. In fact, the *Symposium*'s carefully crafted critique of self-sufficiency culminates with Socrates's speech, a speech portrayed as superior to Aristophanes's in its turn away from the self to the beautiful and good, which are eternal.

Unlike Socrates, Levinas, in *Totality and Infinity,* argues that desire is not a type of need.[11] In striking contrast, though, he does so to underline, not deny, fundamental human vulnerability to the other. As a result, the two philosophers' views of desire are not as different as they seem since they share a common aim. Socrates underlines human vulnerability by rejecting heroic male self-sufficiency. Levinas, in a similar vein, does so by rejecting the return to the self that, according to him, dominates Western philosophy. Western philosophy, Levinas says, most often is ontology, "a reduction of the other to the same" (*TI* 43/13). Like Aristophanes and Socrates, Levinas rejects the idea of human invulnerability. Like Socrates and unlike Aristophanes, however, Levinas rejects the idea that love aims at fusion. "Man's relationship with the other," Levinas says, "is *better* as difference than as unity: sociality is better than fusion. The very value of love is the impossibility of reducing the other to myself, of coinciding into sameness. From an ethical perspective two have a better time than one [*on s'amuse mieux à deux*]!" (EI 188). Aristophanes's mistake, he says, is thinking that love "can be reduced to . . . fundamental immanence, be divested of all transcendence, seek but a connatural being, a sister soul, present itself as incest. The myth Aristophanes tells in Plato's *Symposium,* in which love reunites the two halves of one sole being, interprets the adventure as a return to self" (*TI* 254/232). Desire, for Levinas, is about the other, not about the self. The objective of desire's movement is "the other, the Stranger." Desire "is absolutely non-egoist" (*TI* 63/35).

For Levinas, desire is metaphysical and need ontological where ontology is comprehension of beings and metaphysics is respect for exteriority, that is, respect for the other as other (*TI* 42–43/13). Desire is not a species of need, he says, though it is customarily interpreted that way, interpreted to "be at the basis of desire" such that desire is thought to "characterize a being indigent and incomplete or fallen from its past grandeur" and to "coincide with the consciousness of what has been lost." When understood as a type of need, desire is "essentially a nostalgia, a longing for return" (*TI* 33/3).

For Levinas, however, desire is not a longing for return and "does not rest on any prior kinship" (*TI* 33–34/3). It is not about the self—not about returning to it, nourishing it, or completing it: "The metaphysical desire has another intention; it desires beyond everything that can simply complete it. It is like goodness—the Desired does not fulfill it, but deepens it" (*TI* 34/4). The other deepens desire, or even hollows it out (*le creuse*). The other does not feed me: "The other metaphysically desired is not 'other' like the bread I eat, the land in which I dwell, the landscape I contemplate" (*TI* 33/3). Ontology, for Levinas, promotes freedom, specifically "the freedom that is the identification of the same, not allowing itself to be alienated by the other" (*TI* 42/13). But I am not essentially defined by freedom. In metaphysics, the other critiques my freedom: metaphysics "discovers the dogmatism and naïve arbitrariness of its spontaneity, and calls into question the freedom of the exercise of ontology." It "calls into question the exercise of the same" (*TI* 43/13).

In metaphysical desire, then, I am confronted by my vulnerability. The other, who cannot be integrated, who cannot be consumed by me or reduced to me, disrupts me, disrupts my sense of my self as all there is, a sense I achieve at the very same time that I achieve a self—an I, an egoism, a psychism—namely, in the atheist stage, as Levinas calls it, the stage in which I resist the totality of what is to form a self. Atheism, for Levinas, is separation. Resistance takes place through a process of taking in and feeding on what is outside myself while at the same time remaining distinct from that on which I feed (*TI* 112/84, 122/94). Atheism is accomplished, concretely, in a home, since a home, with its doors and windows, enables me to connect to what is outside while retreating to recollect and retain myself (*TI* 154/127, 156/129). In the atheist stage, I move from enjoyment, and sensibility broadly speaking, to perception to consciousness, that is, comprehension, representation, intentionality, or knowledge. In comprehension and representation, I dominate the other by capturing him or her in a concept, a concept that reduces the other and prevents me from seeing that other as other (*TI* 163–68/137–49).

But the other, like myself, resists the totality and cannot be fully integrated or reduced. The other contests me (*TI* 171/145), opposes me (*TI* 197/171), masters me (*TI* 176/146). The other breaks the ceiling of the totality, breaks totality's closed circle (*TI* 171/146). For Levinas, as for Socrates and Aristophanes, desire is not a sign of heroic mastery but an indication of fundamental human vulnerability. And, as with Socrates, the vulnerability is not harmful since, to use Levinas's term, the other as such is a marvel (*TI* 292/269). The other who disrupts me opens a new dimension (*TI* 171/146). The opposition is pacific (*TI* 197/171), the resistance nonviolent (*TI* 197/171), the opposition nonhostile (*TI* 171/146). The other is a master who does not conquer but teaches (*TI* 171/146). What the other teaches is his or her very otherness, sometimes referred to by Levinas as height (*TI* 171/146), sometimes as surplus (*TI* 97/70). The teaching of the critique of heroic or Western self-sufficiency is that there is a type of vulnerability, a type of openness, that does not leave me vulnerable to harm, but instead is positive—positive, though, in different ways for Socrates and for Levinas as we have seen in chapter 1 and will see again in this chapter though delineated in a different way (section 2).

Desire, according to Levinas, is accomplished in the face to face relation with the other and in fecundity. The face to face relation, the relation in which I relate to the other as other and the other relates to me as other, takes place in language—not in the content of language but in language's function of direct address, not in the speaking about but in the speaking to, not in the said but in the saying, as Levinas says in *Otherwise Than Being*. Language, Levinas says, is "contact across a distance" (*TI* 172/147), where *distance* is metaphorical and suggests that I can never know or represent the other in his or her otherness, that the other's otherness can never be a given for me. The personal other for Levinas is infinite where *infinite* means indefinite but in such a way as to be contrasted with the way in which the elemental world is indefinite and which Levinas designates with a Greek term for indefinite, *apeiron*. What is *apeiron*, such as a forest of which I only see a part or a sea all of whose elements I cannot perceive from my current position, can be disclosed. What is infinite, the other, cannot (*TI* 158–59/132, 192–93/166–67). The infinite can only be revealed, where revelation for Levinas is distinct from disclosure. The one who speaks is not disclosed. He or she is not placed in the light of another but, in articulating the world, is announced across what he or she presents (*TI* 65–66/37).

Fecundity, the second accomplishment of metaphysical desire, is a type of relation with the future that is "irreducible to the power over possibles" (*TI* 267/245). The biological sense of fecundity is the father's production of the child but fecundity is broader than that (*TI* 247/225). Fecundity in general is found in relations between one person and another and between the I and itself (*TI* 306/283). In fecundity, we surmount the passivity to which our will is exposed. Our will is free—the possibility of its freedom is produced when, in the atheist stage, we resist the totality to form an egoism—but the will is immediately exposed and vulnerable. The work of the will can be taken or sold (*TI* 227/202–3). The will itself, because of its necessarily material manifestation, is subject to violence, and we are subject to death (*TI* 229/205, 224/199). This suffering and death are surmounted in fecundity (*TI* 236–40/213–17). Human existence, for Levinas, is not, as Heidegger avers, being toward death but is the *not yet* or a way of being against death (*TI* 224/199). We surmount our passivity and death in fecundity, in the production of inexhaustible youths. "Fecundity," Levinas says, "continues history without producing old age." In fecundity, he goes on, the I "meets with no trammels to the renewal of its substance" (*TI* 268/246). In this way, the I exists infinitely, since fecund desire produces another who desires: "Here the desire which in the first pages of this work we contrasted with need, the desire that is not a lack, the desire that is the independence of the separated being and its transcendence, is accomplished—not in being satisfied and in thus acknowledging that it was a need, but in transcending itself, in engendering desire" (*TI* 269/247)

2.

How, then, are Socrates's and Levinas's views of love and desire different? Each, as we have seen, rejects the idea that love is a return to the self: for Socrates, love is, first of all, a desire to have the good for oneself forever—but then it is the desire to generate and reproduce and, by doing so, to produce immortality; similarly, for Levinas, love in one respect is need—but in another is fecund desire and exists infinitely, beyond death (*TI* 254–55/232–33). Each sees love as a sign of human vulnerability, an example of the central other-directedness of human beings and of human subjectivity or soul. Each, then, in his understanding of love, is a philosopher of the other.

The difference is in what the generativity or fecundity is like. Here is a real difference between the two philosophers, not that one is a proponent of self-sufficiency or autonomy and the other of vulnerability or heteronomy, but that one sees immortality in the persistence of form while the other sees it in a series of creations ex nihilo. One draws a relation between immortality and the eternal while the other connects what is beyond death to the upsurge of something new. Levinas is wrong when he states that the way in which he differs with Socrates on love is that Socrates thinks immortality is the object of love while he, Levinas, thinks love's aim is the other, the stranger: "love as analyzed by Plato does not coincide with what we have called Desire. Immortality is not the objective of the first movement of Desire, but the other, the Stranger" (*TI* 63/35). Instead, both philosophers believe love defeats death and, as we have seen, both believe love is, fundamentally, a directedness to something outside oneself. The difference in their views is, instead, the difference between the eternal and the new.

Levinas says "desire in its positivity" is "affirmed across the idea of creation *ex nihilo*" (*TI* 04/77–78; see also 63/35). By associating love and desire with creation ex nihilo, Levinas does not mean to refer to the creation of the universe and its contents in six days. Instead, he wants a "rigorous concept of creation" (*TI* 292/268–69) by which he means a philosophic idea that carries its own weight and is not grounded in appeal to religious text. The other in his or her singularity is a creation ex nihilo for Levinas because singularity is lack of determination (since determination implies generality) and production out of anything determinate (that is, out of anything whatsoever) would be production of something determinate. Creation ex nihilo is not the development of potential, not the realization of projected possibility: "This future is neither the Aristotelian germ . . . nor the Heideggerian possibility" (*TI* 267/245). Instead, it is the production of something that is its own beginning.

How can that be? Creation ex nihilo is found, in the most concrete case, in the production by the father—or, dare we say, by the father and mother—of a child who in some way, nonetheless, is his or her own beginning: "the separated and created being is thereby not simply issued forth from the father, but is absolutely other than him" (*TI* 63/35); in fecundity, being is "produced not as the definitiveness of a totality but as an incessant recommencement" (*TI* 270/248). Every human being begins as a child who is immersed in the totality of what is and not clearly distinct from it due to an original inability to distinguish subject from object. Each one produces his or her self, ego, psyche, or singularity by resisting the totality: "The psychism constitutes an *event* in being" and "is already *a way of being*, resistance to the totality" (*TI* 54/24). The resisting is a resistance to all concept, all determination. In that respect, the self is not composed of or produced out of anything, but is instead a resistance to everything determinate. The resistance continues throughout life since the self, though essentially its contents, always remains distinct from them (*TI* 112/84, 122/94). This is Levinas's core metaphysical idea, of a self that constantly emerges in or offers a variety of forms while, at the same time, resisting the forms in which it emerges or which it offers, a self that is essentially in relation while, at the same time, absolving itself from the relations (*TI* 110/82).

Both in its biological meaning and in its extension to the relation of one person to another and of the I to itself, fecundity denotes a relation to another's future that is not a power: "The relation with such a future, irreducible to the power over possibles, we shall call fecundity" (*TI* 267/245). Fecundity, the very accomplishment of desire, is not heroic. Like Socrates, Levinas is a critic of the heroic masculine ideal, in his case perhaps best represented by aspects of Heidegger's philosophy, for example, resolute and authentic being toward death. The erotic relation involves "a characteristic reversal of the subjectivity issued from position, a reversion of the virile and heroic I" (*TI* 270/248). The erotic subject is initiation not initiative (*TI* 270/248).

Similarly, for Socrates, love is not heroic. In the *Phaedrus,* as we saw in chapter 1, the helmsman or governor of the soul, who is identified with reason (specifically with *nous*), falls on his back at the sight of the beloved and as a result loves him and serves him. The helmsman is knocked out by the sight of the youth and no longer in the things of himself (*Phdr.* 250a6–7). He even serves like a slave to his beloved (*Phdr.* 252a1–b1). The lover's nonheroic service to his beloved, though, is differently characterized than the relation to another that is not a power described by Levinas. The lover, according to

Socrates, at the sight of the beloved ascends to the place beyond the heavens up to the very forms themselves, a process Socrates calls recollection of those eternal forms, and then descends and, in the best cases, joins together with the beloved in philosophy, that is, in a sharing of the very eternal forms the sight of the beloved has spurred him to recollect. The lover and his beloved youth come together over an eternal third that they share in common (*Phdr.* 248d2–4, 252e11–253b1). Similarly in the *Symposium,* as we have seen, immortality is illustrated by Diotima's example of matter that changes while form persists and is exemplified by the production of a child who shares human form and by the educative function of sharing with a youth speeches about what is good in the hopes that the youth will be affected by such conversations to become beautiful and good, that is, to share in those forms (*Sym.* 206c1–212a7).

For Levinas, to the contrary, the effect of fecundity is not to reproduce eternal form. Instead, fecundity involves relating to an other in such a way as to facilitate the arising of something that has not in any sense been before. The ability to relate in this way to the future is fecundity, and the way of relating is contraction—"contraction that leaves a place for the separated being" (*TI* 104/77). For Levinas, the fundamentally ethical way of relating is a contraction that enables the wholly other and his or her projects to be. Fecundity plays this role not just in erotic relations narrowly speaking but in all desire, since fecundity is the accomplishment of desire, and in our face to face relations to others and our relation to our self, since fecundity extends from the biological to both of these. Antiheroic reversion, initiation, and contraction play a role in all desire for Levinas, then, since all desire is a type of contraction in relation to an other that allows the other and his or her future projects—in their newness—to be. For Levinas, love and desire are generative vulnerability to what is fundamentally other or new.

3.

But Levinas is not consistent in contrasting his view of love and desire with Socrates's. Though he contrasts his creation ex nihilo or absolute upsurge with the informing of matter in the *Timaeus,* he nonetheless identifies Socrates's good beyond being in the *Republic* with his own *metaphysical separation.* If they were the same—that is, if Socrates's good beyond being were the same as Levinas's—the distinction between Socratic and Levinasian love and desire would collapse. If they were the same, Socratic eros would have to be for the new not for the eternal since the object of Socratic eros is the good (or the beautiful, a closely related transcategorial). But it is not for the new, as

Diotima's example of the matter that changes while the form persists indicates. Socrates must mean something else, then, when he says that the good is beyond being.

There is more reason to think that Socratic transcategorials are different than Levinas's good beyond being than just this textual argument. For one thing, if the object of desire for Socrates were the good beyond being in Levinas's sense—that is, radical singularity—then we would expect Socratic virtues to be different than they are. We would expect Socrates to discuss virtues of the same general type as kindness, compassion, and faithfulness—virtues that go past knowledge of an individual's characteristics and are directed instead to the singular individual him- or herself. Virtues of this type do not in fact play a central role in the Platonic corpus. Instead, the whole point of Socratic virtue seems to be to critique the heroic male ideal of power or force and replace it with knowledge—not with what is beyond or before knowledge, but with knowledge. A central argument for Socrates regarding virtue is that we all desire good and so virtue is not desire but knowledge or wisdom: we all desire what is good, Socrates argues, so if we do not pursue it, it must be that we do not know what it is (*Meno* 77b2–e2). Of course, Socrates's goal is to replace the ideal of virile force with knowledge understood as wisdom, not merely with being intelligent or smart (as the suggested rejection, at *Meno* 88a6–b6, of the equation of virtue with *eumathia* demonstrates) so that someone could object that the idea that virtue is not simply knowledge but wisdom could be translated into the claim that virtue is the encounter with the other as singular. Justice, they might say in support of their objection, could be equated with wisdom in this sense. What, though, I want to reply, about moderation and courage? These seem to have nothing to do with singularity and more to do with awareness of what is appropriate or best. We perhaps are asking too much of Socrates if we ask both that he endeavor to eradicate an old ideal of virtue as power and replace it with virtue as knowledge or wisdom and, at the same time, that he introduce the ideal of response to human singularity. Moreover, if he had introduced that ideal, wouldn't it be likely that Aristotle, his follower and great critic, would respond to such a crucial conceptual innovation? He does not respond to any such idea but instead responds to what he thinks is an overly intellectualist idea of virtue in Plato that he moderates by stressing the importance of emotional development. Virtue, for Aristotle, is not simply knowledge, as it is for Plato, but also requires suitable emotional development.

What, then, is the good beyond being according to Socrates?[12] It comes up during a discussion in the *Republic* of the mathematical and eidetic or formal aspects of beings, aspects that are known, respectively, by discursive rationality (*dianoia*) and by rational intuition (*nous*) (511d2–5).[13] As a result of this location in the dialogue, the strong suggestion is that the good beyond being is not a nonbeing but a hyperbeing or second-order being—beyond (*epekeina*), hyper, or second order because it is beyond the mathematical and the eidetic aspects of beings (as I have argued elsewhere), that is, beyond both what we might call the *this* and the *what.*[14] Beings, in the *Republic,* are called *originals* to distinguish them from images. In images, such as the image of a tree on water, the mathematical and formal or eidetic aspects are very separate. In originals, such as a tree, they are more together. The good is responsible for their being together. The good is the togetherness of the *this* and the *what,* the mathematical and the eidetic, and, as such, we may call the good *the fitting* meaning the fit between a thing and its qualities or the conformity of a thing to its type.

That Socrates identifies the good with the fitting, or with related terms such as *sufficient, proper, complete,* or *perfect,* is indicated by numerous passages: in book 1 of the *Republic,* Socrates suggests that only if *owed* means *fitting* (*prosēkon*) is justice giving the owed to each (332c2); in book 4, that justice is doing one's thing or doing the proper (*to ta hautou prattein, oikeiopragia*) (433b4, 434c8); in book 8, that the best for each is also what is most proper to it (*oikeiotaton*) (586e2); in the *Gorgias,* that moderation is doing the fitting (*ta prosēkonta*) concerning gods and people, that justice is doing the fitting concerning people, and piety doing the fitting concerning gods (507a7–b3); in the *Philebus,* that two signs of the good are the complete or perfect (*teleon*) and the sufficient (*hikanon*) (20d1–6). All these terms have to do with the fit of *this* to *what,* mathematical to eidetic, with *complete* and *perfect* indicating that something entirely fits while *sufficient* or *proper* are deficient cases of the complete or perfect: the sufficient just meets the mark, we could say, while the perfect meets it entirely.[15]

The beautiful, for Socrates, would be another such second-order being or transcategorial (to use a somewhat Aristotelian term) but one that emphasizes another aspect of mathematico-eidetic beings than togetherness. Instead, the beautiful points not to the togetherness but to the separation of the mathematical and the eidetic, to the transcendence by a *this* of its *what.* In the case of a painting of a tree, the painting in one sense simply is shapes and colors on a surface, but those shapes and colors point beyond themselves. The beauty of something is beyond that something's qualities, as the use of the term *surpassing* (294b2) in the *Hippias Major,* the dialogue on the beautiful, indicates. Since the *Hippias Major* has not been commented on as extensively as other Platonic dialogues such as the *Republic,* I will now give a detailed interpretation of it. The interpretation will show that the beautiful, for Plato, is a transcategorial. In addition, I will return to discussion of the *Hippias Major* in chapter 7, where I will show how it contributes to a discussion of Plato's views on human vulnerability.[16]

In that dialogue, Hippias's first definitions of the beautiful fail because they reduce beauty to a beautiful being (maiden) or to a beautiful quality (gold) rather than seeing that beauty is in and through the qualities of a being but beyond them (*Hipp. Maj.* 287e4, 289e3). So also in the case of every being—every original, to use the term from the *Republic*—form not only is together with thing but transcends it, as the generality or universality of form indicates. The beautiful for Socrates, then, indicates an aspect of the puzzling phenomenon of the relationship between *this* and *what,* between the mathematical and the eidetic, in all beings, with the good, as I have argued elsewhere, indicating their togetherness and the beautiful indicating their separation.

Consider the *Hippias Major* as a whole. The dialogue is full of *twos.* Socrates doubles himself. He talks to himself. The first Socrates, the one who talks the most to Hippias, seems to need the second Socrates, who is not fine or beautiful at all but trashy: "not refined (*kompsos*) but trashy (*surphetos*), giving thought to nothing other than the truth" (288d4–5). At the end of the dialogue, Socrates indicates that he needed Hippias, as well, for what he learned in the discussion (304e6–7). What he learned is not on the surface clear, of course, since the dialogue is aporetic. It ends without an obvious answer to the question, what is the beautiful. Socrates does say, though, that he seems to himself to know, as a result of his conversation with Hippias, what the proverb means that says that fine or beautiful things are difficult: "For I seem to myself to know (*eidenai*) what the proverb means that says, 'the beautiful things are difficult'" (304e7–9). Not surprisingly, the ending suggests that Socrates has gained some knowledge (he seems to himself to *know*) of ignorance (that beauty is difficult). So there is something difficult—dare we say permanently difficult?—about beauty, but there appears to be some knowledge, too. What exactly is the difficulty? What is the knowledge? And what is their connection to the twos that are found in the dialogue?

One way to approach the question is to ask what is the dialogue's answer to the question, what is the beautiful. Despite the fact that the dialogue is aporetic, some answers are suggested. The dialogue, read in a zealous way, does provide some knowledge. As is often true in a Platonic aporetic dialogue, the mistakes in or halting parts of the argument suggest directions Socrates might have wanted to take, or directions of argument Plato is leaving for us to take. For example, one definition in the dialogue remains unrefuted, as commentators have pointed out.[17] It is the definition of the beautiful as the fitting (*to prepon*) (293e2–4). Gold is only beautiful when it is fitting, they conclude in the refutation of gold as the beautiful. So perhaps the beautiful *is* the fitting. The proposed definition runs aground, though, when Socrates asks Hippias whether the fitting is what makes something *be* or *seem* beautiful (293e11–294a2). Hippias's answer is that it makes something *seem* beautiful. Hippias tends to focus on seeming, but if we follow his lead completely, the definition does not work. Whatever the beautiful may be, it must make that which it qualifies *be* beautiful not merely seem beautiful.

Hippias gives his answer, that the fitting is what makes something *seem* beautiful, because he is thinking of an external beauty that attaches to something and hides that something's own lack of beauty. It is superficial beauty that hides something, not a beauty that qualifies something that still shows forth in and through the beauty. Still, there is something important about the discussion of this definition even though Socrates and Hippias leave it behind. Socrates—and the reader—learn something from it. It is important to note that the term I have translated here as *fitting* is not the term translated as *fitting* in the *Republic, to prosēkon,* but instead is *to prepon,* which can also mean *the seemly.*[18] If we translate that way, then Hippias's reluctance to go Socrates's way is not surprising since the seemly can be something you attach to something else to hide what is not attractive or not appropriately exposed. A good suit on a homely man, for example, is seemly, as is a towel that hides one's intimate parts (or, even, the phrase "intimate parts" itself).

We know early in the dialogue that Hippias is not averse to hiding things, that he is not an entirely honest, or at least frank, person. For example, he thinks he has surpassed his contemporaries and the ancients in power and wisdom (281d1), but confesses that he does not usually say so because he pays heed to the envy of the living and fears the wrath of the dead (282d6–8). For another example, early in the dialogue, we learn that though Hippias claims to teach virtue, when Spartans will not allow him to do that, he is satisfied instead to teach them what pleases them most, namely, stories about ancient things such as heroes and human beings who founded cities (285d3–5). The first of these two examples shows his deceptiveness; the second both his deceptiveness and, as Socrates implies, his lawlessness since to be lawful is not simply to do what is allowed but to do what is good (284e5–7). It is not surprising, then, that beauty for Hippias has to do with how things appear and is deceptive.

But Socrates in the end takes up Hippias's idea that beauty has something to do with appearance. Is this what he needed Hippias for—to learn that beauty has something to do with appearance? We know that in the *Phaedrus,* Socrates refers to the beautiful as that which most appears, which shines forth most or which most comes to light—*ekphanestaton* (*Phdr.* 250d7). What Socrates means there is that the beautiful is the one form that appears to everyone. Not everyone will see prudence or the good. But everyone sees the beauty of a beautiful youth or child or beloved. Maybe what Socrates needed from Hippias was a spur to think more about appearing and not as much about being. Can we square that idea with the rest of the dialogue?

We can if we consider the idea that the seemly is what makes things not just seem but be beautiful. Then beauty might in fact be appearance itself—or, to be more complete, the appearance of form. How would that work? At one point in the dialogue, Socrates apparently identifies the beautiful with the surpassing (*tōi hyperechonti,* 294b2). It is just an example, but as is not unusual in Plato, the example is more of a paradigm or parallel. Things are great by the surpassing, Socrates says, in giving a paradigm or parallel of how to answer regarding the beautiful. Just as the good is beyond being, so the beautiful is the surpassing. Just as the good is in the brightest or shiniest part of being (*to phanotaton, Rep.* 7.518c9) so the beautiful is that which shines *forth* most (*ekphanestaton, Phdr.* 250d7). Just as the good is the fitting (*to prosēkon*), so the beautiful is the seemly (*to prepon*) (that is, the kind of fitting that specifically has to do with appearance). What is the difference? In the case of the good, Socrates is talking about what we might call *realization,* an ontological change into form or whatness, whereas in the case of the beautiful he is talking not about realization but about shining forth or appearing to us, which is an epistemological change, or at least a change for a knower.

Both of these have to do with a two. In one case, one thing realizes another. In the other case, one thing discloses another or brings it to light. Hence it is not surprising, in retrospect anyway, that Socrates goes on to talk about the general idea that sometimes when there are two things, both together are something different than each is separately. In the ontological realm, when the head of the hammer is with the hammer's handle, then the head can *be* a head rather than simply an interestingly shaped piece of metal. In the realm of beauty, when a patch of the color red is together with the more predominant grays, greens, and browns of the painting—Georgia O'Keefe's *Lake George Barns,* for example—the grays and greens are more vivid. They were there all along, but they show up more or stand out more. Without the red patch, the other colors do not stand out *for us.* So as Socrates in the *Theaetetus* and Aristotle in the *Metaphysics* suggest regarding ontology that the whole is something different than a heap of parts (*Tht.* 201d8–206b12; *Met.* 1041b11–33), Socrates here suggests regarding appearance that when two are together, something else arises *for us.*

Once again, though, the example is left hanging. With the example of the surpassing, Socrates appears to push Hippias toward, or at least set things up to allow for, the idea that in beauty, both together are different than each is separately (300b6–8). If that is true of beauty, and I am arguing that Socrates thinks it is, Socrates likely was waiting to see if Hippias would agree. But Hippias is so far from agreeing that he does not even move in the general direction Socrates leaves open to him, namely, the direction of thinking that beauty has something to do with twos, that is, with something new that results when both of two things are together.

This, perhaps, though, is part of the point of the dialogue. The dialogue is frustrating because Hippias does not seem to get it—to get much of anything Socrates is saying. The dialogue, in other words, is not just aporetic, but frustratingly aporetic. Does Hippias resist?[19] Or does he just not get it? We can compare Hippias to other interlocutors, such as Theaetetus or Meno. Theaetetus is refuted again and again, but keeps coming back with suggested alternative answers. Meno, to the contrary, resists many (though not all) of the refutations Socrates makes. His resistance appears in the form of an attack on Socrates (as like an ugly stingray that immobilizes what it contacts) or, in some cases, his willfully changing the subject, bossing Socrates around by pushing him to consider something other than Meno's answer. Give me another answer about color, he orders when Socrates has defined shape. Can you teach me that learning is recollection? he asks, when Socrates has just argued that there is no teaching but only recollecting.

Hippias is not like either of them. Unlike zealous Theaetetus, he does not really push to find another answer that responds to Socrates's criticisms. He gives definitions, but they do not really respond to Socrates's objections. What is important, though, is how his definitions fall short. When Socrates's coarse double asks Hippias the first time to define the beautiful and makes it clear that he does not want the answer to the question what is *beautiful* but what is *the* beautiful, Hippias responds in such a way as indicates that he is ignoring the distinction on which Socrates has clearly insisted and answers that a beautiful maiden is beautiful (not *the* beautiful, but *beautiful*).[20] Socrates indicates that he thinks Hippias cares more about giving answers that seem or look good rather than ones that are adequate when he replies, "You answer beautifully at least, by the dog, and reputably [*eudoxōs*]" (287e5–6). Mere beauty, then, is delineated by Socrates as being a positive seeming (*eu* + *doxōs*) that goes no further. Hippias goes on to say that the answer cannot be refuted because it seems so (*dokei*) to everyone (288a4). Anyone, he continues, who asserted that "what you say" is not beautiful would be ridiculous (288b1–3). The point is to say something that is beautiful and will *seem* beautiful to everyone. This becomes clear when Socrates proceeds next to list examples. Hippias is fine with the idea that a beautiful mare praised by the gods is beautiful, and with the idea that a beautiful lyre is beautiful but not with the third example, a beautiful pot. His response is that the answer is a base answer about a dignified topic (Socrates "dares to name base—*phaula*—names regarding a dignified—*semnōi*—matter") (288d1–3). In reply, Socrates in the guise of the double says that he is not refined but trashy, caring for nothing other than the truth (288d4–5). Hippias and Socrates's double make quite a fine pair—or, should I say less ironically, a comical or ridiculous pair—with Hippias caring only that his answer seem so to others and Socrates's double caring only that the answer be true. The difficulty here is not, as some commentators say, that Hippias thinks beauty cannot be defined but can only be understood through examples.[21] Instead, the difficulty is that he cannot allow an answer that indicates that beauty is besmirched by any touch of the ugly or the plain. It must be dignified. As a result, he does not understand the very power of the beautiful, namely, to raise the ugly or plain to a higher level, specifically, to a level on which it is beautiful or to a level on which the beautiful is beautiful in and through what is by itself ugly or plain. It is this combination of what is beautiful with what is ugly that characterizes Socratic wisdom or, more generally, Socrates himself as the representative of specifically human wisdom and of all that is in between: knowledge of ignorance, resource and poverty, beauty and ugliness, and, more generally, ability and vulnerability. Even this discussion of beauty in the *Hippias Major* is a critique of the heroic ideal, since the discussion critiques the ideal of self-sufficiency that would not be touched by anything low or plain, just as Achilles would not reenter the battle because he had been disrespected or a soldier was not to return without his beautiful shield even if, despite losing it, he had won the battle. In comparison with the gods, Socrates says, a beautiful maiden is ugly, so that the example of beauty that Hippias started out with was no more beautiful than ugly. Things, Socrates indicates in the *Republic,* tumble about between being and not being—in this case, between being and not being beautiful (*Rep.* 5.478e1–479d6). Or, as Heraclitus says, and as Socrates quotes him here, "the wisest human being, in comparison with a god, will appear an ape both in wisdom and in beauty and in all other things" (289b3–5).

Given that his first answer was refuted on the grounds that things are a mixture of beauty and what is not beautiful, and given that Socrates is looking for the form due to whose presence things are adorned and appear beautiful, Hippias's next answer is gold. Gold is not a thing. When it is present, things are adorned and appear beautiful. The problem with Hippias's answer is not simply that it is an example rather than a definition. Even more, it is problematic because once again it is an answer that would not allow for the combination of beautiful and the ugly or plain that is found in things. Gold covers over what is ugly or plain. It is as if Hippias were to say, "You want beauty? Add some gold." The word translated here as "adorned," *kosmeitai,* has two different meanings. One is related to *kosmos* as beautiful order. One is related to beautification in cosmetics. An order or arrangement of things that by themselves are not beautiful allows those things both to show themselves as what they are and to be beautiful. Cosmetics, instead, covers things that are not beautiful and, by doing so, makes them beautiful.[22] Once again, Hippias does not understand the power of beauty, which is to be beautiful in and through what is by itself ugly or plain. Socrates's double responds with the example of the eyes of Pheidias's statue of Athena, which were not made of gold but of ivory, as were the face, feet, and hands, and the middle of the statue's eyes, which were not made even of ivory but of stone (290a8–d4). Even stone is beautiful, Hippias agrees, when it is fitting (*prepōn*) (290c7).

The fitting (*to prepon*) is what strikes the senses in such a way as to be conspicuous or clearly seen. The fitting, thus, has to do with appearance, and can denote either the shining forth that makes something susceptible to being clearly seen, or the being seen itself, that is, either the appearance or the perception. The conspicuous is not just what is seen, but what is clearly seen. The conspicuous stands out for us, is obvious or striking. Another meaning of *to prepon* is the fitting or seemly. What is fitting is appropriate or suitable to something else. What is seemly is what is of good or pleasant appearance, or what conforms to propriety. What is true of beauty as *to prepon,* then, is that it involves something that can be seen standing out so that it can be seen clearly; it involves my perception of that which stands out; and it involves the fit of one thing to another such that something stands out. Socrates utilizes the third sense of *to prepon* and goads Hippias by suggesting then that when we fill the pot he mentioned previously with beautiful soup, a ladle of fig wood would be more beautiful in the pot than one of gold. The homely answer irritates Hippias, but he is forced to agree with it.

Frustrated, Hippias attempts one more definition. You might think his definition would reflect what was learned in the discussion of the last example. If it did, it could include the simple idea of seeming or appearance, the idea of something that appears standing out even more, or the idea of the fitting or suitable. All of that could be encompassed by the idea of *to prepon* perhaps best translated as *the seemly,* should we strain the resources of the English language to put all this in one word in this context. For Hippias, it would be easier, as he could simply say *to prepon.*

Instead, ignoring what could be learned from their discussion so far, Hippias reverts to another example of beauty as a cover-up of what is not beautiful at all. If you are wealthy, healthy, and honored, it is beautiful to give your parents a beautiful funeral and for you to be beautifully and magnificently buried by your children. What a grim answer! Death is not so beautiful for a Greek, given what existence is like in Hades or the familial tomb. The funeral covers over an eternal discomfort that awaits both parents and children. To what end are wealth, health, and honor if we are all simply to end up as insubstantial, flitting shades. The greatest human beings would not be covered by this definition, as Socrates points out in a question using the example of Achilles, son of the immortal goddess Thetis (292e8). Clearly, he would not bury her. In response to the refutation, Plato makes sure we will think about the inescapable bleakness of death, when he euphemistically tells Socrates to go to Hades. "Go to blessedness!" Hippias says. "The human being's questions are not even respectful (*euphēma*)" (293a2–3). Not only is Hippias's third definition too narrow—it does not cover stone, wood, human being, god, activity, learning—but once again it is beauty as something that hides something else rather than fitting it or bringing it out or making it conspicuous. Hippias cannot even speak of our eventual residence in the bleak afterlife without using a euphemism ("blessedness").

Hippias, then, is not like Theaetetus who pushes past every objection to try to find an answer. Hippias's whole approach is euphemism. Nor, though, does Hippias attack Socrates or simply push him around like beautiful, bossy, lazy Meno. Instead, Hippias just gives some pretty answer. The beautiful for him could be characterized as the pretty, where the pretty is what is on the surface and is appealing because it hides something. The beautiful is not for him something that enables what it qualifies to shine forth, to be manifest or conspicuous, and at once to change or attain a different level. Similarly, Hippias's answers hide something about himself. They hide the fact that he does not know, that he is ignorant. They hide it, and they prevent him from changing as a result. They prevent him from looking for the answer. Hippias does not admit to his vulnerability—in this case, his ignorance—and so he is not as a result of admitted vulnerability or ignorance plunged into the search for an answer. Hippias repeatedly says he has the answer or could get it if he were just alone to come up with it. Hippias, then, does not see the importance of the two—that is, of Socrates and him together, forming a pair that could change Hippias and bring something, in this case the beautiful, to light. He does not see the importance of publicly admitting his own vulnerability. Instead, he hides it by saying something pretty, something seemly in the lower sense of that term.

Hippias, then, since for him beauty is only a surface covering, is not comfortable with anyone noticing his vulnerability or ignorance. Instead, he is all about power. He makes more money than the renowned intellects of the ancient world, he says early in the dialogue, because he has wisdom and power. When Socrates, in his second definition, suggests beauty is power, Hippias not surprisingly goes along emphatically with the idea (*Sphodra,* he says—295e10). Socrates, having found a point of agreement with Hippias, then goes on to make one of his usual points about power. The beautiful, he says, cannot simply be power, but must be power for something good, since power for something that is not good is not beautiful but ugly. Power for something good, he says, is the beneficial (*to ōphelimon,* 296e5). Then he makes an unexpected point, that the beautiful as the beneficial is the cause of the good. The reader wonders about the sudden turn in the dialogue. Why is the beautiful the cause of the good? The reader of the *Republic* might think instead that for Socrates the good is the cause of the beautiful since the good is the cause of truth. One imagines, or hopes, that Hippias, too, is surprised at the claim.

Moreover, we know from other dialogues, such as the *Meno* and the *Republic,* that Socrates thinks that the greatest human power is knowledge or wisdom. He says that as well in this dialogue. The powerful is most beautiful, Socrates says, and so wisdom is the most beautiful of all (295e). Wisdom is knowledge of the good, as we can conclude from, for example, the development in the *Republic* of the knowledge that is needed for virtue that takes us all the way up the divided line to the idea of the good. Hence, Socrates's claim that the beautiful is the cause of the good implies that wisdom is the cause of the good. Once again, this seems to contradict the *Republic* where Socrates argues that the good is the cause of truth and knowledge. Socrates, then, must mean something different here, namely, that when we are wise, we become good, as indicated in the *Republic* as well as the *Phaedrus.* As noted in chapter 1, we learn from the *Phaedrus* that when we are wise by recollecting the form of the beautiful, we become good to our beloved. As noted in chapter 2, from the *Republic* we learn that when we are wise by having knowledge of all time and all being all the way up the divided line to being and ideas, to all time and all being, and to the brightest of being, the form of the good in the *Republic,* we acquire virtue and will serve the city.

Infuriatingly, Hippias does not take Socrates's bait. When Socrates says that the beautiful is the cause of the good, we can assume that he wants Hippias to ask about the claim. Socrates's counterintuitive claim shifts the subject from ontology to human beings. But Hippias will not show vulnerability by asking Socrates what in the world he means. Surely Hippias knows that beauty can cause evil, as any Athenian would know by thinking about treacherous Alcibiades or Meno. Socrates goes off as a result instead into what appears to be a bad argument that since the beautiful is the cause of the good, the beautiful is not good. We want Hippias to ask or say, Socrates, don't you see you have only shown that the beautiful is not *the* good, so that the beautiful could still be good? But Hippias, true to form, does not.

Hippias is not wise, then, because forms do not show up for him. The opening of the dialogue is heavily ironic, we can conclude, when Socrates starts off by addressing his interlocutor as "Hippias, the beautiful and wise" (281a1). Hippias's beauty is a beautiful covering that does not allow for vulnerability, that is, for awareness of one thing's need of being accompanied by another that can make what is present in the first shine forth, a shining forth that the first could not accomplish by itself. Hippias needs Socrates but does not know it, and covers his need with an anxious, but showy, prettiness. Socrates, on the other hand, needs a blunt Socrates who can keep him thinking about the good and the useful, which are crude, and a beauty-conscious Hippias who can get him to realize how important seeming is for beauty.

Socrates's last significant attempt to make progress is his definition of beauty as the pleasure that accompanies sight and hearing (298a6–7). With it, he pushes toward the view that beauty has something to do with form, for he rejects the possibility that what is crucial to the definition of beauty is what is crucial in each part of the definition—pleasure that accompanies sight, pleasure that accompanies hearing. Instead, what is crucial for the definition of the beautiful is something else common (*koinon*) to the two parts and something that is missing from, for example, pleasure from sex (300a10). Socrates mentions form (298b4), but Hippias as usual does not take him up on the hint.

The hint is that the answer might *be* form itself (or might centrally involve it). Specifically, Socrates brings in two examples of beautiful things from which we would not ordinarily say we derive pleasure through sight or hearing—namely, beautiful practices and laws—and asks whether they are beautiful through some other form than pleasure through sight and hearing. Hippias concurs, twice, presumably because the beauty of human beings; decorations, paintings, and sculpture; voices and music; and speeches and stories *is* different than the beauty of practices and laws. In fact, the last two examples on the list itself are different from the others. The beauty of speeches and stories, like the beauty of practices and laws, is different from the beauty of human beings; decorations, paintings, and sculpture; voices and music. Socrates is pushing for the idea that the beauty of material things is not something material. He pushes for that idea by gradually bringing in examples of beauty that are not material: the beauty of speeches, stories, practices, and laws. The movement of the argument is reminiscent of Socrates's claim in the *Philebus* that there is no such thing as bodily pleasure. The point there is that what we call bodily pleasure is pleasure experienced by the soul. The point here seems to be that the beauty even of material things is not material.

Hippias agrees with Socrates's claim that the beauty of practices and laws is different than the other examples. We should not be surprised, since we know that it was the example of beautiful practices that led Socrates to ask Hippias what is the beautiful in the first place. Hippias in that early part of the dialogue swears by Zeus and declares that he has achieved a great reputation regarding beautiful practices, specifically by describing in detail what a youth ought to pursue, pursuits that are both beautiful and lawful (286a3–b7). At this point, having gotten Hippias where he wants him, Socrates indicates that what he is looking for is the perception that comes *through* hearing and sight (298d1–3). So it is not only that Socrates is looking for one form that covers (or is common to) all cases, but that the form he is looking for is form itself. He starts this movement of the argument by distinguishing the pleasures of food, drink, and sex, which have more to do with being filled and emptied, from the pleasure that accompanies sight and hearing, which have to do with discernment or perception of form.

Another hinted point that Hippias misses is that, in beauty, both together have something that each separately does not. Hippias ought to pick up on this point given the earlier discussion of the fitting (*to prepon*) where they agreed that gold, stone, or ivory are or are not beautiful depending on what they are with. Socrates's point, of course, is not that the pleasure from hearing and the pleasure from sight have something in common that each does not but that two things can have something in common, beauty, that each does not have (303a2–3). Hippias also misses another suggested point in the same passage, namely, that it would be very irrational (*pollē gar alogia,* 303c3–6) if in the case of beauty, both together are something that each separately is not. Much like the *Meno,* the quest for an answer stalls here not because the interlocutor does not have the resources for an answer. Instead, it stalls because Hippias does not draw on the resource that they have, namely, the recollection from their previous discussion that two things together can have a beauty that each separately does not. Hippias has a good memory and is smart, but he does not seem very philosophic in the Socratic/Platonic sense. He does not seem to be able to draw an argument out of the discussion of an example. In other words, he has a good memory but does not excel at Socratic recollection. Like Meno, he has a good memory but cannot philosophize. The reason for it is different, though. Meno has a decidedly tyrannical personality, perhaps due to his beauty and the power it gives him. He will not inquire, but demands that pleasing answers be given him. Hippias, on the other hand, has an impulse to cover over anything plain, ugly, or threatening. He cannot philosophize because he cannot linger over what is ordinary or ugly until the beauty within it becomes conspicuous.

The dialogue comes near to its end when Hippias expresses frustration with Socrates for engaging in unseemly arguments by making fine distinctions or by chopping up "great and continuous bodies of being" into pieces. Interestingly, though, it is Hippias, not Socrates, who at least in argument is unable to comprehend wholes, for it is Hippias who adamantly denies that there are cases in which both together are different than each separately. If he were right about that, there would be no wholes, only heaps, since in a whole, a material quality becomes a part, rather than a mere quantity of matter, when it is together with other parts. There is in the case of wholes a kind of increase or, to use Socrates's term, a whole that surpasses its parts.

What Socrates knows, then, when he says he seems to himself to know what the proverb means that says "the beautiful things are difficult" is that there is such a thing as the visibly surpassing or transcendent. He knows that in the realm of appearance both together are something other than each separately. Though this is, in one sense, irrational, he sees and knows that it is true. When both are together, there is something other than just both together. When both are together, something else arises, called *beauty*. It is irrational because indeterminate, not easily countable. Is beauty some third thing separate from the original two? No. It is in and through them. Is beauty nothing but each of the two? No. For separately, the two are not beautiful. Both together should be two. Instead, they seem to be three. Following Socrates, we could call beauty, since it is something other that arises, the surpassing or transcendent. In the case of the beautiful, that something other that arises is form. Beauty is form that arises or comes to light *for us* when two things are together. Beauty, in other words, is the appearance or perception of form. Socrates, then, has knowledge and a difficulty since what he knows is itself difficult, namely, that in some cases, both together are different than each is on its own.

For Socrates in the *Hippias Major*, then, the beautiful has to do with the fundamental ambiguity of being. Being is double, for it consists of formed beings. The good, as I have argued elsewhere, is the presence of form in beings. Hence, the good is, as Socrates says in the *Republic*, the cause of truth and knowledge—where truth is *alētheia* or the unhiddenness, showing through, or disclosure of form. Only if form is in a thing can there be truth since truth is the unhiddenness or disclosure of that form. The beautiful, too, is about twos. Beauty results when one thing causes the form of another to appear. Beauty is close to truth where truth refers more to the process by which form becomes unhidden and beauty more to the result of that process, namely, the appearance of form or the surpassing. When two things are put together in a certain way, a form that was already present and realized in the first changes its manifest state: it shines forth and is seen. The good and the beautiful, then, are not outside of being for Plato. Instead, they are hyperbeings or second-order beings—or, to use a different language, transcategorials.

The beyond being in Plato, then, is not the same as the beyond being in Levinas. For the beyond being in Plato, whether it is the beyond being of the good or the surpassing of the beautiful, has to do with form—with form, the immanence of form, and the shining forth or transcendence of form. The beyond being in Plato is in the realm of the light, form, and generality not, as it is in Levinas, in the realm of what is before or beyond the light because it has to do with the singular. This type of interpretation of Socrates's beyond being fits more the overall Platonic problematic than Levinas's interpretation does and, in addition, makes it possible to preserve the difference between Socrates's and Levinas's views of love and desire that section 2 of this chapter delineates.

We are left once again, then, with two types of vulnerability to the other, one a Levinasian open vulnerability, a vulnerability not to the form but to the singularity of the other, and the other a Socratic-Platonic vulnerability to the other's form that involves responding to *what* things or persons are and relating to them based on what fits them as a result of what they are. Each type of vulnerability is important, I assert, because each is necessary both for our good dealing with ourselves and with other people. It is necessary and good both to respond to people based on what fits them and thus to play a role in enabling them to be what they are and, as well, to respond to them beyond or without reference to what they are at any particular time and by so doing to participate in enabling them to be or do something that is utterly new. Leaving this gesture toward an argument for a more comprehensive notion of relationships to the other aside, this chapter's consideration of desire and need has shown us that both Plato and Levinas, in discussing desire, delineate an essential human vulnerability to the other while the chapter's attention to the concept of creation and to the distinction between the eternal and the new indicates that the essential vulnerabilities on which their concepts of desire rest are significantly different in kind.[23]

CHAPTER 4

Knowledge

Crucial to Levinas's thinking about relating to the other is the distinction he draws, in *Totality and Infinity,* between the interiority of learning understood as Socratic recollection and the transitivity of what he calls *teaching* or *instruction:* "The transitivity of teaching," he says, "and not the interiority of reminiscence, manifests being" (*TI* 101/74). As a result, teaching, not maieutics, is the precondition of knowledge where the precondition is "a *pure* 'knowledge' or 'experience'" that, unlike the rest of knowledge or knowledge in an ordinary sense, brings me more than I am capable of, brings me an other beyond the capacity of the I. Teaching, Levinas says, "does not operate as maieutics." Instead, the soul is "capable of containing more than it can draw from itself" (*TI* 180/155).

Operative in the distinction between maieutics and teaching is Levinas's view that in knowledge we wish to approach the known in all its otherness without marking it: "Knowledge or theory designates first a relation with being such that the knowing being lets the known being manifest itself while respecting its alterity and without marking it in any way whatever by this cognitive relation" (*TI* 42/12). But Socratic knowledge cannot achieve this goal since it fundamentally involves simply bringing out what is already present. Socratic maieutics awakens what is already in me (*TI* 69/44). The Socratic master does not genuinely teach but "simply arouse[s] the reminiscence of former visions" (*TI* 86/58).

But is Levinas right about Socratic maieutics? Socrates does tell Theaetetus, in the dialogue by the same name, that he is a midwife of souls and that some of those who associate with him discover in themselves and bring forth many fine things (*Tht.* 150d2–8). At the same time, though, Socrates indicates that some offspring are true and others false (b9–c3) and that he is ready to deprive Theaetetus of the latter kind of offspring just as midwives sometimes deprive women of theirs. This complication in the metaphor of psychic midwifery suggests something less than the Levinasian claim that Socratic knowledge is the simple explication of what is already inside us. For its being in us is not sufficient for its being knowledge.

It is for a different reason that Socrates suggests for knowledge both that we must search within and, at the same time, that what we discover in such a search may not be sufficient. In the *Meno,* where the topic is not maieutics but recollection, the point of Socrates's exhorting the interlocutor to turn to himself is clear. Knowledge is not placed in you by another but requires real and zealous inquiry. Think, Socrates suggests there; don't just absorb. That is what he means by searching within. Meno really is recalcitrant to genuine inquiry. He perceives it as slavish. He puts up roadblocks to its success such as the famous eristic argument (the *Meno* argument) that it is not possible to seek either what you do or do not know. There is no need to seek the former and no way to seek the latter since you wouldn't know it if you found it. Socrates's response to the argument is that in between complete knowledge and complete ignorance is a state of partial knowledge, metaphorically described as knowing something but having forgotten it.

Theaetetus is quite a different personality than Meno, however. While Meno would render inquiry impossible, Theaetetus is eager in argument and too sanguine about its possibilities. (For example, he defines knowledge as perception though irrational magnitudes, about which he made discoveries, cannot be perceived.) As a result, one of Socrates's main activities in the *Theaetetus* is to show Theaetetus problems and engender in him some epistemological caution. The two dialogues are companion dialogues—after all, one is about virtue and the other about knowledge and, according to Socrates in an argument never successfully refuted in the *Meno,* virtue is knowledge—with one suggesting a need for boldness in inquiry and the other a need for caution. Both dialogues indicate, in their imagery, that the knowledge we seek both is and is not inside us. In the *Meno,* we have but have forgotten what we seek. In the *Theaetetus,* knowledge is the result of the move from merely possessing knowledge to actually having or holding it. Similarly, we can contrast birds that we have in a birdcage with those we take out and hold in our hands. To make the difference with Levinas complete, the image further suggests that some of the birds are true and others false knowledge, just as when we are pregnant, we in a sense do and do not have what we have conceived but, even after bringing forth, some of what is brought forth is true and the rest merely an image. The point suggested in the *Theaetetus,* then, is that there is a method of inquiry but it is not veridical or foolproof. The method is one of explicating what is both immanent and transcendent to thought, that is, of making the implicit explicit, but doing so may simply bring out wind eggs, that is, false opinions or suppositions.

If we are right to bring together all the conclusions about Platonic inquiry and recollection into one account here as I have done, including the claim made in the *Phaedrus* that recollection is moving from many perceptions to the one idea implicit in them, then Levinas is wrong to say that maieutics brings me only what I contain. Instead, it brings me what I both do and do not contain. Knowledge for Plato is not of what is immanent, but of what is both transcendent and immanent. In addition, not every opinion immanent to my soul is knowledge, since some are false. What then is the real difference between Socrates and Levinas on the preconditions for knowledge?

An answer lies in what is absolutely other or absolutely foreign: "The absolutely foreign alone can instruct us," Levinas says, and only human beings are absolutely foreign (*TI* 73/46). They cannot be captured in a concept, comprehended by a theme, located in a category. They are "refractory to every typology, to every genus, to every characterology, to every classification" (*TI* 73/46). Our relation to the absolutely other is not disclosure but truth. Truth is "a modality of the relation between the same and the other" (*TI* 64/35), specifically, with the absolutely other: "a relation with the absolutely other [*l'absolument autre*], or truth" (*TI* 29/xvii). Sometimes Levinas refers not to otherness but to exteriority and calls our relation to it *respect:* "the respect for this metaphysical exteriority," he says, "constitutes truth" (*TI* 29/xvii). Truth is not disclosure because "to recognize truth to be disclosure [*dévoilement*] is to refer it to the horizon of him who discloses" (*TI* 64/36). For Levinas, then, in addition to an ordinary knowledge and truth, there is a pure knowledge understood as bringing me more than I contain as well as truth understood as relation with what is absolutely other. It is because of knowledge and truth understood this way that teaching, not maieutics, manifests being. Levinas's point here, and his rhetorical approach, is to critique knowledge by showing that only the ethical can achieve what knowledge aims to achieve, thus justifying his periodic description of ethical ideas in epistemological terms (*truth* for our relation to the other as such and *teaching* for what we receive from the other in such relations). If things are best understood or characterized in terms of their goal, then ethics can be construed in epistemological terms. For it is ethics that achieves the fundamental epistemological goals.

The same point can be made in a different way, however. Rather than constructing the ethical in epistemological terms in order to show the difference between ethics and knowledge in some ordinary or Platonic sense, sometimes Levinas simply contrasts the two, that is, he simply contrasts knowledge and the ethical. A formative contrast for Levinas, then, is the contrast between maieutics and knowledge, on the one hand, and teaching and revelation, on the other. Using this rhetorical strategy, *knowledge* denotes not the ethical constructed in epistemological or pure terms as Levinasian pure knowledge but instead simply denotes knowledge in some ordinary or Platonic sense. At the same time, *revelation* in this strategy does have a pure Levinasian meaning. As a result, it does not mean disclosure or unveiling but has a Levinasian pure or absolute sense of "manifestation of the Other," that is, "the manifestation of a face over and beyond form" (*TI* 66/37). The one who manifests himself "at each instant undoes the form he presents" (*TI* 66/37). For Levinas, unlike Plato's Socrates, form does not show but betrays the other, congeals him or her. Form is not adequate to the other since form "incessantly betray[s] its own manifestation, congeal[s] into a plastic form" (*TI* 66/37). Not revealed through form, the other instead is revealed through speech. "The interlocutor alone," Levinas says, "is the term of pure experience" (*TI* 67/39).

In his discussion of knowledge and the ethical, then, we have a set of *pure* epistemological terms—ethical ideas constructed in epistemological terms—including *experience, knowledge, truth,* and *revelation.* To round out the list, another term to consider is *meaning.* As Levinas gives each of the preceding terms an absolute or pure sense, so he does with *meaning. Experience, knowledge, truth,* and *revelation,* in their absolute or pure sense, all have to do with something like reference. In the realm of absolute knowledge, what then would *meaning* or *sense* convey? "The way of undoing the form adequate to the Same so as to present oneself as other is to signify or have a meaning [*un sens*]," Levinas says (*TI* 66/37). The closest the other can come, in other words, to having what we would ordinarily call *meaning* is to have a particular way of undoing forms presented and showing herself independent of them. This brings us back to speaking since "to present oneself by signifying is to speak" (*TI* 66/37). In speaking, the other presents himself without giving himself: "to signify is not to give" (*TI* 66/37). To speak is to offer forms without being identified with them. To *experience, knowledge, truth,* and *revelation* we must, then, add Levinas's other absolute epistemological terms, *meaning* or *sense, signification* and *speech.* All of these absolute or pure terms are needed if we are to think about how Plato and Levinas do and do not differ on knowledge.

In what follows, I will show that knowledge, for Plato, is not of what is immanent but of what is both immanent and transcendent and that as a result Platonic maieutics and recollection are more similar to Levinasian teaching than Levinas thinks since both respond to something beyond or transcending the self (section 1); and, after discussing and delineating the variety of absolute epistemological terms Levinas uses to talk about our relationship with what is utterly beyond us (section 2), I will show that the real difference in their epistemological standpoints is Levinas's idea that we are taught only by what is absolutely foreign or absolutely other, that is, by an other who utterly transcends and cannot be experienced as immanent (section 3). If I am correct about that difference, then once again we can conclude that, though both Plato and Levinas are philosophers of the other, their philosophies of the other are of significantly different types.

1.

There are many questions we can ask about Platonic forms (even leaving aside not the least among them, the question whether we are fully justified in referring to them as *the forms* as if they were reified entities or things). We can ask, for example, what they are and also what is their relation to things. A common answer Plato's Socrates gives to the first question is that a form or idea is a *one over many.* In the *Meno,* for example, Socrates says about virtues that "even if they are many and various, all of them have one and the same form due to which they are virtues" (*Meno* 72c6–8); in the *Republic* that "we are accustomed to posit some one particular form for each of the *manys* to which we apply the same name" (*Rep.* 10.596a6–7); and in the *Parmenides,* Parmenides says, "when some many seem to you to be large, perhaps there seems to be some one idea that is the same when you look over them all, hence you believe that the large is one" (*Prm.* 132a2–4). In each of these examples, the form is an ontological principle, something by virtue of which things that are many are, in another respect, one. Forms are, as well, epistemological principles or that by virtue of which we know things. In the divided line passage in the *Republic,* knowledge of the forms is the highest type of knowledge, called *noēsis* or intellectual intuition. Other types of knowledge are derivative of it. *Dianoia,* or thought, for example, depends for its own reasoning on the assumption or hypothesis of forms. Finally, in the *Parmenides,* after showing Socrates a number of problems in explicating forms, Parmenides suggests not only that forms are epistemological principles but also that they are dialogical or conversational principles. If a person does not distinguish forms for things, he says, "he will not even have anything to which to turn his thought," and "he will utterly destroy the power of dialogue" (135b8, c1–2).

In taking this approach, Plato's Socrates—or, with more historical accuracy, Plato—follows Heraclitus who, preceding Plato, posits a nonmaterial principle of things called the *logos.* It is an ontological principle since, according to Heraclitus, "all things happen according to this logos," and I use it to "distinguish each thing according to its nature and say how it is" (1). So that according to which things come to be what they are is also that according to which I say what they are. I use the logos to collect things together and select them out as different from other things. Plato would say I do this not in accordance with their logos but in accordance with their form or idea, which is the character that things different in number have in common by virtue of which we appropriately call them by the same name.

In addition, according to Parmenides in the dialogue named after him, that according to which things are what they are and by virtue of which we know them as what they are is also that by virtue of which we can communicate what they are one to another. The logos, Heraclitus says, is common but hidden: "the logos is common," he says (2), but "nature likes to hide itself" (123). We can understand the logos if we will really listen to it: "listening not to me but the logos" (50). We, to an extent, already know the logos: "The Lord whose oracle is at Delphi neither speaks nor hides but gives a sign" (247). We know it and don't know it. It is hidden but indicated.

So, too, for Plato, we know it and do not know it. As the *Phaedrus* definition that we have looked at in previous chapters suggests, we perceive the form in many things, but do not understand those things according to form. When we do—when we move from many perceptions to what is one through reasoning—we are recollecting. What is implied in the *Phaedrus* definition of recollection is that the form is implicit in our perceptions and that recollection is making that form explicit.

Utilizing the *Phaedrus* definition alone is not adequate due to the other, different definition in the *Meno.* It may be compatible with the *Phaedrus* definition, but there is not enough explanation of it to be sure. But we may utilize the *Republic*'s discussion of knowledge on the divided line to make our case. The line is, as others have pointed out, a proportion suggesting an analogy. There's more than one analogy to be drawn, though, since the middle sections of the proportion are equal. One is, as images are to things, so things are to forms. We do not know an image if we do not know the thing of which it is an image. Similarly, we do not know a thing unless we know the form the thing images. Imagination is seeing an image as an image. Trust, on the other hand, is simply seeing something of a certain kind: I see a tree. I see a person. I see a flower. I do not deduce a tree, a person, a flower. Trust is not a discursive reasoning process. It is immediate. That is what makes it analogous to *noēsis.* It is, however, not utterly immediate. For implicit in my trusting seeing is the form of tree, the form of human being, the form of flower. Trust, then, plays the same role in the divided line that perception does in the definition of recollection in the *Republic.* It is a type of cognition that is immediate and has knowledge of a form implicit within it. Recollection, in the *Phaedrus,* or movement up the divided line, in the *Republic,* is a process of making the form explicit, or of moving from many perceptions to the form, that is one, through reasoning.

A form or idea, then, is a one over many in more than one way. It is one form for many particulars or instances, as in one form of virtue for many instances of virtue. It is one form for many people who are thinking it. It is one form for a number of people who talk about it. A form is common to many. When we dialogue—when we communicate—we share among ourselves that common form.

How, then, do transcendence and immanence come in? Does Socrates think forms or ideas are in things? Or beyond them? Immanent? Or transcendent? The common view of Plato is that ideas for him are transcendent while they are immanent for Aristotle. In the *Parmenides,* however, Parmenides points out to Socrates that if the idea is in one thing that is separate from another thing the idea is in, then the idea is separate from itself, which, if we employ ordinary uses of the terms *in* and *separate,* is absurd: "being one and the same, it will be present at once and as a whole in things that are many and separate, and thus it would itself be separate from itself" (131b1–2). However, in response to Socrates's suggestion that idea could be like day that is in different places at the same time, he also argues that idea cannot be over things without the idea being sectioned, like a sail a part of which is over each of a number of people (131b7–9). He also claims regarding the specific idea of unity that "it is nowhere" since "it is neither in itself nor in another" (138a2–3). What are we to conclude from these claims? That ideas are neither in nor beyond things? Why not conclude, instead, that the relation between ideas and things is a unique relation, one that is somewhat like the relationship we call *in* and somewhat like the relationship we call *beyond* or *over*? It can be in many things without being separate from itself. And it can be beyond or over a number of things and still retain its whole nature. Then we could say the idea is both immanent and transcendent though not in the way the water is in the pail nor beyond or over in the sense that the sky is beyond or over the trees. This, presumably, is the point of Parmenides's particular way of questioning Socrates—to push him to more adequately characterize ideas.

What would that mean in practice? It would mean that the form both is in a thing and transcends it since it also is in other things; it is both in me and in others with whom I communicate since I know it but they know it as well; it is in me but beyond me since when I know it what I am knowing is the form of something outside me. Even more, the form is transcendent in a sense we have seen in a previous chapter, namely, the form limits me. In answering the question, what is virtue, I cannot give just any answer, not correctly anyway, but am limited by the form itself. As we saw about the *Meno,* what is suggested there is that virtue is knowledge and knowledge is being limited by and following the forms. We do not conduct our reason as the full title of Descartes's *Discourse on Method* suggests. Instead, reason is a type of following or being limited by something—something of which we have an inkling, but which we do not know in all clarity. It is not so hidden that we have no guide, nor is it so evident that we need not make an effort to find it. Hence, our relation to forms is a mixture of effort and response, of doing and suffering. We must act, because what we seek is hidden. We must be responsive since what we seek is partially known to us and known in such a way that our responsive relation to it may guide us to what we seek. Hence, as stated before, Socrates uses images that suggest what we seek is partially known—known but forgotten in the *Meno,* in a birdcage but not in our hands in the *Theaetetus.* None of these images, however, suggests that what we know when we know is, simply, ourselves. In the *Meno,* for example, what we know are things—all things—which we knew before but forgot. In the *Phaedrus,* what we know is the beauty of the youth, which beauty simply knocks me on my back, a physical posture that suggests awe before the boy and before the form of beauty the boy makes manifest. The beauty we know is meant by Socrates to be transcendent. The process of our knowing it is an ascent up to the hyperouranian place—the place beyond the heavens—where the beautiful is described as sitting on a throne.

2.

What I am suggesting, as in previous chapters, is that there is greater kinship between Levinas and Plato than Levinas maintains. Neither endorses the modern idea of the self that can only return to itself. Supposing that what I have outlined in the previous section of this chapter is correct, then Levinas is wrong to say that knowledge, for Plato, is simply a return to the self. And Levinas does say it, numerous times. Let us pay attention to what he in fact says.

"Teaching," Levinas says, "is not reducible to maieutics; it comes from the exterior and brings me more than I contain" (*TI* 51/22). Here is the idea familiar to us by now that in the maieutic process we do not leave the self. What is Levinas's point in making this claim? About teaching, Levinas goes on to say, "In its non-violent transitivity, the very epiphany of the face is produced" (51/22). One point then is nonviolence. Teaching, through its transitivity, is nonviolent. But so, as we have seen in chapter 1, is understanding, at least as Plato conceives it. Understanding of form is, for him, the very source of nonviolent relations, of relations that do not reduce to self-assertion, to outrage or assault, to a zero-sum game, to *hybris.* Levinas goes on to contrast maieutics with the transitive action in which reason "is found to be in a position to *receive*" (51). As stated before, however, what is the helmsman falling on his back if not an image of the receptivity of intellectual intuition (*nous*)? We cannot properly give Levinas his place in the history of thought if we do not remember that the modern self closed in on itself is a departure from premodern ones that center around the self's fundamental receptivity to or dependence on what is. To the extent that they are proponents of receptivity, we can see Levinas and Plato as companions, both arguing for our fundamentally other-directed nature. In reading Levinas, it is important to remember that Bacon, with his rape metaphor for our understanding of nature (forcing nature to give up her secrets) and Descartes, with his emphasis on mastery (mastery and possession of nature being for him the goal of science or knowledge) see themselves, correctly, as introducing something new or different with their idea of the autonomous, masterful self.

Levinas does repeatedly conflate premodern and modern conceptions of the self when, for example, he accuses Plato of believing in a sovereign soul: in "rational thought," Levinas says of Plato, "the sovereignty of the soul is manifest" (*TI* 114/86). The Platonic contemplative soul's relation with its objects, according to Levinas, "confirms the same . . . in its sovereignty" (*TI* 114/86). But what of the philosopher we have seen described in the *Republic* as having perceived all time and all being—all the way to the first beings, the forms, and the first among them, the form of the good? This philosopher, because of his experience of a goodness beyond him, is beyond injustice, beyond the desire to have more for himself. Like the lover in the *Phaedrus,* the philosopher who perceives all time and all being including the idea of the good then proceeds to serve others.

Levinas is convinced, though, that Socrates conceives of a self that can only return to itself: "The ideal of Socratic truth . . . rests on the essential self-sufficiency of the same, its identity in ipseity, its egoism. Philosophy is an egology" (*TI* 44/13). At this point, we could question this picture of Socratic truth, described in the *Meno* as a type of slavery or following and in the *Phaedrus* as falling on your back in awe. But there are more, and less metaphorical, passages than these—passages indicating that one of Socrates's main points is the non-self-sufficiency of truth.

In the *Gorgias,* for example, one of Socrates's main points is that speeches are not about speeches. This dialogue about rhetoric progresses from the easygoing and pleasant Gorgias to the enthused and not too dialectically skillful Polus to the utterly selfish Callicles, portrayed as the dark and dangerous result of the views put forth first and more pleasantly by Gorgias. For Callicles, justice is for the strong to rule the weak and have more. How does this utterly egocentric view unfold out of the views of Gorgias? The whole point of Socrates's confrontation with Gorgias is to push him to show that speeches are about something—that they have content and are other-directed, not simply turned in on themselves.

It is to emphasize this point—that speeches are other-directed, not self-sufficient—that Plato has Socrates promote the question, what is rhetoric about. It is about speeches, Gorgias responds (*Grg.* 449e1). This amounts to saying that speeches are about speeches. This self-directedness is not adequate to Socrates. Speeches about what subject, he wants to know. But all the other subjects—health and disease, good and bad bodily fitness, and so on—are taken. Doctors have the art of speaking about the former, trainers about the latter, and so on. Eventually, Gorgias claims, with a little nudging by Socrates, that rhetoricians persuade, in the courts, about what is just and what unjust (*Grg.* 454b5–7). But, Socrates points out, if so, why does Gorgias say that rhetoric is a neutral tool to which knowledge of justice has to be added—and for whose unjust instrumental use rhetoric should not be blamed? For if the rhetor knows justice, he will be just and no additional knowledge of justice need be added (*Grg.* 460b6–7). Gorgias cannot have it both ways, Socrates suggests. Either rhetoric is a neutral tool to which justice must be added, and then it is not clear what its subject matter is, or it is about justice, that is, it is knowledge of justice, in which case it is unclear how it can, in some cases, be unjust.

Socrates's point is that speeches are about something other than themselves. There are options for what they might be about in the case of rhetoric. Gorgias, probably out of shame, picked justice. Socrates, to the contrary, suggests later in the dialogue that rhetoric is about flattery. It is to justice what cookery is to medicine: it does not know about and produce some good but, instead, knows about and produces pleasure in the listener through flattery. Rhetoric, instead of producing a beneficial correction in a sick soul, makes the sick soul feel good through feeding it what pleases it.

Speeches have a subject matter, Socrates indicates. They do not simply turn in on themselves. They are guided, shaped, and limited by their subject matter. Gorgias does not seem to see—or does not want to admit—the potentially unjust consequences of his view to the contrary, that is, his view that speeches are not about anything but are content- and value-neutral tools. Callicles makes the implications evident. Impervious to conventional views, he is an utter proponent of the view that the best life is one in which we are unrestrained and unshaped by any limit or guide. According to Callicles, justice is not a type of response or receptivity, but unrestrained rule. It is for the stronger to rule the weaker and have more (*Grg.* 483d5–6). In addition, virtue and happiness, according to him, are luxury, unrestraint, and freedom (*Grg.* 492c4–5). He rejects the idea even of moderation understood as self-rule and says, in response to Socrates's suggestion of it, "How can a man be happy if he is a slave to anything?" (*Grg.* 491e5–6). According to Socrates responding to Callicles's whole train of thought, the good man will speak looking toward something (*Grg.* 503d6–8). The best rhetors aim at improving their fellow citizens. They do not simply gratify themselves and look to their own interest (*Grg.* 502d10–503b5). The best speeches and speakers, then, do not look unrestrainedly to themselves but are limited by and attempt to produce what is good.

As, for Socrates, speeches are not simply about speeches but are of something, so, for Socrates, ideas are not mere thoughts. Socrates, as a young man, learns this from Parmenides. To solve the problem that we posit a form to account for many things that are great and so we must posit another form to account for the increased many that are great (the things plus the form, ad infinitum), Socrates suggests that a form might simply be a thought in our soul (*Prm.* 132b3–6). Parmenides, in good Parmenidean fashion, asks him whether a thought is of nothing or of something. It's impossible for it to be of nothing, Socrates says. It must be of something—and, he says prompted by Parmenides, it is of something that is not something that is not. Specifically, Parmenides suggests and Socrates concurs, it is of something thought thinks of as some one character or look (*idea*) for many, and the character or look is the form. As the historical Parmenides states that "the same thing is for thinking as for being,"[1] so here Plato's Parmenides teaches Socrates that a thought is not an independent entity in the soul—as an idea will, later, be for Descartes—but instead is fundamentally other-directed. Specifically, thoughts are of ideas. Ideas are not mere thoughts.

Similarly, love—even the gods' love—is other-directed according to Socrates, not turned in on itself. Love is directed toward an other that has apparent value. Love itself does not determine value. Euthyphro thinks his prosecution of his father for murder is holy because the gods have engaged in similar actions and what is loved by the gods is holy. But, Socrates famously asks, is it holy because the gods love it? Or do the gods love it because it is holy? (9e11–12) The latter of course is his answer. It is the nature or being of something that determines its value, in this case, its holiness, and love is and should be in response to that value. Love does not determine value. Value determines love. Love is other-directed.

Speeches, thoughts, and love. All are other-directed. All are shaped, limited, determined by what they are not. This is one of the main types of point made by Plato's Socrates. What they are limited by are the ideas. Rhetorical speeches should be about justice. Love of a certain type should be of the holy. Repeated similar thoughts are of some one form. Truth, then—whether the truth of speeches, of thoughts, or of love—does not result from a turn to the self. It results from a turn to and beholding of what is.

3.

My reading of Levinas's claims about the Platonic return to the self, though, so far has been one-sided, disclosing only similarities in the two philosophers' views and not differences. Their views are similar in that both in Platonic recollection and in Levinasian teaching, we respond to something beyond or transcending the self. What are the differences? In what language does Levinas delineate them?

We can begin by looking in a different light at passages we have already seen. Levinas, as we have seen, says that teaching does not operate as maieutics but, instead, the soul is "capable of containing more than it can draw from itself" (*TI* 180/155). I have argued that the soul, for Plato, too, is receptive of something outside itself—that it is shaped, limited, and determined by something outside itself, namely, being. But Levinas wants to say more than that. He wants to say that the soul can be directed to something that it can never contain, to something that will always escape it. How to say this? For, if we are in relation to something, haven't we in some sense contained it? And, if we have not contained it, how are we in relation to it? This is the linguistic problem Levinas faces in discussing the non- or precognitive relation we have to the other—the other who is unique or singular or new and, thus, in an absolute sense, other.

He takes different linguistic paths to solve this problem. The problem, again, is how to speak of a relation to what we cannot contain, cannot hold, cannot grasp, cannot limit, cannot comprehend. One way he deals with the problem is to speak of the other placing in me the idea of infinity: "It [teaching] does not operate as maieutics, but continues the placing in me of the idea of infinity" (*TI* 180/155). What is infinite, of course, is what lacks boundaries or limits. How, then, can it be *in* me? In fact, the infinite is not in me. What is in me is the idea specifically of what cannot, because boundless, be in me. He goes on: "The idea of infinity implies a soul capable of containing more than it can draw from itself" (*TI* 180/155). What I am in relation to actually is exterior to me: "It [the idea of infinity] designates an interior being that is capable of a relation with the exterior, and does not take its own interiority for the totality of being" (*TI* 180/155). The other is not really in me, is not really contained in me. The other is outside me—irremediably so. I have in me, in other words, the idea of something that cannot be in me, cannot be contained by me, cannot be drawn from me, is separate from me. Separation, he says, is "a break with participation" (*TI* 180/155). What then is our relation to it like? It is, he says, "a relation extending over the irremediable abyss of this separation" (*TI* 180/155).

He goes on to say something that elucidates the real difference between Levinas and Plato: "Separation not being reducible to a simple counterpart of relation, the relationship with the Other does not have the same status as the relations given to objectifying thought, where the distinction of terms also reflects their union" (*TI* 180/155–56). But this is just what we do get in Plato. Even though being is beyond me, for Plato, it is for him also in some sense in me—it shapes me, for example, or determines me. For Levinas, the other remains absolute in the relation: "The terms remain absolute despite the relation in which they find themselves" (*TI* 180/156).

We may, thus, call the terms Levinas uses for delineating the relation to that which remains irremediably other "absolute terms." The other, for Levinas, transcends me—not in the way that forms transcend me in Plato (since forms both transcend me and are in me), but in an absolute transcendence, a transcendence that never becomes immanence. The other "appears but absents itself from the apparition" (*TI* 181/156). The other appears, in other words, in an absolute appearance, not in the way that forms appear. When I am taught, my soul opens—but not in the way my soul opens to take in form. Instead, "the soul opens," Levinas says, "in the marvel of teaching" (*TI* 181/156). There is an absolute openness, a directedness to what can never be reached or encompassed. The other who gives a sign, the other who in an absolute sense appears, cannot be signified: "The signifier, he who gives a sign, is not signified" (*TI* 182/157).

My relation to the other is "a relation with a being that maintains its total exteriority with respect to him who thinks it" (*TI* 50/20–21). Though Levinas speaks of the "infinite in the finite, the more in the less" (*TI* 50/ 21), he does not mean by that something in me that I can encompass, thematize, contain. For these are accomplished by the idea of infinity. Instead, he makes clear, my relationship to the other who is exterior to me is conversation. In conversation, the other overflows idea: "To approach the Other in conversation is to welcome his expression, in which at each instant he overflows the idea a thought would carry away from it" (*TI* 51/22). If I welcome the other's expression, I "*receive* from the other beyond the capacity of the I," I am taught. That is, "I receive something more than I contain" (*TI* 51/22). The soul, for Levinas then, is directed toward something it cannot contain, toward something that always escapes it, namely, the other.

These two passages indicate, though, that there are in fact two ways that Levinas utilizes linguistic resources to delineate the relation we have to that which escapes us. One is to say that though I relate to the other, the other is absolved from the relation. Another is to say that in my relation to the other I am in a position truly to *receive.* In other words, there are two basic ways Levinas uses language to speak of the relation we have to the other: one is to say the other is separate from me; the other is to say I receive the other. Regarding the latter, Socrates is criticized for receiving nothing, since maieutics brings me only what I already contain while Levinasian teaching brings me what I do not already contain, and since I do not contain it already, I in fact receive it. Socratic sovereign reason "knows only itself" (*TI* 43/14) and receives nothing. On the contrary, Levinas says, the other is strange to me, irreducible to me (*TI* 43/13). In my relation to him or her, then, I can truly receive, I can "*receive* from the other beyond the capacity of the I" (*TI* 51/22).

The reason for these two seemingly contradictory ways of describing my relation to the wholly other is that there is no mediation. There is no third term used to connect or mediate the other two: no concept, no sensation, no being (*TI* 42/13). Since there is no term that connects me to the other, the other is separate from me. Or, to conceive it differently, since there is no term between me and the other, I truly receive the other. The other, to presage terms more clearly delineated in *Otherwise Than Being,* is far and near—or, we might say in the context of *Totality and Infinity*—my relation to the other is either absolute separation or absolute receptivity. This rhetorical strategy is similar to Plato's strategy of constructing the forms as both in and beyond the things that share in them where *in* and *beyond* are given an unusual sense.

That to which I have a relation of absolute separation or absolute receptivity is, for Levinas, the absolutely other or the absolutely foreign. Only such a person can teach us: "The absolutely foreign alone can instruct us. And it is only man who could be absolutely foreign to me" (*TI* 73/46). Here, too, we have two absolutes, for *teaching* indicates not ordinary but absolute teaching in which what I learn is something I cannot integrate, cannot comprehend or contain, namely, the other who is, absolutely, foreign. The terms are *teaching* for absolute receptivity and *absolutely foreign* for absolute separation.

I do receive, in others words. Despite the idea of asymmetrical responsibility that in *Otherwise Than Being* is so central, in my relation to the other, absolutely other, I do receive something. There is, in other words, a directedness to the other. Such a directedness really does exist and really is accomplished, though not in the ordinary or Husserlian sense fulfilled. I do have an intentionality toward the other, but it is an unfulfilled intention, an intention that moves toward but never reaches its object. Levinas calls it, as we have seen, "an intentionality of a wholly different type" (*TI* 23/xii) or an "'intentionality' of transcendence" (*TI* 49/20) and maintains that describing it is the very goal of *Totality and Infinity:* "But it is a 'vision' without an image, bereft of the synoptic and totalizing objectifying virtues of vision, a relation or an intentionality of a wholly different type—which this work seeks to describe" (*TI* 23/xii).

"Teaching is not reducible to maieutics; it comes from the exterior and brings me more than I contain. In its non-violent transitivity the very epiphany of the face is produced" (*TI* 51/22). We have heard this statement before. Teaching brings me something. That is what it means to call it *transitivity.* The absolute terms in this statement, which we have seen before, are *brings me something* for absolute receptivity and *from the exterior* for absolute separation, or *transitivity* for absolute receptivity and *more than I contain* for absolute separation.

We are considering that which makes the receptivity in Socratic recollection and the receptivity in Levinasian teaching different, namely, the other. The other is absolute, according to Levinas, because he or she refuses concepts: "the refusal of the concept is not only one of the aspects of its being," Levinas says, "but its whole content; it is interiority" (*TI* 118/90). Similarly, in *Toward the Other,* Levinas says, "The Other as Other is not only an alter ego: the Other is what I myself am not. The Other is this, not because of the Other's character, or physiognomy, or psychology, but because of the Other's very alterity" (*ToO* 83/75). The other's very alterity. The otherness of the other is not a content we can grasp. Instead, it is resistance to content. It is otherness itself.

The point in this is that I have a relation to the other—an absolute or pure relation of receiving the other without marking him or her—without the relation cancelling out the fact that I am separate, absolutely separate, from the other: "The relation with the Other does not nullify separation. It does not arise within a totality nor does it establish a totality, integrating me and the other" (*TI* 251/229). Absolute otherness, unlike qualitative otherness, cannot be integrated. It has no content: "alterity does not determine the other in a formal sense, as where the alterity of B with respect to A results simply from the identity of B, distinct from the identity of A. Here the alterity of the other does not result from its identity, but constitutes it; the other is the Other" (*TI* 251/229). Alterity is not the otherness of different qualities: "The alterity of the Other does not depend on any quality that could distinguish him from me, for a distinction of this nature would precisely imply between us that community of genus which already nullifies alterity" (*TI* 194/168). My relation to the other is different from the Platonic relation to form or content because the absolute otherness of the absolute other is "absolute difference, inconceivable in terms of formal logic" (*TI* 195/168).

4.

If the difference between Socratic maieutics and Levinasian teaching is not receptiveness or directedness to something outside the self but is instead the type of directedness, with maieutics leading to receptiveness to concept or form and teaching leading to directedness to that which we can never fully contain, then how can we characterize the result? The result, in the case of Plato, is knowledge—but knowledge cannot be the result for Levinas since otherness is resistance to form, concept, idea. The result, instead, is revelation.

Revelation, for Levinas, is another absolute or pure term. By revelation, Levinas does not mean the unveiling of what is hidden. He certainly does not mean insight into what is clear and distinct, as with Descartes. But neither does he mean the gradual coming to light of form that is obscure but dimly lit. If I am right, Plato *does* mean that. For Plato, the acquisition of knowledge is the movement from trust (I see a tree) to discursive reason (this is a tree) and then the intellectual insight that is explicitly presupposed by discursive reason (the idea of tree). Or it is the movement from many perceptions (many cases of "I see a tree") to what is gathered together into one by reasoning (the idea of tree).

For Levinas, such a movement is called, in order to make a connection to Heidegger, *disclosure.* Revelation is not disclosure, according to Levinas. Instead, the experience I have when I am taught by the other is an absolute experience: "*The absolute experience is not disclosure but revelation:* a coinciding of the expressed with him who expresses, which is the privileged manifestation of the Other, the manifestation of a face over and beyond form" (*TI* 66/37). Form does not reveal but betrays, congeals, or alienates the other. The other as such has no form—the other resists form—and so what we are taught when the other teaches us is not form but is the very one who expresses. In revelation, what is expressed is nothing other than the very one who expresses. In revelation, what is expressed *is* the other. When we are taught, we do not comprehend or know that other, but we are directed to him or her—directed to them across the forms that he or she presents, forms that he or she undoes, stays separate from, resists: "The life of expression consists in undoing the form in which the existent, exposed as a theme, is thereby dissimulated" (*TI* 66/37).

Revelation is not the revelation of an object: "Revelation, by relation to objectifying cognition, constitutes a veritable inversion" (*TI* 67/39).[2] The relation to the other who teaches me—a relation that takes place in language—is not an objectification: "language does not consist in invoking him as a being represented and thought. But this is why language institutes a relation irreducible to the subject-object relation: the *revelation* of the other" (*TI* 73/45).

Platonic maieutics and knowledge and Levinas's teaching and revelation, then, are more similar than Levinas thinks since both involve the learner's responsiveness or receptivity to the other outside herself while they are, at the same time, significantly different: in maieutics and recollection I direct myself to something both transcendent and immanent, namely, form—form that is hidden but indicated; when I am taught by an other, I direct myself to what can never be immanent, can never be comprehended, can never be an object for me, namely, the other—the other absolutely foreign. I cannot know the other because whatever I know about the other is content the other offers me, forms the other presents to me; what I know is not the other who offers something to me, the other who presents something to me. I cannot know the *who.* Knowledge is of the *what.* With regard to their epistemological standpoints, then, the difference between Plato's and Levinas's philosophies of the other is the difference between what is hidden and what is foreign.

PART II

Otherwise Than Being

CHAPTER 5

Time and the Self

Perhaps, though, the contrast between Levinas and Plato is surpassed in *Otherwise Than Being.* Certainly, it is not thematic in the latter work as it is in the former. Moreover, there are a host of differences between the two works. Is the contrast I have been drawing eliminated in Levinas's more mature writing? If so, the points I have made would be primarily of historical or biographical interest. We need, then, to change focus in the next two chapters—from Plato/Levinas comparisons to the relation between Levinas's two major works. Then, in our final chapter, we will compare Plato and Levinas one last time.

1.

I maintain that the kind of contrast I have sketched between Plato and Levinas is there in *Otherwise Than Being* but that it is drawn in metaphysical terms not as a contrast between two thinkers. Rather than contrasting Plato's *recollection* with Levinas's *teaching, Otherwise Than Being* makes a similar point by speaking of that of which there is no reminiscence, no recollection. Specifically, it speaks of "a temporality beyond reminiscence" in a *diachrony* (*OB* 30/39), of temporality that refuses "to be assembled into a representation" and is an *anarchy* (*OB* 51/66). *Anarchy, diachrony*—these are Levinas's terms for thinking of a time in which there is no reminiscence, representation, rediscovery, recall, reuniting, recapture, retention; in which there is no "recuperation in which nothing is lost" (*OB* 28–29/36). It is under the heading of two types of temporality, one in which what is lost is recovered or recuperated and one in which what is lost is irrecuperable, that something similar to the Plato/Levinas distinction is expressed in *Otherwise Than Being.*

The important role of time is a central difference between Levinas's first and second major works. The title of the second of the two works, *Otherwise Than Being or Beyond Essence,* suggests that. It suggests that Levinas intends to spell out the spatial language he uses in *Totality and Infinity,* suggested by the term *Beyond,* in terms of temporal activity or what he calls *temporalization,* suggested by the adverb *Otherwise.* Following Bergson and Heidegger, Levinas hears a temporal quality to the term *being.* He wants, but says he does not venture, to write being as *essance,* a form that indicates the temporalizing of being, rather than using the usual, static form, *essence* (*OB* xlvii/ix).[1] Even though he follows the two philosophers in hearing such a temporal resonance of being, his own main point is that more is needed for a critique of presence than just that. What is needed is something *otherwise* than being where *otherwise* (*autrement*) is not an adjective but an adverb ("not *to be otherwise* but *otherwise than being,*" *OB* 3/3). What is needed is a way that is not *be*ing—a way of showing up or being present that is not showing up or being present at all. According to Levinas, human beings—whether ourselves or others—have the way that is other than being. What is that way? When we find it, we will find a central metaphysical similarity between *Totality and Infinity* and *Otherwise Than Being* and see the continuity between Levinas's earlier and later views.

First, though, it is important to note the obvious differences between the two works. One of the most striking is that in the later of the two, Levinas speaks not of the welcoming of the other by the same but of the other *in* the same. That, together with the adverbial quality of the other in *Otherwise Than Being,* could lead one to think that the second work is in part a critique of the overontologizing of the other in the first—especially if you add to that the fact that, in the second of the two works, Levinas uses numerous new terms to capture his insights, terms such as *hostage, substitution, for-the-other, proximity.*

On the other hand, the fact that there is a problem in Levinas's formulations in *Otherwise Than Being* need not indicate a simple problem-correction model for the difference between the two books. Instead, what if there are inescapable problems in talking about our relations to others? What if, to use Levinas's language, Hebrew cannot be made effortlessly and unproblematically to speak Greek? In reading Levinas, the extraordinary, and extraordinarily rich, terminology can become routinized over time, and we can forget how much of it functions to give us the experience, in a deep, metaphysical way, of something at least striking and puzzling if not problematic.

For example, in *Totality and Infinity,* when Levinas wants to say that the other shows up but does not show up—that is, that the other does something that takes the place of or is in some way parallel to showing up but does not show up—he uses the term *epiphany.*[2] So the other does not *really* show up, is not *really* present to us or in the light. The other is not *really* a phenomenon. Instead, the other is an epiphenomenon. When he wants there to say, to the contrary, that we do take in or receive the other in a certain, deep way, he uses the term *revelation* and uses it as a term of contrast with *disclosure,* a term with resonances of Heidegger's teachings about nature. The term *revelation* itself does not indicate any such contrast, though, since to re-veal is to unveil, the very sort of thing Levinas does not mean for the term to convey. Linguistically, the two terms have roughly the same meaning, of coming out of obscurity to awareness. Nonetheless, by making *revelation* a contrast term to *disclosure,* Levinas intends to denote something we are aware of without the mediacy of anything else. *Otherwise Than Being* has its own puzzles. In it he says the other is in me, denudes me, takes my substance from me, disrupts me—but there is still me. I lose myself or substitute myself, but somehow I am still there. My point is that in *Totality and Infinity,* the central expositional difficulty is that the other is made too separate from me while in *Otherwise Than Being* the other is made too close to me. In the former, the other is made more than it is, while in the latter I am made less, to the point almost of vanishing. If so, then it is not the case that the latter work simply corrects the problems in the former. Instead, it simply substitutes one set of problems for another.

It is not unheard of, however, for a philosopher to utilize puzzling formulations to talk about fundamental metaphysics, specifically to talk about a fundamental term that is sui generis. Both Plato and Aristotle do so, for example. According to Aristotle, Plato utilizes the term *indeterminate dyad* to speak about intimate unity (*Met.* 13.7).[3] An indeterminate dyad is something two but not quite two—not quite two, not quite one. In a culture in which numbers all were counting numbers, this could be an extraordinary idea, though for Plato scholars it has become sedimented and not surprising over time. Similarly, Aristotle uses the term *somehow* frequently in speaking about metaphysics.[4] Centrally, he says that there is nothing more unified than the unity between form and matter where matter is potentiality and form actuality and, in an entity composed of form and matter, potentiality and actuality are somehow one—somehow one, in other words, and somehow not one (*Met.* 8.6 1045b20–21).[5] He also uses the unusual coinage, the *what was being* or *what is being* where the *was* or *is* actually is not a past tense but is an imperfect and suggests what something is imperfectly being or is on the way to being. That, of course, when we desediment it, is puzzling. It is and is not being something? Well, yes, Aristotle does want to say that. The matter is being a certain form—right now, in my body, all the time. And being has a temporal resonance. The matter is be*ing* a certain form. In order to describe an intimate unity, specifically, the intimate unity of any hylomorphic entity, Aristotle must say such things, though we have become used to them and have to reawaken our awareness of them despite translations that obscure them (such as the translation of *to ti ēn einai* as *essence,* which makes form and the relation between form and matter more static than they actually are for Aristotle). After all, the relation between form and matter is for Aristotle a paradigm of activity (*energeia*) where form is the activity of matter and, he says metaphorically at one place, matter according to its own nature desires and stretches out for form (*Phys.* 1.9 192a18–19, 22).[6] All these terms are attempts to indicate something sui generis that cannot fully be captured in any other terms. In an intimate unity, an indeterminate dyad, for example, one entity in a sense is the other—so Aristotle says it *is being* the other, or it *somehow is* the other, or it *desires* the other. We paper over Aristotle's views when we reduce these ideas to *essence* or simply to potentiality.

Similarly, it seems to me the expositional problem for Levinas is to explain or designate something that is like an intimate unity, namely, the relation I have to another human being that, for Levinas, if not quite the same as an intimate unity, is something like one since it is unmediated—for, if it were mediated, it would fail ultimately to relate. If a concept stands in between me and another, then I am not really relating to the other, but bringing the other into my horizon (reducing the other to the same, as Levinas says). So either I say the other is beyond me, and it sounds as though I am talking about a relation to a separate being and thus overontologizing, or I say I substitute myself for the other and nearly vanish in the substitution, making me less than I am. Levinas's challenge is to speak of an unusual sui generis relation. He attempts to meet the challenge, as we saw in the preceding chapter, by speaking of the relation as being *like* our ordinary understanding of what it is for something to be beyond, or *like* the ordinary meaning of something being within. Neither approach is strictly speaking correct—that is, neither is literally true—but each reveals something of the unique relation denoted.

2.

But what is that unique relation? What is the unique relation between myself and another person, between what Levinas calls *the same* and *the other*? What is the self for Levinas? And how does it relate? I have said that the fundamental metaphysical idea of *Totality and Infinity* is of a self that emerges in or offers a variety of forms while at the same time resisting those forms, the self that is essentially in relation while at the same time absolving itself of relation. It is this central metaphysical idea that accounts for Levinas's collection of unusual terms such as *epiphany* or *substitution.* The other is manifest in forms but is not identical to them (epiphany). I take in the other but still remain me (substitution).

We often hear that, in *Otherwise Than Being*, the self—the singular or unique being—is the one who is responsible. This, of course, is correct, but only part of the story and, because it is only part of the story, may make it seem that the singular self as described in *Totality and Infinity* and the singular self as described in *Otherwise Than Being* are more different than they actually are. Specifically, it might suggest the following, misleading contrast: in *Totality and Infinity*, the self resists forms and relation while in *Otherwise Than Being*, the self is fundamentally in relation. To see instead a similarity between the two accounts, we must consider what it means to be responsible according to Levinas. Among other things, it means to be, essentially, for another; it means that the self is fundamentally outside itself; and it means this in a temporal sense. I mean to suggest by this explanation that the account of the ethical self for Levinas must not be separated from an account simply of the self. To be a self, for Levinas, is to be outside oneself directed to another being—and that, fundamentally, is what responsibility is. This is Levinas's critique of the early modern idea of the subject. In the section of *Otherwise Than Being* on *the one*, that is, on the unique or singular self, Levinas identifies uniqueness (*unicité*) with "the non-coinciding with oneself, the non-repose in oneself, restlessness" (*OB* 56/72).[7] It is essential (if that is the right term) to the singular self that it be for another—that is what it is to be (so to speak) a singular self. To bring out this idea, Levinas famously uses the language of pain and exposure. I am outside myself, I am restless, I am exposed, I am denuded. At the beginning of the section on the one, he says, "The exposure to the other is not something added to the one to bring it from the inward to the outside," that is, it is not that there is a self that exposes itself and as a result is moved from its comfortable inside to something outside. Instead, part of what it is to be one is to be exposed, as he goes on: "Exposedness is the one-in-responsibility and thus the one in its uniqueness" (*OB* 56/72). So exposedness is uniqueness.

First, it is important to pause over this very idea—a somewhat shocking idea. *Exposedness is uniqueness*! Often, instead, we think that falling back on yourself, being yourself, being in yourself, is uniqueness. Levinas here denies it: uniqueness is "the reverse of certainty that falls back on itself." Instead, uniqueness is a restless directedness (in time) toward another. And we may call this restless directedness toward another *responsibility*, or to spell the point out, *the one in responsibility*, that is, the one that is one by restlessly directing itself to another, that is, by being responsible.

But why? Is exposure uniqueness? It seems like a ludicrous idea. What in the world can Levinas mean? He says, to complete the quotation above, "Exposedness is the one-in-responsibility and thus the one in its uniqueness, stripped of all protection that would multiply it." Another surprising statement. It means that only what is stripped of all protection, all meaning, all concepts, all form, is one. When put that way, the claim makes sense. Any protection, that is, any particular way of being in relation to another, any particular, conceptualizable way of being at all, makes something plural. Anything formal, conceptualizable, determinately meaningful is plural. As Aristotle suggests, when he says that there is no knowledge of the singular (*Met.* 3.6 1003a12–17) (and, we might say, when we discuss the singular we are not in the realm of Athens/Aristotle but of Jerusalem/Levinas), whatever is formal or conceptualizable is not singular but general and, thus, multipliable. But Levinas says more than this. He says that the singular is restless, that is, that what is singular is not just devoid of concepts but a directedness toward another. This is its peculiar way of signifying. It signifies from noncoincidence, from nonrepose, from restlessness. It is this way of being, this restless being toward another that is devoid of and not guided by concepts, that Levinas describes as *otherwise than being*. Thus he goes on: "The 'otherwise than being' is not a play, it is the relaxation more serious than being." There is no play in this kind of relaxation, this relaxation of all determinateness, of all determinate direction of one's own to be for the other. There is only vulnerability. No playing out this way of being for and that way of being for. Uniqueness (*unicité*) is an utter being for, an utter being open to, an utter vulnerability—and so it is serious to the highest degree. Being—that process of becoming one or another of one's various possibilities—fundamentally is a kind of play. There is no play—there is no such play—in that way of being called *otherwise than being*.

With this exegesis behind us, let us summarize: what it is to be a unique or singular self in *Otherwise Than Being* is to be, fundamentally and utterly openly, directed to another but not just to one particular other or to any other conceived in one or another particular way. But this means that what it is to be a unique or singular self is to be essentially in relation while at the same time absolving oneself of the relations, the very understanding of the self that we saw in *Totality and Infinity*. The accounts of the self in the two books, then, are not as different as casual references to them might indicate ("resistance to the totality," "responsibility to the other"). This is made clear for us when Levinas says, directly, "The absolute exteriority of the exterior being is not purely and simply lost as a result of its manifestation; it 'absolves' itself from the relation in which it presents itself" (*OB* 50/21). The self is manifest—the self is in relation—but the self absolves itself from the relation through which it is manifest. Hence the self cannot be captured in a concept or summed up by the ascription of a number of forms.

3.

What then are the differences between the two books? One difference is that in *Otherwise Than Being* responsibility is stressed while *Totality and Infinity* stresses desire. These are, it seems to me, two sides of one coin. Desire—metaphysical desire, Levinas sometimes calls it—is directedness toward the other conceived of spatially as over there or beyond. I desire that other who is beyond all categories—I direct myself to that other who escapes all determination—when I am ethical. The emphasis in *Totality and Infinity* is on the other. And the other is conceived of, metaphorically, as beyond. In *Otherwise Than Being,* the focus is on the self—on what that directedness of the self without guiding conceptualization, determination, desire, intention, hope, aim, intention is like for the self. It is a scooping out of the self, we could say. A coring out of it. A denucleation, Levinas says sometimes in *Otherwise Than Being.*[8] In *Totality and Infinity,* Levinas stresses the receiving of the other that nondeterminately directed desire suggests.[9] In *Otherwise Than Being,* he emphasizes the loss of self (as ordinarily understood) that nondeterminate directedness implies. The two books look at the same things from different perspectives. Why does nondeterminate directedness lead to a kind of primal receiving of the other? Because, without any category to mediate my relation to the other, I really receive him or her. Why does nondeterminate directedness lead to a loss of the self as ordinarily understood? Because, without any category to mediate my relation to the other, all the possible concrete content of the self has been eliminated—I am denucleated, denuded, stripped bare.

The *Otherwise Than Being* understanding of the self and its relation to other that I have described is found not just in one section but throughout the book. For example, toward the beginning, Levinas refers to man as "a unicity withdrawing from essence":

> A unicity that has no site, without the ideal identity a being derives from the kerygma that identifies the innumerable aspects of its manifestation, without the identity of the ego that coincides with itself (*du moi coïncidant avec soi*), a unicity withdrawing from essence—man (*OB* 8/10).[10]

Unicity has no site. The *me* is outside itself and "does not find any rest in itself either, unquiet, no coinciding with itself" (*OB* 8/9–10). Once again, Levinas gives us the triad of unicity, being outside the self for another, and lack of form, ideality, concept, category.

What we found extraordinary, that our singularity results from our fundamental directedness to another—that exposedness is uniqueness—Levinas, of course, knows is extraordinary, knows violates our ordinary logic: "Despite-me, for-another . . . is the sense of the 'oneself' (*soi-même*), that accusative that derives from no nominative; it is the very fact of finding oneself while losing oneself" (*OB* 11/14). We find ourselves by losing ourselves. Exposedness is uniqueness. The paradoxical assertions proliferate. Levinas refers to "the against oneself that is in the self" (*OB* 51/66); to the self being "too tight in its skin, in itself already outside of itself" (*OB* 104/132). He claims that the "self is out of phase with itself" (*OB* 115/147); that "to be oneself as in the trace of one's exile is to be as a pure withdrawal from oneself" (*OB* 138/176); that "to be torn from oneself despite oneself has meaning only as a being torn from the complacency in oneself characteristic of enjoyment, snatching the bread from one's mouth" (*OB* 74/93); that the self is "a defecting or defeat of the ego's [*du Moi*] identity" (*OB* 15/18); that "the psyche in the soul is the other in me, a malady of identity, both accused and *self,* the same for the other, the same by the other" (*OB* 69/86); that "I, the same, am torn up from my beginning in myself, my equality with myself" (*OB* 144/184). He is aware, too, that the paradoxical remarks do not reflect ordinary logic. He says that "signification is the contradictory trope of the-one-for-the-other" (*OB* 100/126). He says that the psyche's relation to the other is beyond the logic of same and other: "The psyche signifies the claiming of the same by the other, or inspiration, beyond the logic of the same and the other, of their insurmountable adversity" (*OB* 141/180). The self, for Levinas, does not follow the logic of same and other in which same cannot be other and other cannot be same—in which, as he puts it, same and other experience an "insurmountable adversity." Instead, for Levinas, to be a psyche is to be a same that is other—while remaining same.

But in all this discussion, found throughout *Otherwise Than Being,* of the self that is itself by being for another—the self that finds itself by losing itself—one main point is that the self does not become that to which it is in relation. It is essential that the self be in relation—that it be for another—but the self is the self that is in relation. It is not a self that is (or, is essentially) that to which it relates, or fuses with that to which it relates, and so on. "I am not a transubstantiation, a changing from one substance into another, I do not shut myself up in another identity, I do not rest in a new avatar. As signification, proximity, saying, separation, I do not fuse with anything" (*OB* 14/17). To fuse with the other would be to shut myself up in a new identity. The self that loses itself does not simply find itself again. There is a process, a continual process, of being for another—for different others. Levinas calls that process *recurrence:* "I am a term irreducible to the relation, and yet in a recurrence which empties me of all consistency" (*OB* 82/104). In fact, for Levinas, the process of being for other without becoming the other *is* the self. Levinas calls the self *recurrence by contraction:* "this recurrence by contraction," Levinas says, "is the self" (*OB* 108/138). Once again, then, the self in *Otherwise Than Being* is the same as the self that in *Totality and Identity* is described as essentially in relation while absolving itself from relation. The self in *Otherwise Than Being* is the self that relates to an other but then contracts and returns to itself as the starting point from which it relates, again and again—that is, recurrently—to other others.

This points to why being for the other, as we have seen, is signification. What does Levinas mean by this claim? "The subject is for another; its own being turns into for another, its being dies away turning into signification," Levinas says (*OB* 52/67). The question points to the question, how do we reach signification? Our attempts fail, and we only reach the signified—being for this, being for that. But each of those is a particular signification, characterized in its particularity not by signification itself but by what is signified. But someone who is vulnerable, affected (or, as Levinas says, elected), open to recurrently being for recurrent and different others reaches pure signification. For that person's being dies down in the constant and recurrent openness. He or she is not for any one other in particular, but is open or vulnerable to all. Hence, that person's own being—her being one thing or another thing—dies down. What is left is not any particular signified but what precedes it, namely, signification itself.

4.

Before concluding this argument that the central metaphysical idea of *Otherwise Than Being* is the same as the central metaphysical idea of *Totality and Infinity* (discussed in previous chapters), it will be useful to show the location of that idea in the overall ideas of *Otherwise Than Being.* Though the two books develop in different ways, the basic metaphysical location of the idea is the same in each work. As in *Totality and Infinity,* so also in *Otherwise Than Being,* discussion of the self that essentially (so to speak) relates to an other is part of a general discussion of sensibility and corporeality. According to Levinas in the latter work, for the self, something comes before sight, vision at a distance, intentionality, knowledge—and even before directedness to an end by Heideggerian *dasein* that is always already immersed in a field of instrumental connections.[11] What comes before is sensibility, understood in a certain way. For Levinas, what comes first is a taking in of what is without. The self is not closed, as is the self on a Cartesian conception, but fundamentally in relation. This is common to Levinas as well as to Husserl and Heidegger. But there is a difference. Before we conceptualize, according to Levinas, before we give meaning to objects, before we are immersed and use instruments to achieve an end, we are contented. That is, we are given content. At the deepest level, we are an openness to . . . to whatever, and that whatever becomes, for a time, our very substance, our very contents. This, for Levinas, is what is fundamental to subjectivity as bread (and other basic food) is fundamental to our corporeality. At the most fundamental level, our subjectivity is not being—where being is always a being this or a being that. Something precedes being, and when we experience that something, the experience is an experience of a rupture of our being, of a breakup of our essence, an experience of our vulnerability: "This breakup of identity, this changing of being into signification, that is, into substitution, is the subject's subjectivity, or its subjection to everything, its susceptibility, its vulnerability, that is, its sensibility" (*OB* 14/17).

Before we give meaning to contents, in the Husserlian sense, we are contented. It is not the case that sensation "participates in the meaningful only inasmuch as it is *animated* by intentionality" (*OB* 65/82). There is meaning or sense prior to that, a prior type of meaning or sense that Levinas calls *signification.* Husserl uses this type of sense but does not mention it, does not bring it in as a kind of sense: "Husserl imperceptibly introduces into his description of intention an element that is different from pure thematization: intuition fills (that is, contents or satisfies) or deceives an aim aiming emptily at its object" (*OB* 66/83). Being filled is not a species of cognizing or knowing: "A thermal, gustative or olfactory sensation is not primarily a cognition of a pain, a savor, or an odor" (*OB* 65/81). As Heidegger argued that using a hammer is different than cognizing a hammer, so Levinas argues that savoring bread is not the same as cognizing its gustatory properties. Instead, it is a being filled, a being contented. Desire, then, or hunger, is not "a simple consciousness of" (*OB* 66/82). We can call that desire or hunger intentionality, as I above have called it meaning or sense—but only if we mean a different type of intentionality, or meaning or sense, not intentionality, meaning, or sense in an ordinary Husserlian usage: "intention in a sense radically different from theoretical aim" (*OB* 66/83). Levinas will alternate between saying it is not intentionality and saying it is intention of a radical sort.

The example, and then metaphor, often used for this sensibility is hunger, for this radically intentional (or non- or precognitive) desire, and bread, for what fills it. There is a specifically Jewish background to this, deriving from the biblical references to bread for the hungry. Ethics, for Levinas, disrupts me, disrupts any me that has a being—a going on being—or a content. Ethics is being for the other, or responsibility, that directedness toward or susceptibility to any other that empties me out. Levinas refers to it, metaphorically, as giving bread to the hungry: "To give," Levinas says, "to-be-for-another, despite oneself, but in interrupting the for-oneself, is to take the bread out of one's own mouth, to nourish the hunger of another with one's own fasting" (*OB* 56/72).

The fasting to which he refers most is multivalent, referring to the fasting involved in giving bread or sustenance that you have to another who needs it; referring to ethics in general as a type of giving, the type involved in all being for another; and, most likely, referring to the fasting that takes place for a Jew on Yom Kippur, the annual holiday in which the passage from Isaiah referring to giving your bread to the hungry is recited. For Levinas, all ethical activity, all responsibility, is like giving your own bread to the hungry: "It [the one for the other] is the passivity of being-for-another, which is possible only in the form of giving the very bread I eat" (*OB* 72/91). For Levinas, sensibility is enjoyment (*jouissance*) and its frustration, as he says referring to the traditional Yom Kippur morning *haftarah* reading (that is, reading from the prophets and the writings) that, in fact, is read on a day when those who hear it themselves would be fasting:

> The immediacy of the sensible is the immediacy of enjoyment and its frustration. It is the gift painfully torn up, and in the tearing up, immediately spoiling this very enjoyment. It is not a gift of the heart, but of the bread from one's mouth, of one's own mouthful of bread. It is the openness, not only of one's pocketbook, but of the doors of one's home, a "sharing of your bread with the famished," a "welcoming of the wretched into your house" (Isa. 58) (*OB* 74/94).

Here is the part of the traditional *haftarah* reading to which Levinas refers. In it, God says that all the formal ways of being ethical, of doing what is right—even fasting—are nothing without giving of yourself to others. I quote the passage in full since it will be significant in what follows (here and in the remaining chapters):

> [God says:] Cry with a full throat, do not hold back,
> let your voice resound like a shofar:

> declare to My people their transgression,
> and to the House of Jacob their sin.
> Yes, they seek Me daily,
> as though eager to learn My ways,
> as if they were a people that does what is right,
> and has not forsaken the way of its God.
> *When we fast,* you say,
> *why do you pay no heed?*
> *Why, when we afflict ourselves,*
> *do You take no notice?*
> Because on your fast day you pursue your own affairs,
> while you oppress all your workers!
> Because your fasting leads only to strife and discord,
> while you strike with cruel fist!
> —Such a way of fasting on this day
> shall not help you to be heard on high.
> Is this the fast I have chosen?
> A day of self-affliction?
> Bowing your head like a reed,
> and covering yourself with sackcloth and ashes?
> Is this what you call a fast,
> a day acceptable to the Lord?

Is a formal, ritual fast acceptable to the Lord? The Lord goes on to answer his own rhetorical question:

> Is not *this* the fast that I have chosen:
> to unlock the shackles of injustice,
> to loosen the ropes of the yoke,
> to let the oppressed go free,
> and to tear every yoke apart?
> Surely it is to share your bread with the hungry,
> and to bring the homeless poor into your house;
> when you see the naked, to cover them,
> never withdrawing yourself from your own kin.
> Then shall your light break forth like the dawn,
> and your healing shall quickly blossom;
> your Righteous One will walk before you,
> the glory of the Lord will be your rear guard.
> Then when you call,

> the Lord will answer;
> when you cry, God will say, *Here I am.*
> If you remove lawlessness from your midst,
> the pointing finger, the malicious word;
> if you give yourself to the hungry,
> and satisfy the needs of the afflicted;
> then your light shall shine in the darkness,
> and your night become bright as noon;
> the Lord will guide you always,
> filling your throat in parched lands,
> and renewing your body's strength;
> you shall be like a garden overflowing with water,
> like a spring that never fails.
> Some of you shall rebuild the ancient ruins,
> rebuilding the foundations of ages past.
> You shall be called *Repairer of the breach.*
> *Restorer of streets to dwell in.*

What is acceptable, then, is giving. But, as he goes on to indicate, it is not that formal ritual is unacceptable. What is unacceptable is using ritual or ritual time to attain one's own interest:

> If you keep from trampling the Sabbath,
> from pursuing your own affairs on My holy day;
> if you call the Sabbath *a delight,*
> the holy day of the Lord *honored;*
> if you honor it,
> abstaining from your [old] ways,
> from carrying on your own affairs or speaking of them—
> then you shall delight in the Lord.
> I will cause you to ride upon the heights of the earth,
> and I will feed you with the portion of Jacob your father
> —The Lord has spoken (Isa. 58:1–14).[12]

Even fasting, then, is not what is required, not what we are called on to do, if it loses its initial meaning of giving of oneself: "Because on your fast day you pursue your own affairs, while you oppress all your workers!" the Lord says. "Such a way of fasting on this day will not help you to be heard on high." Even the Sabbath is not what God wants if, on it, we are more concerned with ourselves than with others including God. We must give, the passage says. We must not pursue our own affairs. We must free those constrained by injustice. We must share our own bread, open our own home, cover the naked, remove lawlessness, satisfy the needy. If we do all those things, then, even though empty because we have given of ourselves, we will be full to overflowing, like a garden with overflowing water, a spring that never fails: "you shall be like a garden overflowing with water, like a spring that never fails."

The passage perfectly parallels Levinas's own views not only on ethics but also on knowledge as described in the section called "The Reduction." There Levinas refers to affirmation and retraction, thematization and reduction, the said and the saying. The philosopher's effort is to reduce the said back to the saying—but without ever completely eliminating the said, the thematization, the affirmation, the book, the proposition, and so forth. At one point, he suggests that fixation on any one said is idolatry: it is necessary, he says, "that the saying call for philosophy in order that the light that occurs not congeal into essence what is beyond essence, and that the hypostasis of an eon not be set up as an idol" (*OB* 44/56). Similarly in the Isaiah 58 passage quoted above, ritual serving God can, when fixed on the form itself not on the form aiming at the goal of serving the other or God, become idolatry as can any action or expression. Form, whether ritualistic, ethical, epistemological, is fine, and even inescapable, so long as it serves our being for the other rather than serving an effort to fuse with or fix—to fuse with or fix ritual, action, statement, concept. For Levinas, a common theme runs through religion (which for him is any nontotalizing bond with another), ethics, and knowledge. Fusion and congealment are idolatry, whether in ritual, in our relation to others, or in our efforts at knowing. We must, in all these spheres, offer forms—religious forms, forms of the other, conceptual forms—followed by "loosening this grip of being" (*OB* 44/56). This, according to Levinas, is the very effort of the philosopher. It is also, as we have seen, the very effort or nature of the self, the self that relates to the other through forms and then absolves itself of those forms and begins anew. Religion, ethics, knowledge, the self—all, for Levinas, have the same metaphysical, quasi-dialectical, and dynamic structure.

We are locating Levinas's discussion of his central metaphysical idea in his discussion of sensibility. We have seen its location there, and we have seen one of the principal metaphors for it—giving bread to the hungry. We have also seen how his discussions of ethics, religion, epistemology, and psychology all have the same structure. What, though, is the relation, in *Otherwise Than Being,* between sensibility and knowledge? Does Levinas develop the two ideas as he does in *Totality and Infinity*?

For Levinas, in chapter 2 of *Otherwise Than Being,* truth is exhibition of being (23/29), but, as we have seen in that chapter, being congeals in the said

(*OB* 44/56). In chapter 3, Levinas understands the difficulty in a different, but related, way. There is an inadequacy in being's exposition, he says, an inadequacy of being with itself. Specifically, in truth, there is a partition of being, a partition in which part stands for or is an image of whole. He explains this by delineating a hierarchy from sensibility to knowledge, specifically from sensible image and sensible intuition to knowing. Sensible image, Levinas says, is image "immediately welcomed without undergoing modifications" (*OB* 61/77). Even here with passive reception—passivity, immediacy, sensible concretion—and no modification, there is still a problem from the standpoint of truth. For the image conveys only part of the whole, and thus cannot be allowed to remain in its fixity. If it did remain fixed, truth would be incomplete or one-sided. Instead, for truth we must have more. The image must symbolize or reflect the whole.

Sensible intuition, Levinas's next stage, "is already sensibility becoming an idea" (*OB* 61/77). It is the sensible already oriented toward what is beyond it. It is *this* as *that,* for example, seeing this as red. It is not a concept, but it is the sensible conceptualized. Knowing is the next stage. Knowing "is identification which understands or claims *this* as *that*" (*OB* 61/78). Not merely perceiving *this* as *that* but understanding or claiming that *this is that.* As *this is that,* knowing breaks with passivity. Knowing, Levinas says, "does not remain in the pure passivity of the sensible" (*OB* 61/78). Moreover, it is in fact always symbolic. All knowing is symbolic, though we may not ordinarily think of it in that way. It is symbolic because in knowing there is a said and a said is like part to whole or part as a symbol of whole.

We will come back to Levinas's views on knowledge in more detail later. For our purposes now, what is important is the difference between sensibility and knowledge. What is the difference? It is crucial, first of all, that for Levinas there is a difference—crucial to his own views and crucial as well to his critique of Husserl and Heidegger. All knowing is preceded by sensibility. Hence, spirit cannot be summed up under the heading of knowledge. The difference is that sensibility, identified with saying, is "a pure for-another, a pure giving of signs, making oneself a sign, expression of self, sincerity, passivity" (*OB* 62/78).

Sensibility is, according to Levinas, "enjoyment and wounding" (*OB* 63/80). These can be summed up, he says, as *proximity* where proximity "does not belong to the movement of cognition" (*OB* 63/79). Sensation, Levinas says, "is not reducible to the clarity or the idea derived out of it." Instead, "It is vulnerability—enjoyment and suffering—whose status is not reducible to the fact of being put before a spectator subject" (*OB* 63/80).[13] So, once again, what is central here, as in *Totality and Infinity,* is human vulnerability. The vulnerability that is sensibility always opens out to cognition while, at the same time, it is different than cognition. Sensation is passive; knowledge is active.

In *Totality and Infinity,* the move from sensibility or affectivity to knowledge is followed by a relation to what cannot be sensed or known, namely, to the alterity or transcendence of the other. That relationship takes place in language and goes by a variety of names: the face to face relation, for example, or the ethical relationship (*TI* 194–95/168–69). How is it different from sensibility and knowing? Unlike knowing, our relationship to a personal other is passive not active. In addition, unlike both sensation and knowing, our relation to the personal other is not precisely relation to content. In "visual or tactile sensation," Levinas says, "the identity of the I envelopes the alterity of the object, which becomes precisely a content" (*TI* 194/168). In other words, sensible relation to an other reduces the other to content while the face to face or ethical relationship to an other relates to the other as other. This is the work of language, specifically, of language as speaking to, not speaking of, the other. The other may present himself as a theme, but

> his presence is not reabsorbed in his status as a theme. The word that bears on the Other as a theme seems to contain the Other. But already it is said to the Other who, as interlocutor, has quit the theme that encompassed him, and upsurges inevitably behind the said (*TI* 195/169).

The relation to the other in *Totality and Infinity* has, then, the same relational structure we have discussed previously in *Otherwise Than Being*. There is a moment of content or theme and a moment that dissolves the content or theme. The passage just quoted suggests that the dissolving moment is the very speaking to—that is, speaking to an interlocutor—itself. To speak *to* another assumes the content or theme we already associate with the other—content or theme expressed in a said—may be surpassed. Something else may surge up. If not, why would we bother to speak? The other, for Levinas, is "a being not entering into, but overflowing, the sphere of the same" (*TI* 195/169–70).

How, though, is this alternation between content or theme and dissolution different than the similar alternation we might have in knowledge? As we have seen, there is an alternation between affirmation and retraction, thematization and reduction, the said and the saying. The difference, as we have discussed in chapter 3, is in two kinds of indefiniteness, the indefinite that can be disclosed (such as a forest of which we only see a part) and the infinite that can never be disclosed. The other is infinite, beyond my grasp, beyond me. The idea of infinity, Levinas says, "does not come from our a priori depths—it is consequently experience par excellence" (*TI* 196/170)

Following the general differences between Levinas's two major works that I have sketched above, it is not surprising that in *Otherwise Than Being*, the relation to the personal other, called proximity, obsession, the face to face, is more often described in terms of its shocking impact on me than in terms of surplus, surge, or overflow that I receive or experience as it is more frequently in such passages as the one quoted above from the earlier work. The other traumatizes me. "The blow of the affection makes an impact, traumatically, in a past more profound than all that I can reassemble by memory," Levinas says (*OB* 88/111). "The subjective," he goes on, "does not only undergo, it suffers" (*OB* 88/111). The neighbor, he says, "strikes me" (*OB* 88/112). Still, Levinas indicates that he has not abandoned the idea of surplus or overflow when he refers to an increasing debit. Yes, the infinite other is for me debit, but the debit increases, its dynamic increase is glory: "This debit which increases is infinity as an infinition of the infinite, as glory" (*OB* 93/119).[14] In relating to the other, my resources are emptied out. For only in this way do I relate to the other as such. But the alternation of relating to the other in a theme selected by me and the subsequent retraction of the theme that retraction empties me out is endless—an endless process. We will look further at this dizzying emptying-out process in chapter 7.

The overall structure of the self and of human relations in Levinas's two major works, then, is the same. Each assumes a self that emerges in but is not reducible to forms and each compares our relation to the personal other with sensibility and knowledge. Like sensibility and in contrast to knowledge, relation to a personal other is passive. Unlike knowledge, the ethical relation is not conceptual. Though it includes a moment of conceptualization, a moment of approach to what appears and can be disclosed, my relation to an other recurrently dissolves concepts and appearances since the other can never be disclosed but is announced by and beyond what is disclosed. Moreover, though the two works emphasize different themes, in each the other both is traumatic to me and, from another standpoint, ever occurring increase.

Finally, how does this conception of the self relate to the conception of time expressed in *Otherwise Than Being*? We began this chapter by saying that *Otherwise Than Being*, rather than contrasting Plato's *recollection* with Levinas's *teaching*, makes a similar point by speaking of that of which there is no reminiscence, no recollection, no representation, rediscovery, recall, reuniting, recapture, or retention. Instead of synchronic time, in which what is past can be collected, presented, captured, or taken hold of again, time is diachronic. Why? Because synchronic time implies the retention in the present of what was in the past. In synchronic time, what was is retained, collected together, or united with what is present. But the self, in its relation with an other, does not fuse with anything that it can then fuse with again. The self is for the other without becoming the other. The self is for the other without any concepts or themes to guide it in its relation to the other. As a result, there is nothing to capture, nothing to re-present. The self's temporality as a result is diachronic since there is nothing remembered that could be retained and be in the present. There can be relation to an other in the past, but there can be no recollection of it.[15] Hence, we may speak of a temporality "without reminiscence," that is, of a *diachrony* (*OB* 30/39). Similarly, there is no concept or theme involved in my relation to an other and so temporality cannot "be assembled into a representation" by way of a concept or theme once present that can be present again. Hence, we may speak of temporal *anarchy* (*OB* 51/66). The past thus understood is, in a sense, more past than any past (that is, more past than what is past in synchronic time) since it cannot be retained or recaptured in my thought or memory. Whatever is otherwise than being—whatever is in relation without concepts to guide it—cannot be captured in time.

With this, we can conclude discussion of how the difference between Plato and Levinas carries over into *Otherwise Than Being* metaphysically rather than intertextually. We learn in *Otherwise Than Being* that what we can know, we can retain or recollect and know again, now; while what cannot be known—what is without concept, theme, or presence—cannot ever be retained, remembered, or recollected. Synchrony is to diachrony in *Otherwise Than Being* as Plato is to Levinas in *Totality and Infinity*. We will discuss knowledge—along with violence, freedom, and creation—in greater detail in the next chapter.

CHAPTER 6

Violence, Freedom, Creation, Knowledge

What about the main concepts treated in our discussion of *Totality and Infinity*? Do they make an important appearance in *Otherwise Than Being*? How are they handled? Are they handled in such a way that the themes I have brought out in my discussion of the earlier book carry through into the later?

Answering these questions in this chapter will advance this book's themes in two ways. First, since the Plato/Levinas distinctions I have drawn are derived from *Totality and Infinity,* showing that the concepts on which the distinctions rest play an important role in *Otherwise Than Being* extends the preceding chapter's argument that the Plato/Levinas distinction continues to be applicable to the later book (sections 1 through 4). Second, once that is shown, it is possible to solidify and amplify the account of how Plato and Levinas differ on knowledge—on what knowledge is and on how it is related to the ethical (section 5). Knowledge is passive or receptive for Plato while it is active for Levinas. As a result, for Plato the ethical is a type of knowledge, while for Levinas it is a non- or precognitive movement toward the other; moreover, in Plato's ethics there is a central ontological concept, variously described as the idea of the good or of the beautiful while, as we will see in our final chapter, Levinas's ethics gestures toward something beyond ontology and without concept, the glory of the infinite.

1.

Let us begin with violence. If anything, the language of violence in *Otherwise Than Being* is even stronger and more evident than the similar language in *Totality and Infinity.* Responsibility, the key term for ethics in *Otherwise Than Being,* is understood in the later work in terms of exposure, wound, outrage, suffering, trauma, subjection, contraction, breakup, fission, denucleation, excision, dispossession, immolation, being gnawed away, biting in on oneself, oppression, persecution, being a hostage, bearing the weight of the universe, bearing the weight of the other—just to name a few.

For example, in the key, central section entitled "Substitution," Levinas refers to the oneself's responsibility as "exposure to wounds and outrages" and says the goal of responsibility is for the oneself "to offer itself, to suffer and to give" (*OB* 105/134). He also understands the self there, as we have seen, as recurrent contraction: "this recurrence by contraction," he maintains, "is the self" (*OB* 108/138). He often uses language regarding the self or ipseity, though, that is even stronger, even more violent: "The recurrence of ipseity, the incarnation, far from thickening and tumefying the soul, oppresses it and contracts it and exposes it naked to the other" (*OB* 109/138). He describes the passivity of the responsible self as "the passivity of a trauma," "a deafening trauma," and "the passivity of being persecuted" (*OB* 111/141). "A subject," he says simply, "is a hostage" (*OB* 112/142).

In a related but different vein, he speaks of the recurrently contracting self as "identity gnawing away at itself" (*OB* 114/145) and, similarly, of the self in responsibility as "involved in the *gnawing away at oneself*" (*OB* 121/155). The psyche, he maintains, signifies "an undoing of the substantial nucleus of the ego that is formed in the same, a fission of the mysterious nucleus of inwardness of the subject" (*OB* 141/180). "Subjectivity understood as self," for him, is excision, dispossession, contraction, self-immolation; it is "the exciding and dispossession, the contraction, in which the ego does not appear, but immolates itself" (*OB* 118/151). The self is "forgetful of itself" but, even more, "forgetful in biting in upon itself" (*OB* 115/147). As a result, the self that gnaws away at itself, that undoes its own nucleus or immolates itself, "impassively under[goes] the weight of the other" and is "under the weight of the universe" (*OB* 118/151, 116/147).

Here, as in both the *Phaedrus* and *Totality and Infinity,* the language of violence is used to convey something that is not, literally, violent, namely, a type of beneficial vulnerability to the other. In the *Phaedrus,* as we saw, love is always disruptive. It knocks you out. Being in love is like falling on your back. But, despite this, love relations need not be assaultive. Instead, in love, you serve the other and the love you experience opens you to the very idea of beauty. In *Totality and Infinity,* Levinas's term for the disruption we experience in love, and in all direct relations to the other, is *essential violence*—a rupture of my going on being that, at the same time, gives me something I do not already contain. Essential violence is a breaking open that opens a new dimension. For Levinas, as we have seen, the self is not harmed but effectuated by its vulnerability to an other: fraternity constitutes ipseity (*TI* 279–80/257).

So also here. The coring out of the ego that is, ultimately, a way of being for an other is, at the same time, not alienation but inspiration where *inspiration* has its root meaning of breathing in a spirit or something divine. Levinas says about the self, "Its responsibility for the other . . . does not signify a submission to the non-ego; it means an openness in which being's ego is surpassed in inspiration" (*OB* 115/146). "I exist through the other and for the other," he says in a similar vein, "but without this being alienation: I am inspired. This inspiration is the psyche" (*OB* 114/146). The psyche, in other words, undoes the ego and lets something divine in: "The psyche can signify this alterity in the same without alienation in the form of incarnation, as being-in-one's-skin, having-the-other-in-one's-skin" (*OB* 114–15/146). Moreover, it is when the ego is cored out that I am most my self. "The oneself," Levinas says, "has to be conceived outside of all substantial coinciding of self with self" (*OB* 114/145). "The word *I*," he says in a biblical allusion, "means here I am, answering for everything and everyone" (*OB* 114/145).

Recurrent being for different others *is*, then, identity: "Recurrence becomes identity in breaking up the limits of identity" (*OB* 114/145). Being for an other *is* being a self: "The self is on the hither side of rest; it is the impossibility to come back from all things and concern oneself only with oneself. It is to hold on to oneself while gnawing away at oneself" (*OB* 114/146). To repeat a phrase from above: "I exist through the other and for the other" (*OB* 114/146). In *Otherwise Than Being*, Levinas's name for the disruption that gives me my identity and, at the same time, lets the divine in is *good violence* (*OB* 43/56). Responsibility, he says, "is an interruption of essence, a disinterestedness imposed with a good violence" (*OB* 43/56). The violence of being for other is not ordinary, harmful violence but, instead, good violence for two reasons: first, in this type of violence, I am or become myself; second, this good violence lets in the other.

So the point in chapter 1, that the language of violence used to delineate the self in its good relation to other is a common feature of both Plato's and Levinas's thought, does carry through to *Otherwise Than Being* and the conceptualization of the self found in it. There is a type of vulnerability to other that is not a threat, that does not diminish me, even though it does dramatically disrupt me. And, as in *Totality and Infinity*, it is an open vulnerability—not a vulnerability to form or being, as in Plato, but an open vulnerability since for Levinas, the job of the philosopher is not to take in form or connect to being, but to loosen the grip of form or being. Moreover, the nonthreatening openness or vulnerability that Levinas in *Otherwise Than Being* calls *good violence* is, like love in Plato's *Phaedrus*, divine. As Plato's Socrates calls love a type of divine madness since it is a way of relating to the divine, so Levinas calls our relation to the other *good violence* or *inspiration* since, in contracting the self, the divine comes to pass in us.

2.

What about freedom? We have seen in our discussion of the *Republic* and other dialogues and of *Totality and Infinity* that both Plato and Levinas may seem not to favor freedom, since each of them emphasizes a kind of being ruled or being for another, while in fact they do favor a surprising kind of freedom that comes from being in response. For Plato, as we see in the *Meno,* to be virtuous is to be limited by form but, as we see in the *Republic,* limitation by form is a type of liberation. Similarly, for Levinas, the other calls my freedom in question but, at the same time, my relation to him or her is temporary and I remain free in it.

Similarly in *Otherwise Than Being,* our freedom is an unusual kind. Referring to the passivity found in substitution, Levinas calls it "a different freedom from that of an initiative" (*OB* 115/146). Why is substitution, that particular form of being for an other that breaks up our own identity, freedom? How is being in response in this particular way not a form of being limited, broken, or unfree? Levinas's answer is "Through substitution for others, the oneself escapes relations" or, even more, "In this most passive passivity, the self liberates itself ethically from every other and from itself" (*OB* 115/146). Levinas means by these statements that only through ever-recurring and constantly changing relation to others called *substitution* do we free our self from any particular way of being ourselves and from any particular relation to particular others as well. Substitution is an ever-recurring breaking open of oneself and one's current way of being to be for another and then a breaking open of that relation to be for another, and another, and another, and so on. It is only this loosening up, this unfixing of what currently is, that is freedom. This view, expressed first in Levinas's *On Escape,* is consistent throughout Levinas's work. For Levinas, ethics is the most freeing activity there is—well, not activity but passivity, we must say, since ethics for him is recurrent, open response, a being in response not a doing in the ordinary sense at all. Nonetheless, for Levinas, ethics is the most freeing. When, out of the blue, we break up what we are, and what we are doing, to do or be for the other who is before us, we are more free, less constrained, less fixed, less chained to ourselves—and to any other—than in anything else that goes on in our lives.

3.

What about creation in *Otherwise Than Being*? Does it play the same role there as in *Totality and Infinity*? In chapter 3, I argued that though the Platonic Socrates identifies love and desire with need while Levinas contrasts desire and need, their differences on desire and need are not as great as they seem since Socrates introduces need for the same reason that Levinas rejects it, namely, to highlight human vulnerability; that each sees love as a sign of human vulnerability, that is, of the central other-directedness of human beings and of human subjectivity or soul; and that the real, nonterminological, difference in the two concepts of desire results instead from the presence or absence in them of a concept of creation ex nihilo. Each thinker believes love starts with self-concern but then changes and is directed to the other: for Socrates, love first is a desire to have the good for oneself forever but then becomes a desire to generate and reproduce and, by doing so, to produce immortality; for Levinas, love in one respect is mere need while in another it is fecund desire and exists infinitely, beyond death. The difference between the two thinkers instead, I argued, is in what love's generativity or fecundity is like: Socrates connects immortality with eternity; Levinas connects what is beyond death to the upsurge of something new. In other words, both think that love is directed to something outside oneself and that love defeats death, but they differ in that Socrates thinks lovers together share in and produce something immortal (immortal forms; a child who shares human form; a beloved who, through education, shares in the forms of the good and the beautiful) and Levinas thinks the productivity or fecundity of love is the facilitation of the arising of something not eternal, but new—that is, of something that has not in any sense been before, namely, the other. For Plato, in other words, the new other is a reproduction of eternal form, and thus not essentially new, while for Levinas, the other as such is something genuinely new—not an example of a form, an instance of a type, a particular of a universal, but instead something singular or new.

In *Otherwise Than Being*, Levinas carries the contrast with Plato forward. He associates the idea of creation both with the Jewish religious themes of the book and with the idea of absolute passivity that is another of the book's central themes. Absolute passivity, he says, is contributed by the idea of creation. Creation, he maintains, should not be understood in ontological terms since it is not a function of preexisting and indestructible matter. Speaking about ontology, he says, "It is not by chance that Plato teaches us that matter is eternal, and that for Aristotle matter is a *cause;* such is the truth for the order of *things.*" Connecting this idea to passivity, he goes on: "Western philosophy, which perhaps is reification itself, remains faithful to the order of things and does not know the absolute passivity, beneath the level of activity and passivity, which is contributed by the idea of creation." Continuing, he sums up his critique: "Philosophers have always wished to think of creation in ontological terms, that is, in function of a preexisting and indestructible matter" (*OB* 110/140).

Creation, in other words, is not like our ordinary making out of preexisting matter—a table out of wood, for example, or a pot out of clay. That conception of making—the one that in *Totality and Infinity* Levinas associates with Plato—involves the idea of form and the potential for form. When I make something, on this kind of account, I actualize the forms that are potential in the particular matter I have selected to utilize. The matter, then, is not utterly passive. It has its own activity and limits. It acts to constrain what I can do with it. I must be responsive to the matter in this kind of making, for the matter is active in certain ways. It acts to facilitate and limit my own activities on it.

In creation, to the contrary, what is acted on is utterly passive, with no activity whatsoever. In the process, the created being plays no active role at all, and the creator is neither facilitated nor constrained by that which he or she creates. On this account, what is created cannot in any way be responsive. The creation precedes any possibility of response, facilitation, limitation. Sometimes, as above, Levinas speaks of a passivity that precedes or is "beneath the level of activity and passivity." Other times, he refers to a passivity that cannot revert into an assumption (*OB* 113/145). What Levinas intends to convey by these terms is a passivity that has no form to it at all. When I make a table out of wood, the wood is passive; it is acted upon. However, the wood has form that gives it some activity, the activity of limiting and facilitating what can be done with it. When God created heaven and earth out of nothing, the created things were utterly passive. They neither facilitated nor constrained God's (pure) activity. Thus, Levinas says, "in the concept of creation *ex nihilo,* if it is not a pure nonsense, there is the concept of a passivity that does not revert into an assumption. The self as a creature is conceived in a passivity more passive still than the passivity of matter" (*OB* 113–14/145).

The self, then, is called into being without contributing anything to that call and is, as a result, utterly indebted to that call, since contributing nothing. Here, we should read Levinas as *utilizing* the biblical concept of creation to characterize the relation of self and other. He is not simply invoking the Hebrew Bible or simply promoting the idea of the creation of the universe out of nothing in six days. Instead, he is suggesting that I am created by the other without my having anything to do with it. This is evident when Levinas associates the idea of creation and the idea of obeying before hearing. "We will do and we will hear," the Hebrews say at Sinai, reversing the usual or Greek order of the activities. Ordinarily, we would think it is necessary to hear something first, and understand it, before we do it. Instead, doing comes first and is not a function of understanding. For Levinas, response to the other is not a function of understanding. We do not respond to the other because he is of a certain type or involved in certain types of activities. We respond to the other as such. We respond to the other in an utterly passive way of response that is not facilitated or limited by any conceptual or formal content. And why do we do so? Because we are creatures, ourselves created beings. The other, as we have seen, contents me, or is my content. I am, "essentially," the other—and another, and another, and another. I contribute nothing, and thus am indebted. My relation to the other is debit—though the debit is a continually or infinitely increasing one, and one that from another perspective is inspiration or glory since the emptiness or openness is not only continually recreated but also continually "filled." "But in creation," Levinas says, "what is called to being answers to a call that could not have reached it since, brought out of nothingness, it obeyed before hearing the order" (*OB* 113/145). He goes on, here again in the section on "Substitution," to refer to other ideas from the Hebrew Bible that suggest ultimate passivity both in responsibility or ethics and simply in the structure of the self: "The word *I* means *here I am,* answering for everything and everyone," he says, referring a repeated common response to direct address in the Hebrew Bible. "Here I am (*hineni*)" suggests the pure making oneself available that the phrase's lack of real content suggests. I am always here, so what does the phrase mean? Levinas is fascinated by such phrases of pure response not guided by any concepts, for example, also "bonjour" (*OB* 143/183). But, as he goes on to say, though I am utterly passive, utterly for an other, I am not alienated, but inspired, or, as he puts it differently, my debit is glory. "I exist through the other and for the other, but without this being alienation: I am inspired" (*OB* 114/146). Later, he connects the *here I am,* sincerity, and *bonjour* with glory. Sincerity is as simple as *hello* (*OB* 143/183) and is connected, in its passivity, with the glory of the infinite: "Glory," Levinas says, "is but the other face of the passivity of the subject" (*OB* 144/184). Passivity and inspiration, like debit and glory, are for Levinas simply two sides of one coin. Creation, then, plays a similar role in *Otherwise Than Being* as in *Totality and Infinity* and, in addition, points us toward the glory of the infinite. We will discuss the glory of the infinite further in the next chapter.

4.

Finally, we come to knowledge. Of the four concepts treated in this chapter, it is the one least treated in *Totality and Infinity* and most—and most excitingly—expanded on in *Otherwise Than Being.* As with other topics in the latter book, so also with knowledge, the emphasis is on the self, in contrast to the emphasis, in *Totality and Infinity,* on the other. As absolute desire, the moral figure of *Totality and Infinity,* is about the self while responsibility, the moral figure of *Otherwise Than Being,* is about the other, so also absolute receptivity, the epistemological figure of *Totality and Infinity,* is about the self, while interruption of self or of essence, the epistemological figure of *Otherwise Than Being,* is about the other. The interruption referred to is the interruption of essence that, as we have seen before, is *good violence:* "an interruption of essence, a disinterestedness imposed with a good violence" (*OB* 43/56). As I desire something for myself but am responsible to the other, so I also receive something for myself but am interrupted by the other. The latter two formulations are two formulations of one phenomenon, namely, the phenomenon of relating to the known without marking it: I receive the other, but it is absolute reception; my set of marks—categories, descriptions, standpoints, and so forth—give way to the other. They loosen up or uncongeal.

In chapter 4, I argued that for both Plato and Levinas, knowledge is directedness to what is other, not a return to the self. In this way, their views of knowledge are the same. At the same time, I argued, their views of knowledge differ in that, for Plato, the known is both immanent to and transcendent of the self while, for Levinas, the known utterly transcends the self. In *Totality and Infinity,* I detailed, the utter transcendence in Levinasian pure knowing is described as absolute receptivity. In *Otherwise Than Being,* as I will now delineate, utter transcendence is characterized instead in terms of interruption or violence.

The interruption or violence in question is achieved through what Levinas calls the *reduction:* the reduction of the said back to the saying. We reduce the said to the saying, he says, so that what is beyond essence does not congeal into essence or, put differently, so that hypostasis does not become idolatry. The job of the philosopher, Levinas says astonishingly enough, is to loosen the grip of being—or, to be more complete, first to show being and then to loosen its grip—again and again and again. And why do we do this? Because only absolute knowing is absolute receptivity. Ordinary knowing is active. It marks what it knows. As a result, all ordinary knowing is idolatry—is taking a perspective to be the thing itself, taking a part that I have selected to be the whole from which it comes, taking ideology to be truth.

This stunning idea of a ceaseless positing and taking back is an astonishing new way of thinking about what philosophers ought to do. It is animated not by relativism, but by Levinas's *epistemological humility,* as I shall call it. Our aim, in knowing, is to approach the known without marking it. But we cannot achieve our aim fully and must be content instead with a back-and-forth process of speaking the other, and respeaking, and respeaking, without end.

The point is that our responsibility to the other whom we would know, whom we would approach without marking, is only achieved by speaking—by what Levinas calls *the saying* (*le dire*)—but speaking inevitably marks the other, depriving the other of singularity. Speaking results, Levinas says, in *the said* (*le disant*).

Our attempt to achieve our aim inevitably fails of complete achievement but the attempt can only take place in such an activity that must in part fail: "But is it necessary," Levinas rhetorically asks, "and is it possible that the saying on the hither side be thematized, that is, manifest itself, that it enter into a proposition and into a book? It is necessary," he answers (*OB* 43/56). Here, thematization, manifestation, proposition, and book all are ways of describing the said. Our attempt to go beyond the said to the other must take place through the said. The said is necessary. But why? Because the said contains a saying—a directedness to the other as other. By itself, the saying does not mark—but, of course, the saying never is by itself. Hence the need for the to-and-fro process we are invited now to call *philosophy.* Levinas describes the saying as *responsibility:* "The surprising saying which is a responsibility for another is against 'the winds and tides' of being, is an interruption of essence, a disinterestedness imposed with a good violence" (*OB* 43/56). He goes on to describe the back-and-forth process of philosophy further. I shall quote him at some length, to show how the process of philosophy—philosophy as a back-and-forth process—works. Referring to the saying, Levinas says,

> It must spread out and assemble itself into essence, posit itself, be hypostasized, become an eon in consciousness and knowledge, let itself be seen, undergo the ascendency [*l'emprise*] of being. Ethics itself, in its saying which is a responsibility requires this hold [*emprise*]. But it is also necessary that the saying call for philosophy in order that the light that occurs not congeal into essence what is beyond essence, and that the hypostasis of an eon not be set up as an idol. Philosophy makes this astonishing adventure—showing and recounting as an essence—intelligible, by loosening this grip [*emprise*] of being (*OB* 44/56).

Saying cannot, in other words, accomplish its goal. It becomes a mark, a fixation: essence, position, hypostasis, eon, light, being. Philosophy must loosen the hold of being, must unfix what is fixed, as Levinas goes on:

> A philosopher's effort, and his unnatural position, consists, while showing the hither side, in immediately reducing the eon which triumphs in the said and in the monstrations, and, despite the

> reduction, retaining an echo of the reduced said in the form of ambiguity, of diachronic expression. For the saying is both an affirmation and a retraction of the said (*OB* 44/56).

A new type of philosophy is required, then. One that knows and reflects its own limitations. One that includes assertion and retraction or, in more nuanced fashion, that features types of assertion that contain their own retraction or point to their own limitations: intentional ambiguity, diachrony.

If philosophy from its inception has been fundamentally motivated by recognition of the difference between nature and convention, Levinas here requires of philosophy that it apply its own founding recognition to itself. As philosophy results from the desire to disentangle the known from the knower, Levinas requires of philosophers that they accept and, even more, take steps to deal with, the fact that our knowledge of nature is never free of convention, that the known is always marked by the knower. For us, there is no nature without convention, no known without marks of the knower, no truth without theme. We reflect this by gesturing from one theme to another, diachronically. The reduction is such gesturing:

> As the truth of what does not enter into a theme, it [the reduction] is produced out of time or in two times without entering into either of them, as an endless critique, or skepticism, which in a spiraling movement makes possible the boldness of philosophy, destroying the conjunction into which its saying and its said continually enter (*OB* 44/57).

Thus, Levinas delineates a new, bold philosophy, not satisfied with convention but also not satisfied with itself, a spiraling movement of critique and self-critique without end. The movement is back and forth but, even more, it is spiral. For, after the first, each saying is a resaying and there is no return to a beginning—a pure beginning, an absolute *archē*, unmarked being, nature conceived without convention: "being is inseparable from its meaning!" Levinas says in good phenomenological fashion. He goes on: "it is spoken. It is in the logos" (*OB* 45/58).

5.

Where does this leave us in our reflections on Plato and Levinas on knowledge? What is the problem, really, that leads Levinas to say that philosophy must be spiral, must be endless critique, critique without ultimate resolution as opposed to critique with a terminus? The two questions are connected. For Levinas, as we have seen in chapter 5, knowing is active not passive since knowing is always understanding or claiming that *this is that:* knowing "is identification which understands or claims *this* as *that*" (*OB* 61/78). Knowing, then, is not passive but active: it "does not remain in the pure passivity of the sensible" (*OB* 61/78). All knowing is preceded by a moment of pure passivity, the purely passive reception of sensible image, of sensible image "immediately welcomed without undergoing modifications" (*OB* 61/77). Knowing, in other words, is preceded by a moment of passive reception—of passivity, immediacy, or sensible concretion. Such sensible image, though, quickly becomes sensible intuition or sensibility becoming idea, *this* as *that,* and sensible image quickly is followed by knowledge, *this is that.* Knowledge, thus, is active, not passive. It is, in other words, in good part about us, our standpoint, our theme, our take, our ascendency, our hold. Though there is a moment in knowing that is passive—and so spirit is not identical with knowing—that moment is inseparable from idea and thus from activity (*OB* 61/77–78). For Levinas, then, the locus of passivity—of open, human response to what is other—is sensibility, not knowledge, while for Plato, as we have seen, it is in knowledge that pure responsiveness is found. Ascent to the forms and to the highest of the forms is figured as falling on your back or as a type of slavery.

This, then, delineates a major difference between Plato and Levinas, a difference Levinas increasingly characterizes in *Otherwise Than Being* by expressing passivity in terms that derive from and reflect the concerns and categories of the Hebrew Bible and those that reflect activity and knowing in terms that derive from Greek thought. For Levinas, knowing is active and, thus, risks idolatry. Idolatry, I would say, is taking as perfect what is not perfect. In knowing, taken as a static act, we claim to comprehend, we take ourselves as comprehensive or perfect. In knowing, we take our limited perspective to be what is, to be the whole, to be the truth. But it is not the truth. It is, instead, symbolic, since the said is like part to whole or part as symbol of whole.

We can compare Plato and Levinas by looking at the passage in Plato's corpus that is the most similar to Levinas's reflections on sensible image, sensible intuition, and knowledge. It is the well-known divided line section of the *Republic* (*Rep.* 6.509d1–511e5). In it, the highest knowing—which is the type of knowing needed for virtue—is passive or receptive, rather than active. It is a simple knowing—a simple beholding—rather than a discursive process of seeing *this* as *that* or taking *this* to be *that.*

In the divided line passage, Socrates outlines levels of knowing by arranging each type of knowing on a line cut in a specific proportion of segments: "take a line cut in two unequal segments," he says, "and go on and cut each segment in the same ratio" (509d6–8). Corresponding to the levels of knowing arranged on one side of the line are levels of being arranged on the other. Because of the particular proportion in which the line is cut—the two segments of the line are cut in the same ratio in which the whole line has been cut—the two middle segments are equal and, as a result, the lowest segment has to either of the middle segments the same ratio that either of the middle segments has to the highest segment.[1] The proportion is important because Socrates uses the mathematical proportion to draw an analogy. In Greek, *analogia* means both *analogy* and *proportion.* Crucial for our purposes in the analogy is the fact that knowledge on the lower level of each of the two main segments is double (of *this* as *that*) while knowledge on the higher level of each of the two main segments is simple (of *this*).

The lowest level of knowing is imagination (*eikasia*). Socrates's examples of images are shadows and appearances (specifically, appearances produced in water or in close-grained, smooth, bright things), and so on. Imagination in this context is not fancy but is seeing an image *as* an image—for example, seeing the image of a tree on water *as* the image of a tree. The next level up is trust (*pistis*), which is a simple, nondiscursive kind of seeing. Socrates's examples of what we trust are animals, growing things, artifacts, and so on. An example of trust, then, would be simply seeing a tree—not seeing something *as* a tree or judging it to be a tree, but simply seeing a tree. Together, imagination and trust constitute seeing in general.

The next two levels, which together constitute intellection or knowing in general, are thought (*dianoia*) and intellectual intuition (*nous*). Socrates's examples of the objects of thought are those utilized by people who do calculation and geometry, namely, odd and even in calculation, and figures and forms of angles in geometry. Thought, in other words, knows the mathematicals, roughly divided into the number and shape. Finally, the highest level of knowing is intellectual intuition (*nous*). Its objects are forms (*eidē,* 510b8, 510d5, 511a3, 511c1–2).

Ontologically, the central analogy Socrates wants to draw is between things and images. Given the proportion he utilizes, the implication is that as images are to the things that are their originals so things are to forms. For example, a tree has to the form of tree the same relation that an image of a tree has to a tree: things are like images of the forms. Similarly, thinking is like imagination. For, just as to know an image one must know the original of which it is the image and, even more, know the image through the original, so also to know a thing one must know the form of the thing and, even more, know the thing through the form (as we saw in chapter 1, knowing things according to their forms is what Socrates, in the *Phaedrus,* calls *recollection*).

Socrates's example of knowing a thing through its form is knowing a triangle or square you draw through the form of triangle or the form of square. Socrates says, "They make the arguments for the sake of the square itself and the diagonal itself," by which he means the form of square or the form of diagonal, "not for the sake of the diagonal they draw, and similarly with the others" (510d). A soul, he says, "uses as images those very things of which images are made by the things below" (511a). In other words, in higher-order thinking, we treat things as images, that is, we understand things through or according to their forms. His example is a geometer who, for example, uses a visible square to think about square itself, that is, about the form of square, or what we might call squareness.

Similarly, as imagination is to trust, so thought is to intellectual intuition. Intellectual intuition—*nous*—is unmediated or nondiscursive knowing, that is, the simple taking in of form. Similarly, then, trust is a simple—unmediated, nondiscursive—seeing. Because trust is nondiscursive, one might think it is passive, but it is not. Just as imagination has an obvious discursive quality and a double structure (seeing the colors and shapes on the water *as* a tree), if things are like images of the forms then, following the analogy, our trust in the case of seeing a tree must also have implicit discursiveness based on an implicit double structure: nondiscursive seeing of a tree (an example of trust) implies the possibility of making explicit what is implicit in it (and in all trust), namely, that *this* is a *tree* (that *this* is a *what*). Such discursive taking *this* as a *tree* is thought (*dianoia*) that, as the analogy suggests, is in fact discursive in the same way as imagination is discursive, namely, by reflecting and drawing out or articulating an implicit double structure: thought sees *this* thing in front of us as a *tree.*

Following the analogy and the examples, we can understand Plato to be spelling out our ordinary, trusting relation to things in the world (seeing a tree, seeing a human being, etc.) in terms of two aspects involved in it: a mathematical component (*this* tree, singular; or *these* trees, plural) and an eidetic component (this *tree,* or these *trees*), reflecting the two highest levels of the divided line. *One* tree, *the* tree, *these* trees—all these indicate the mathematical, or the *that.* One *tree,* the *tree,* these *trees*—all these indicate the eidetic or the *what.* For Socrates in the *Republic,* the ascent from imagination and trust to discursive thought and intellectual intuition is the ascent from opinion and sensation to knowledge, from convention to the truth, from marking what is to approaching it without marking it.

That is why Socrates refers to a form as unhypothesized ("an unhypothesized beginning," 510b6–7). A hypothesis is a putting (*thesis*) under (*hypo*). In a hypothesis, something is put under something else or, more specifically in this case, something is supposed by or utilized in our knowing of something else. Knowledge of trees is supposed by seeing an image of tree; you cannot see shapes and colors on water as a tree if you do not know trees. Knowledge of the form of tree, similarly, is supposed by our knowledge of trees; you cannot see this thing as a tree without knowing what it is to be a tree, namely, the form of tree. When we imagine a tree on water, we see a certain colored shape on water *as* a tree. When we know a tree, we see a certain thing *as* a tree.

Both trust and knowledge of forms, however, are simple. They are not seeing something as something, but simply seeing something. In the case of trust, the simplicity is somewhat illusory or a matter of degree. In the case of a form, the simplicity is real. I simply see the form. I simply take in the form. I do not bring anything to it. In other words—and most importantly for the purposes of our comparison with Levinas—for Socrates, the ascent from sensation to knowledge is the ascent from activity to passivity or responsiveness to what is. The highest type of knowing—*nous* or intellectual intuition—is the most passive. It is the type of knowing in which we bring the least to our knowing, the one in which we least mark what we know. It is a simple beholding of what is.

In addition, the ascent from sensation to knowledge is the ascent to the ethical. This is crucial for this book's main task, namely, comparison of Plato and Levinas. For both Plato and Levinas, to be ethical is to be vulnerable or open in a certain way. For Levinas, that vulnerability or openness is pre- or noncognitive, a directedness toward something gloriously beyond our attempts to limit it and take it in. For Plato, as we are seeing in this section, that vulnerability is a simple beholding and being affected by what is, more specifically, by the highest ("brightest") of what is, the idea of the good. When I intellectually intuit all time and all being all the way up to the brightest part of being, the idea of the good, I am fundamentally affected, according to Socrates. Specifically, I love that by which I have been affected, the good, and now orient all my life and activities in relation to it. This is the more complete working out of the claim made (and never refuted) in Plato's *Meno,* namely, that virtue is knowledge or, to be more precise, a kind of knowledge: "wisdom (*phronēsis*) is virtue" (*Meno* 89a3). But wisdom is knowledge of what? the reader of the *Meno* asks, noting Socrates's immediate qualification: "either entirely or a certain part" (89a4). Of the idea of the good, the *Republic* answers. Ultimately, in the *Republic,* virtue is not harmony of the parts of the soul. That, instead, is civic virtue, a second-order virtue possessed by those who do not make the ascent to complete knowing. For those who do make the ascent, virtue simply is knowledge. That is, once I have seen all time and all being including the brightest part of being, the idea of the good, then I simply will do what is good. The good I intuit affects me, changes my whole pattern of affectivity. It has the effect of turning me around, and I then follow it by being good and just. Let me substantiate these claims by a reading of the relevant texts.

As mentioned in chapter 2, Socrates's argument that virtue is knowledge is that virtue is good; there is nothing good that is not knowledge or wisdom; therefore, virtue is knowledge or wisdom. Socrates says, "do we say this hypothesis remains for us, that virtue is good?" Meno responds, "Certainly" (87d2–3). Socrates continues, "If then there is anything good that is other and separate from knowledge, virtue might well not be a type of knowledge, but if there is nothing good that knowledge does not comprehend, would we be right to suspect that it is a type of knowledge?" Meno responds, "These things are so." (87d4–8).

It is a counterintuitive but simple argument. It gets its strength from the arguments Socrates uses to show that other seeming external goods—health, strength, beauty, and wealth—are good only when they are guided by internal goods toward correct use, and that seeming internal goods, certain qualities of soul, are only good if they are knowledge or wisdom. Socrates says regarding external goods such as health, strength, beauty, and wealth, "Isn't it the case that, whenever correct use guides them, they benefit us, and when it does not guide them, they harm us?" (88a3–4). For example, overvaluation of beauty can lead to deception of self and other (as in the case of beautiful Alcibiades who, as Socrates well knew, misled many and, as well, was misled by them). Unguided strength can lead to harm of self and others (as in the case of powerful Athens that, as Socrates in the dialogues often suggests, frequently uses its strength for improper ends destructive of other cities and of itself).

External goods are guided well, Socrates then indicates, by goods of the soul. He lists them: "moderation, justice, courage, quick thought, memory, befitting greatness, and all such things" (88a6–b1). Such qualities of the soul, he goes on to indicate, only are good qualities of the soul if in fact they are knowledge, and so he mentions in that light " 'courage' when it is not wisdom (*phronēsis*) but a kind of recklessness" (88b3–4). "Courage" that is not wisdom is not courage at all but a kind of recklessness, Socrates implies, thereby making his argument complete. Virtue is knowledge—or, better, wisdom—because virtue is good and there is nothing good that is not knowledge; external goods are not good unless guided well; they are guided well only by good qualities of soul; and good qualities of soul are good only if they are knowledge.

Nonetheless, readers might think the question what is virtue remains unanswered in the *Meno* since at a certain point in the dramatic and argumentative unfolding of the dialogue, Socrates questions his own argument's conclusion. He asks, "Therefore, true opinion is not at all a worse guide to correct action than wisdom?" (97b9–10). After all, true opinion in fact is true. So maybe knowledge is not needed for virtue. The question is, dramatically, one of the most important moments in the dialogue. It is the moment that Socrates finally seems to have an impact on Meno, the moment when he finally seems to be able to get Meno—who does not say what he believes but what Gorgias, his teacher, says—actually to inquire and to wonder. "So that I wonder, Socrates," Meno says, "these things being so, why knowledge is much more worthy of honor than correct opinion, and how they are different one from the other" (97c11–d3). We know, of course, that philosophy begins in wonder.

Meno's soul hangs in the balance. If virtue in fact is knowledge, Meno's own virtue is at stake because at this point he finally seems to want to make an effort to achieve knowledge. He finally seems to want to inquire. Socrates, at this point in the dialogue, has Meno just where he wants him, not thwarting inquiry, but finally engaging in it, not spouting opinions he derives from others, but actually asking a question and, even more, a question about the very value of knowledge in comparison with that of mere true opinion.

Socrates responds to Meno's uncharacteristic open inquisitiveness at this point in the dialogue by telling him that true opinions are like statues of Daedalus, statues so lifelike that if you do not chain them down, they run away. True opinions, if you do not chain them down by reasoning about why they are true, run away from the soul.[2] Virtue, we might then say, is not just good, but it is a relatively settled good, because knowledge, unlike true opinion, is relatively settled since one who has knowledge knows the reason for his or her views. Virtue is knowledge rather than mere true opinion because one who only has opinion can be easily swayed by others or by circumstances. Opinion is, in a sense, put in your soul, while knowledge is something you yourself must establish through reasoning—you must tie it down, but once you do, it tends to remain. Socrates's innocent question, about the relative value of true opinion and knowledge, leads to the most important question, both for the argument of the dialogue and for the drama, namely, what is virtue? Socrates's question pushes Meno to see that knowledge is what he needs if he is to acquire virtue, as his opening and persisting questions in the dialogue indicate he very much wants to do—not, presumably, to acquire virtue in the sense of morality, but to acquire virtue understood as the strength of soul that any up-and-coming young Greek man would want to be known for and to have.

Of course, it turns out that this crucial dramatic moment does not represent a lasting change in Meno—Meno who we know, historically, became quite a vicious human being after the dramatic date of the dialogue.[3] Meno will not consistently inquire. He will not consistently follow an argument. Earlier in the dialogue, for example, Meno persists in asking Socrates to answer his question how virtue is acquired even though Socrates has argued that we cannot answer that question until we know what virtue is: "Socrates, I would be most pleased to investigate and hear the answer to what I asked first, whether to go after it as teachable or by nature or as something that comes to human beings in some other way" (86c7–d2). He also, for another example, earlier in the dialogue asks Socrates to teach him that all learning is recollection—"Can you teach me that this is so?" he asks (81e5)—even though what he wants Socrates to teach him is that there is no teaching, only recollection. For a third example, right after that, Socrates says he will loosen his rule and let Meno rule him. The way he lets Meno rule is by bringing in a hypothesis that includes, as a part, *virtue is teachable:* "If, at least, virtue is a type of knowledge," Socrates says, "then it is clear that it would be teachable?" Meno replies, "For how could it not be so?" forgetting Socrates's previous claim that there is no teaching, only recollection (87c5–7). Meno just does not want to recollect. He just does not want to inquire.

We might initially be inclined to say that Socrates had an impact on Meno, though, and that he changes and becomes inquisitive since after the three examples, as we saw, Meno does ask questions, such as the one we looked at, namely, why is knowledge valued more highly than true opinion for virtue. The other question Meno asks in that dramatically most important section of the dialogue is "whether in fact there are any good men" (96d2–3). Socrates puts together everything he needs to answer Meno's questions: good men are those who have virtue, and virtue, because it is knowledge, is acquired by reasoning about why opinions are true. Nonetheless, later in the dialogue, after the point of Meno's induced inquisitiveness, openness, or vulnerability, when Socrates brings in arguments with premises they have already refuted and rejected, Meno nonetheless accepts them rather than asking about them. Socrates seems to bring them in intentionally, to see if Meno has progressed. For example, he says at one point, that they thought "it was wisdom if it could be taught" (98d12). Has Meno simply forgotten Socrates's claim that there is no learning or teaching, only recollection? Again, Meno agrees to the claim that "since virtue is not teachable, it no longer seems to be knowledge" (99a7–8). Socrates seems to be giving Meno time and repeated opportunity to remember the story—unforgettable to us—and accompanying argument that there is only recollection, no teaching and learning. It just appears impossible to get Meno consistently to recollect, consistently to inquire, or, to put it bluntly, consistently to think for himself rather than absorbing what he hears from authoritative others, whether they be Gorgias or Socrates.

For our purposes in this chapter, however, Meno's seemingly unchangeable character is not of the greatest importance, while the lack of refutation, in the dialogue, of Socrates's argument that virtue is knowledge is more central. Virtue is knowledge or wisdom, and not true opinion, because knowledge or wisdom remains in the soul since when we have knowledge, we know why our opinions are true. It is only when he relaxes his rule somewhat that Socrates could seem to think otherwise, and he gives Meno ample opportunity to bring Socrates back to his claim that virtue is not teachable but, instead, is recollected.

Virtue is what kind of knowledge, though? Socrates's vacillation in the *Meno* between the term for knowledge, *epistēmē,* and for wisdom, *phronēsis,* suggests Socrates is aware the question needs an answer.[4] So does the fact that quick thought, *eumathia,* like courage, is on Socrates's list of goods of the soul that are not really good unless they are in fact wisdom. Virtue is not just smartness or intelligence, if we may think of *eumathia* that way. It is wisdom or *phronēsis,* Socrates suggests. As to what wisdom or *phronēsis* is that makes it different than mere smartness or intelligence, there the *Meno* leaves us in the dark.

The issue is, however, taken up in the *Republic.* According to Socrates, the most complete education ends with turning around from consideration of what is coming into being and to know being and the brightest part of being, namely, the idea of the good. To achieve that education, one's soul "must be turned around from what is coming into being with the whole soul until it is able to endure looking at being and the brightest part of being." What is the brightest part of being? Socrates goes on: "And we say that this is the good, don't we?" (*Rep.* 7.518c6–d1)

It is knowledge of this, all time and all being including the brightest part of being, that is virtue. He sometimes calls it not knowledge, *epistēmē,* but wisdom, *phronēsis.* "Therefore," Socrates says, "the other so-called virtues of a soul are perhaps somewhat nearer to those of the body. For they are not in fact present beforehand and are produced later by habits and practices, while the virtue of exercising wisdom (*tou phronēsai*) is in fact something more divine than anything, it seems; it never loses its power" (518d9–e4). The other so-called virtues he is talking about are virtues as understood in the parts-of-the-soul account of virtue in book 4. It is easy for a reader of the *Republic* to think that Socrates's final account of virtue in the dialogue is the one based on the tripartite soul. There are, however, a number of indications in the dialogue that this is not the case.

First, when Socrates gives that account of the virtues, he states clearly that it, and the account of the soul it rests on, are provisional. Regarding his way of proceeding in thinking about the soul in book 4, Socrates says, "know well, Glaucon, that in my opinion, we will never get a precise grasp of it using procedures such as those we are now using in the argument. There is another longer and further road leading to it" (4.435c9–d). The longer, further road is one that leaves convention and heads toward being and its brightest part, the idea of the good. Virtues of the soul understood as tripartite are a type of persisting lawful opinion. Courage, for example, on that account, is "the preservation of lawful opinion produced through education about what is fearful and what is not" (4.429c7–8).

Another sign that the parts-of-the soul account of virtue is not Socrates's final account is that the rational part of the soul is called "*to logistikon*" (the calculative) rather than something like wisdom. The three parts are *to logistikon* (the calculative), *thymos* (spiritedness), and *epithymia* (desire) (4.439c9–441c3). Calculation is only the first level of Socrates's list of studies that ascend up to the best and most complete studies (7.521c1–526c10), so we can take an account of the soul that identifies reason with it to be at best provisional.

Another sign is that, in the story in book 10 of human beings' afterlife choice of a future life, Socrates says that the one who in his life practiced virtue "by habit without philosophy" in the afterlife will choose "the greatest tyranny" (10.619c7–d1, b8). The point of a number of these passages is the same as the chaining-down-true-opinion passage in the *Meno,* namely, that the only true way to achieve virtue is through recollecting, inquiring, thinking for yourself, since only through doing so do you achieve the lasting true opinion that is found in wisdom. Only wisdom will remain. Virtue understood as true opinion, to the contrary, will depart when external constraints are removed.

Finally, to complete this argument that virtue for Socrates is wisdom understood as the knowledge of all being including the brightest part of being, namely, the idea of the good, it is important to refute an obvious point against my claim, namely, that there is another three-part account of the soul after the discussion of virtue as knowledge of the good or wisdom in book 6, namely, the account, in book 9, of the soul as a complex beast composed of three beasts—a human being, a lion, and a many-headed beast with tame and savage heads in a ring. The three beasts are designated as learning-loving and wisdom-loving (*philosophon*); victory-loving and honor-loving;

and money-loving and gain-loving (9.581a3–c5). Right away, however, we note a difference in how the three are characterized in comparison with book 4's parts-of-the-soul account, namely, that the rational part or beast is associated with wisdom, not just calculation, and, even more, it is described as wisdom-*loving,* thus showing that, in it, passion and reason are combined or connected. In the tripartite soul of book 4, reason—understood as calculation—is separate from passion and at best can only control it. For example, "moderation is a certain type of order and control of certain pleasures and desires" according to Socrates (4.430e6–7). Reason is strategic and conventional and it controls emotion, whereas in book 9 reason is of the good and is not separate from but an object of passion or love.

What accounts for this difference is the context of the second three-part account. It occurs after the discussion of the education that goes all the way out of becoming and convention into being including the good. And it occurs in a section that has had to do with decline—for example, the decline of the regimes. The suggestion, then, is that the three-animal soul is a soul that has glimpsed or seen some of being and the good, but has not advanced—or has not lastingly advanced—to the height of knowledge that is wisdom, that is, knowledge of the good. It is influenced by it enough as not to be an entirely habit- or convention-driven soul, but not enough to be fully suffused with it and simply follow it. If so, then, the argument is complete that virtue, according to the *Republic,* is wisdom where wisdom is understood as knowledge of being all the way up to knowledge of the brightest part of being, namely, the good.

Once I have that knowledge, I simply am good. Nothing else has a strong enough appeal to me to cause me to act otherwise. Bodily pleasure and money pale in comparison to the good, so I am moderate. Illiberality and petty speech do not appeal by comparison to one who is reaching out for all of being. Life itself does not seem great in comparison with all time and all being so such a one is courageous. And a person with all these virtues—moderation, liberality, and courage—will be just. In other words, once I have seen all time and all being all the way up to the brightest part of being, the idea of the good, everything else pales in comparison so that I simply am motivated by the idea of the good (6.485c2–486b12).

For Socrates, then, the ascent from sensation to that particular type of knowledge called wisdom and understood as knowledge of all time and all being including the idea of the good is an ascent from activity to passivity or receptivity, that is, from marking things to seeing them without marking them. The ascent from sensation to wisdom is, in addition, the ascent to the ethical. The good I intuit affects me, changes my whole pattern of affectivity. It has the effect of turning me around, and I then follow it and do what is good and just.

Moreover, the claim is not an isolated one in Plato's dialogues. For example, as we have seen regarding the *Phaedrus,* when I ascend to the idea of the beautiful—to the hyperouranian place beyond the heavens where it is seated on a beautiful throne—I fall on my back in awe and, upon my return to earth, want to love the beloved and serve him. For Plato, then, I maintain, the ultimate in passivity or being affected is knowledge. Hence, the high value he places on it. When I know the highest beings I am affected to engage in the highest or best activities in relation to myself and to others. To know the good is to be good and just. Even in the *Meno,* where the argument is truncated since it does not include an argument for what type of knowledge is virtue, virtue understood as knowledge is following, or even slavery, as we have seen. That is, virtue understood as knowledge is passive or responsive, not active.

Hence, the great difference between Plato and Levinas. For Levinas, to know is to affect, not to be affected, and thus it is not ethical. The ethical is what precedes knowing, it is that moment of being affected, of responding to the other. For him, knowledge is not responding but doing, not reaching but marking that which I would reach. Sensibility, on the other hand, is the moment in my relation to others in which I am affected. Plato is to Levinas as Athens to Jerusalem because Plato places affectivity in knowledge while Levinas places it in non- or precognitive sensibility.[5]

Another way to think about the two philosophers' differences on knowledge is by way of the concept of will. The concept of will does not play a role in Plato's ethical views. This is a corollary of some of the interpretive claims in the previous chapters' discussions of various dialogues. Virtue, for Plato, is a disposition to be affected in a certain way. Specifically, it is a disposition to be affected by the good or the beautiful, and the being affected takes place in knowledge (specifically, knowledge of the good).

Plato's central ethical claim, *aretē epistēmē estin* (virtue is knowledge), itself indicates that will is not central for him—especially because, as we have seen, that knowledge is responsive rather than active. There just is no concept of will in Plato. Ethics, for him, centers on our response to what is and the best of what is, the idea of the good. Some might think that *thymos* (spiritedness) in the *Republic,* or the *thymotic* dark horse of the soul in the *Phaedrus,* is a candidate synonym for will, but it is not. *Thymos* is a passion. It is associated with anger and often accompanied by love of honor or shame (*Phdr.*

253d3–6). It forms a pair, together with *epithymia* (desire) or eros (love), of principal passions for Plato, one a connective passion, the other a separating one, as symbolized in the *Phaedrus* by the fact that one horse goes forward to jump on the beloved while the other pulls the chariot back in order to say *no* to such a union or in the *Republic* by the fact that desire and eros lead to a violation and surpassing of the ideal birth number that would keep the city orderly by limiting the number of citizens while spiritedness makes a clear distinction between friend and enemy and welcomes the former while keeping the latter out. For Plato's Socrates, then, there are two principal passions, and they are related to the connection/separation theme that runs through the Platonic corpus constituting its secondary metaphysical theme (after the first-order theme of ideas): How do forms connect to things? How are they separate from them? How are parts connected in a whole? How are they separate? *Thymos* is a separating passion—separating friend and enemy in the *Republic*—and eros a connecting one. Of course, in a fully developed ethical soul, the psychological tendency is neither a simple tendency away (separation) nor a simple tendency toward (connection), not a simple *no* or a simple *yes,* but a tendency toward what is good and away from what is bad: once we comprehend the good, we move toward it and away from its opposite.

Levinas, to the contrary, sees an element of will in knowledge. Speaking of intentionality, he says, "The recurrence of persecution in the oneself is thus irreducible to intentionality in which, even in its neutrality as a contemplative movement, the will is affirmed" (*OB* 111/142). Levinasian affectivity is not intentionality, the statement indicates, because intentionality even in its most contemplative form or movement involves will: What do I contemplate? From where? How much of it? In relation to what? The responsiveness of contemplation is never separate from a voluntaristic component. Pure affectivity—here figured as persecution—is not contemplation, but something less active, more completely responsive, even a vulnerability. For Levinas, contemplation involves will. For Plato's Socrates, contemplative types of knowing are the highest kind—the kind that knows ideas—and are, thus, the most responsive as well. It is in this, really, that the most important difference between Plato and Levinas on knowledge resides—the difference between knowledge construed to be passive and knowledge construed to be active.

For Levinas, even the most contemplative intentionality is a form of auto-affection—not a being affected by the other, but auto-affection:

> In [intentionality] the fabric of the same, self-possession in a present, is never broken. When affected the ego is in the end affected only by itself, freely. Subjectivity taken as intentionality

> is founded on auto-affection as an auto-revelation, source of an impersonal discourse (*OB* 111/142).

In intentionality, I affect myself. For intentionality does not imply, simply, that consciousness is consciousness of an object, but that consciousness is consciousness of an object by way of a meaning—and that meaning is determined by me. In bringing meaning to an object, I am affected by myself. Levinas goes on:

> The recurrence of the self in responsibility for others, a persecuting obsession, goes against intentionality, such that responsibility for others could never mean altruistic will, instinct of natural benevolence or love. It is in the passivity of obsession, or incarnated passivity, that an identity individuates itself as unique, without recourse to any system of references, in the impossibility of evading the assignation to the other without blame (*OB* 111–12/142).

It is in the ethical, specifically in responsibility, that I am most responsive, not in intentionality. Ethics does not center on knowledge, Levinas indicates, but it also does not center on will. Responsibility is not even an altruistic will. Responsibility is passivity—incarnated passivity, since it is in sensibility, not knowledge, that I am most passive, and sensitivity is bodily. So, if Plato is to Levinas as Athens to Jerusalem or Greek to Hebrew, it is due to a very specific construction of Jerusalem or of Hebrew. It is not the Jerusalem or Hebrew of the Cain and Abel story in which we hear that "Sin couches at the door" and "Its urge is toward you, Yet you can be its master" (Gen. 4:7). For Levinas, virtue is not knowledge, but it is not mastery or will either, the most common contrast term to knowledge in ethics. Instead, ethics for Levinas is vulnerability and responsiveness—specifically, non- or precognitive responsiveness to the other. Ethics for him is not mastery of the desire of sin but "Here I am," which Levinas construes to imply a fundamental vulnerability indicated by the fact that, both in Hebrew (*hineni*) and in French (*me voici*), *I* is in the accusative. Ethics is not something I do but something I suffer. In ethics, for Levinas, I suffer the other.

This concludes our demonstration that the main concepts undergirding this book's Plato/Levinas comparison continue to play a role in Levinas's second major work and that a central difference between Plato and Levinas on the human vulnerability that constitutes the ethical is Plato's view that it is wisdom or knowledge of the good that constitutes the ethical and Levinas's view that no kind of knowledge constitutes the ethical since all knowledge marks what it knows and carries the mark of the one who does the knowing. Instead, for Levinas, as we shall see in the next and final chapter, the ethical is openness or vulnerability to something gloriously beyond ontology and knowledge, namely, the infinite.

CHAPTER 7

Glory and Shine

In this final chapter, we return to comparison of Levinas and Plato, beginning with Levinas in order to complete our discussion of the contributions *Otherwise Than Being* makes to this book's topics, and concluding with a return to Plato. For Levinas and Plato, there is an extraordinary quality to the ethical. For Plato, it is the shine of the beautiful and the good—with the good described, as we have seen, as what shines most and the beautiful as what shines forth most. The shine of the beautiful is part of the grace of our existence, but part of its peril, as well. Beauty can draw us to the best and highest things, and it is accessible to all, but it can also keep us from what is best if it keeps us from seeing our deficiencies and our need to remedy them. Similarly, glory, through its immanence, gives us a bit or a trace of the infinite but must be treated with care as well, since any time we think we have grasped an other whole we are overestimating ourselves and falling into epistemological idolatry by taking an imperfect account to be a perfect one. Beauty is different than the infinite, of course, because beauty falls in the realm of the ontological, on my account, while the infinite does not. Each, though, is conceived as the most accessible good and, as such, problematic because of our inevitable tendency to overidentify ourselves with goods in which we can share.

I will begin by discussing interpretive problems that come up about giving some emphasis to the glory of the infinite, given that Levinas does not give it central placement in his work. I will resolve the problems by showing affinities between Levinas's work and Jewish liturgy, Talmud, and Midrash. In doing so, I am not arguing for the reduction of Levinas's work to Jewish religious doctrine nor that his work is derived from Jewish religion or text. Instead, I am showing affinities that his work has with that religion, text, and liturgy—religion, text, and liturgy with which Levinas is increasingly familiar as the years pass. There is, I will argue, an affinity between Levinas's sidelining of glory and the de-emphasis of immanence in Jewish thought and practice. To show that will require turning our attention to that thought and practice and some of its most glorious components. The beautiful in Plato, however, will not be downplayed as a result since its remarkable shine will be discussed in detail in this chapter as well.

1.

"Holy, holy, holy! The LORD of Hosts! His glory fills all the earth!" (Isa. 6:3).[1] This passage from the Prophets—found also in the common Jewish liturgy recited on the Sabbath and festivals—indicates the contrast commonly drawn between holiness (*kedushah*) and glory (*kavod*). What is holy is separate while glory is present on earth. In origin, *kavod* (glory) means weight and comes from the intransitive verb *kaved,* to have weight or be heavy. During the service, those praying perform the distinction between holiness and glory by going up on their toes three times, once for each repetition of the word *holy* (*kadosh*), and coming back down in time to affirm, in the last word of the prayer, God's glory: *Kadosh, kadosh, kadosh adonai tzevaot, melo chol haaretz kevodo.*

For a Jew, though, glory, as the worldly presence of God, is both important and problematic: important because God is present in some way and we wish to be in or have God's presence; problematic because of the risk of idolatry. It is too stark to say that for a Jew, God is only separate. After all, according to the Psalms, the heavens declare God's glory: "The heavens declare the glory of God [*kevod-el*], the sky proclaims His handiwork" (Ps. 19:2–3). Created things, in other words, speak about or testify to God's glory, and, in that way, God is present. But the problematic character of the presence is indicated in the fact that the speech is of an unusual sort, as the next lines indicate: "Day to day makes utterance, night to night speaks out. There is no utterance, there are no words, their sound is not heard" (19:4).[2] Translators are not sure what to make of this passage. The heavens declare and proclaim, day utters and night speaks, but their sound is not heard? The point seems to be that there is utterance or speech that in some sense is not utterance, is not words, and is not heard. One translator, to bring out the contradictory character of the lines, turns it the other way, to indicate that there is no speech or words but there still is voice: "Without speech and without words, nevertheless their voice is heard."[3] Robert Alter translates the line this way, "There is no utterance and there are no words, their voice is never heard" and comments, "The heavens speak, but it is a wordless language."[4] Whichever we choose, the point is that there is a declaration of glory by the heavens, the sky, by each day and each night, and most especially here (as the verse will go on) by the sun, in a type of speech that, in some way, is not speech. God's glory can be expressed, but the expression goes only so far. It is not quite articulate. Perhaps, then, it is not an accident that a following verse, also part of the Sabbath liturgy, connects wisdom with simplicity: "The teaching of the Lord is perfect, renewing life; the decrees of the Lord are enduring, making the simple wise" (19:8). What wisdom do we get from the Lord? Wisdom that can be received by the simple.

In a similar vein, liturgical practice concerning the *Shema*—the central prayer in Jewish liturgy—reflects the relative positions of the holy and glory and indicates concern with problematic ways of articulating God's glory or presence. In reciting the *Shema,* the first line, "Hear Israel, the Lord is our god, the Lord alone" (Deut. 6:4), is immediately followed by "Blessed is the name of his glorious kingdom forever and ever" (patterned after Ps. 72:19). The first of the two lines is read out, loud and emphatically, while the second is read quietly, under the breath, or, in some congregations, silently. God is present—on earth, in the heavens, sun and sky and all things over which God has influence, kingship or reign—but, as we say so, we must be careful of saying so straight out or articulately. Every day, then, a Jew speaks, but does not speak, God's glory, that is, God's presence in the world. Every day, he or she is made performatively aware of the importance and danger of affirming God's presence on earth or, to put it differently, of articulating God's glory.

Of course, there are other passages in the prayer service, including many psalms in praise of God's glory, that do not include these warnings. But the two gestures, in prayers that are liturgically central and frequent, indicate a teaching, namely, that there is something dangerous about asserting God's presence or articulating God's glory, namely, the risk of idolatry, that is, the risk of taking something, whether the sun in the heavens or the rock on the ground that is made into an altar, to be the special location of the holy, the one and only place in which God abides, or, in short, to take something specific to be God.

Because the issue of our relationship to the glory of God cannot be settled—because we can never finally opt to reject the idea of God's presence nor to claim full awareness or articulation of the presence—articulate speech about God is problematic. In a passage that immediately follows one quoted by Levinas to which we shall soon turn, God speaks to a prophet, one who says to God, "Here I am; send me" (Isa. 6:8), and says, "Go, say to that people: 'Hear, indeed, but do not understand. See, indeed, but do not grasp.' Dull that people's mind, stop its ears, and seal its eyes—lest, seeing with its eyes and hearing with its ears, it also grasp with its mind, and repent and save itself" (Isa. 6:9–10). Not surprisingly, translators and commentators once again are puzzled, since God is telling the prophet to keep the people from understanding God and repenting. What if the point, though, is that the repentance God wants is not the one that comes from articulate mental grasping. What is important is beyond or before that. Or, put differently, what is important is something simpler than that. So, in another passage found in the liturgy, we read:

> The earth is the Lord's and all that it holds,
> the world and its inhabitants.
> For he founded it upon the ocean,
> set it on the nether-streams.
> Who may ascend the mountain of the Lord?
> Who may stand in His holy place?—
> He who has clean hands and a pure heart,
> who has not taken a false oath by My life or sworn deceitfully.
> He shall carry away a blessing from the Lord,
> a just reward from God, his deliverer.
> Such is the circle of those who turn to Him,
> Jacob, who seek Your face (Ps. 24:1–6).[5]

Who can experience God's presence? Not the wise or clever, but one who is clean of hands and pure of heart. Not articulate mental grasping, but a kind of moral purity or simplicity, are what God requires. Similarly, in a well-known passage in Micah, in response to the question, "With what shall I approach the Lord, do homage to God on high?" (Mic. 6:6), God responds, "He has told you, O man, what is good, and what the Lord requires of you: Only to do justice, and to love mercy, and to walk humbly with your God" (6:8).[6] What is required of you is not complicated, and does not require complicated specific acts or rituals difficult to understand. No, you already understand. You already know. Now, do it. *Be* just, merciful, and humble.

The passages cited suggest, on the interpretation I have chosen here to take, that God's presence is intellectually elusive and that, as a result, what is needed in relation to him is not complex intellectual connectedness, but something else, specifically, a kind of purity or simplicity.

But could this interpretation be way off? Is not God present in the Hebrew Bible? Isn't he manifest at Sinai, and then in the tabernacle (*mishkan*)? In fact, it is not clear that he is. At Sinai, when Moses went up the second time to get the tablets, he asked to see God's presence, and God denied him that full presence. God tells Moses instead that he will get only a trace of God's presence (his back), not the full presence, not God's face. Moses said to God:

> "Oh, let me behold Your Glory!" And He answered, "I will make all My goodness pass before you, and I will proclaim before you the name LORD, and the grace that I grant and the compassion that I show. But," He said, "you cannot see My face, for man may not see Me and live." And the LORD said, "see, there is a place near Me. Station yourself on the rock and, as My Glory passes by, I will put you in a cleft of the rock and shield you with My hand until I have passed by. Then I will take My hand away and you will see My back; but My face must not be seen" (Ex. 33:18–23).

God does what he promises. Instead of giving Moses God's full presence, God proclaims his goodness. Instead of seeing God's presence, Moses hears God's own self-description, the statement of God's good characteristics, sometimes referred to by Jewish exegetes as the thirteen attributes of God, a list of attributes regularly recited on Yom Kippur and recited by some in their daily prayers:

> The LORD! the LORD! a God compassionate and gracious, slow to anger, abounding in kindness and faithfulness, extending kindness to the thousandth generation, forgiving iniquity, transgression, and sin; yet He does not remit all punishment but visits the iniquity of the fathers upon the children and children's children upon the third and fourth generations (Ex. 34:5–7).

Most of the attributes God mentions are in the general area of compassion (grace, kindness, faithfulness, and forgiveness) and not of justice. That is notable for our purposes because the passage indicates that when we relate to that God whom we are unable to see, that is, whose presence or glory we are unable fully to have and only to glimpse, what we experience instead, primarily, are good characteristics God has that are themselves not forms of articulate knowledge, such as compassion, kindness, and forgiveness. One who is compassionate, kind, or forgiving overlooks what he or she knows about the other person. I do not fully experience God's presence, then, and when God exercises his most predominant characteristics, God does not fully experience mine, either. In compassion and forgiveness, God looks past what, presumably, he knows.

As it goes on, the story of the second reception of the tablets provides more evidence for the problematic quality of God's presence. When Moses comes down to the people after receiving them, his skin is shining, and they cannot look at him. He veils and unveils his face so that he can speak first with God, unveiled, and then, veiled, with the people—veiled so they can look at him. Even the residual presence of the Lord is too much for them:

> So Moses came down from Mount Sinai. And as Moses came down from the mountain bearing the two tablets of the Pact, Moses was not aware that the skin of his face was radiant, since he had spoken with Him. Aaron and all the Israelites saw that the skin of Moses' face was radiant; and they shrank from coming near him. But Moses called to them, and Aaron and all the chieftains in the assembly returned to him, and Moses spoke to them. Afterwards all the Israelites came near, and he instructed them concerning all that the LORD had imparted to him on Mount Sinai. And when Moses had finished speaking with them, he put a veil over his face.
>
> Whenever Moses went in before the LORD to speak with Him, he would leave the veil off until he came out; and when he came out and told the Israelites what he had been commanded, the Israelites would see how radiant the skin of Moses' face was. Moses would then put the veil back over his face until he went in to speak with Him (Ex. 34:29–35).

Moses's skin was shining with God's presence. It radiated out to the people. But it was too much for them fully to take in or see.

Surely, though, God is present in the tabernacle, the *mishkan,* that the people take with them as they travel through the wilderness. The very word *mishkan* is related to the word that later is commonly used for God's immanent presence, *shechinah.* Careful attention to the passages regarding God's relationship to the tabernacle suggests once again a complication of the simple idea of immanent presence. When God tells the people to make the tabernacle, he says, "And let them make me a sanctuary (*mikdash*) that I may dwell among them" (Ex. 25:8). He does not say, "Let them build me a sanctuary that I may dwell *in it.*" Instead, if they build God a sanctuary, then he will dwell among them, that is, be present to them—and be present to them no matter where they are. Two things are going on in this passage about God's presence. First, God will be present among them now wherever they go. God is not just the God who, in the complex way we just discussed, was present at Sinai, but is the God who will be present among them wherever they go. There is no one place of God's presence, but God can be present wherever they go. Second, this presence does not result from the fact that God is present in some one thing, the sanctuary. Instead, he tells the people to make the sanctuary so that he will be present *among them.* God isn't *in* the sanctuary. Instead, the sanctuary makes it possible for the people to access God's presence. So it is that God describes in detail what that sanctuary or tabernacle should be like, and asks the people to bring him gifts for it: "Tell the Israelite people to bring Me gifts; you shall accept gifts from every person whose heart so moves him" (Ex. 25:2). The gifts are gold, silver, copper, linen, wood, oil, and so forth. All these things—the mobile tabernacle, the beautiful materials, the construal of those materials as being gifts to God (who, after all, does not need anything)—indicate not a place in which God is particularly present, but a structure that enables people to be aware of God's presence where that awareness itself is the tabernacle, the *mishkan,* the place in which God resides. For what God instructs is for them to build a sanctuary so that he may dwell *among them.* God, then, can be present to us or in us whenever we direct our hearts to him. He can be present in a variety of material things if only we turn our hearts to him through them.

But perhaps I go too far. Are not some things more suitable to God than others—more suitable to God's presence? The story of Jacob and Beth El suggests to the contrary that the range of suitable things is broad. While on his way from Beer-sheba to Haran, Jacob stops in Luz to spend the night: "He came upon a certain place and stopped there for the night, for the sun had set. Taking one of the stones of that place, he put it under his head and lay down in that place" (Gen. 28:11). While there, he has his well-known dream of angels going up and down a ladder. In the dream, God promises Jacob the land and tells him that God is and will be with him. After that, he becomes aware of God's presence and changes the name of the place: "Jacob awoke from his sleep and said, 'Surely the Lord is present in this place, and I did not know it!' Shaken, he said, 'How awesome is this place! This is none other than the abode of God, and that is the gateway to heaven'" (Gen. 28:16–17). After that, Jacob turns the stone his head had rested on into an altar to God and renames the place "House of God" (Bethel): "Early in the morning, Jacob took the stone that he had put under his head, set it up as a pillar and poured oil on the top of it. He named that site Bethel; but previously the name of the city had been Luz" (Gen. 28:18–19). Even a stone can become an altar, we may conclude, if the stone facilitates our becoming aware of God's presence. It is just a stone. There is nothing special about it. God was there before, but Jacob did not know it. The previous example, of the sanctuary, indicated that we should not think that God is present in the beautiful materials but that they facilitate our being aware of God, and so the example of the stone indicates that even a simple stone can facilitate our awareness of God's presence. For on that stone, Jacob becomes aware of God. There is no one place of the holy, in other words. Places become holy, become filled with God's presence, when they are utilized by us to have the presence of God within.

The line of interpretation I am taking is only one possible line, and in Jewish traditions there are others. It is, however, a central line of interpretation starting at least in the period of the early rabbis when the view of the relation to the temple changes. When that view changes, a certain way of interpreting biblical passages comes to the fore that reflects the change. With the rabbis, in what is sometimes called the "rabbinic revolution," it is no longer the case that the temple in Jerusalem is considered to be the special locus of the holy, nor that hereditary priests have a special relation to the holy, nor that sacrifice is required to have a good relation with the holy. Instead, when two come together to study Torah, the *shechinah* (the immanent presence of God) is with them, and such study or deeds of loving kindness (*gemilut chasadim*) take the place of sacrifice. Similarly, rabbis, who simply are teachers, take the place of a hereditary priesthood.

For example, in the *Pirkei Avot,* a tractate of the Talmud, we learn that the *shechinah* is with those who discuss Torah, with those who study Torah, and with those who eat together if they discuss Torah:

> Rabbi Chanina ben Teradyon said, If two sit together and exchange no words of Torah, then they are like an assembly of scoffers, for it is written, "Nor did he sit in the assembly of the scoffers." [Ps. 1:1] However, [when] two sit together and do exchange words of Torah, then the divine presence [*shechinah*] dwells with them, even as it is written, "Then those who feared *Adonai* [God] spoke the one to the other, and *Adonai* listened and heard and for those who feared *Adonai* and who thought of God, a book of remembrance was inscribed." [Mal. 3.16] This verse applies to two [people]. How may I learn from Scripture that were one person to sit and study Torah, the Holy One would grant a proper reward? From the verse that states, "Though one sit alone and be still, yet will he receive [the reward]" [Lam. 3:28] (*PA* 3:2).[7]

> Rabbi Shimon would say, If three have eaten at one table and have not spoken words of Torah, it is as if they had eaten sacrifices offered to the dead. [Compare Ps. 106:28.] Even Scripture says, "All their tables are filled with filth and vomit without the divine presence." [Isa. 28:8] However, three who have eaten at one table and have spoken words of Torah, Scripture states, "He said to me, this table is in the presence of God" (*PA* 3:4).[8]

Similarly, in the *Avot de Rabbi Natan,* we learn that mercy or deeds of loving kindness replace sacrifice and mitigate the need for the temple:

> Once as Rabban Johanan ben Zakkai was coming forth from Jerusalem, Rabbi Joshua followed after him and beheld the Temple in ruins. "Woe unto us," Rabbi Joshua cried, "that this, the place where the iniquities of Israel were atoned for, is laid waste!" "My son," Rabban Johanan said to him, "be not grieved. We have another atonement as effective as this. And what is it? It is acts of loving-kindness, as it is said, 'For I desire mercy and not sacrifice'" [Hos. 6:6] (*ARN* 6).

Similarly, that there is no one special place of the holy, such as the temple, is made clear in numerous passages. For example:

> you find wherever Israel was exiled, the *shechinah,* as it were, went into exile with them. When they went into exile to Egypt, the *shechinah* went into exile with them. When they were exiled to Babylon, the *shechinah* went into exile with them. When they were exiled to Elam, the *shechinah* went into exile with them. When they were exiled to Edom, the *shechinah* went into exile with them. And when they return in the future, the *shechinah,* as it were, will return with them (*Mech.*, 1.14).[9]

But when will the presence be with them? As we have seen, it will be with them when they turn their hearts to God, when they study or talk about Torah, and when they are merciful or do deeds of loving kindness. We always have the possibility of God's presence no matter where we are, every one of us:

> When the Holy One, blessed be He, spoke to Moses concerning the tabernacle, he said: "Lord of the Universe! Will the Israelites be able to construct it?" He replied: "Even a single Israelite will be able to make it" (*Ex. R.* 33:8).

A *mishkan* is a place where God dwells. No matter what we have or where we are, we can build a *mishkan* for we ourselves can be a *mishkan*, and anything else that is a *mishkan* is one only because we use it to turn ourselves toward God. God does not dwell in the sanctuary. Instead, when we build a sanctuary to God, God dwells among us:

> It says (25.8), "Let them make Me a sanctuary that I may dwell among (or within) them"—in them, the people, not in it, the sanctuary. Each person is to build God a Tabernacle in his/her own heart for God to dwell in.[10]

All these passages—and others as well—suggest that, according to one Jewish interpretive tradition, the holy is separate or, speaking differently, present but mobile and elusive. The holy is present, as glory or immanent presence, but only as a mobile presence that cannot be fixed, cannot fully be grasped, and, to the extent that it can be taken in at all, is glimpsed by us when we relate in a simple or pure way to the plurality of what is.

2.

Two questions come to mind about the chapter subsection entitled "The Glory of the Infinite" (*OB* 140–52/179–94). First, why is a section so important given such an insignificant place in the work? Not only is it not in the center, as one might think it rightly ought to be, but it is close to the end of the work, when much of the work of the book is concluded, as if it were almost an afterthought. It is such an exciting and ecstatic way of approaching the other, but given its placement, one could almost miss it. Second, how can Levinas make the glory of the infinite so important? If the holy is transcendence and glory is immanence, does not the glory of the infinite suggest the very sacred that Levinas rejects on behalf of the holy?

Perhaps, though, Levinas's approach to glory and the holy is not so unique, and instead has strong affinities with the particular Jewish approach to glory and the holy just described. Perhaps, in other words, Levinas's strong anti-idolatry teaching reflects a strong Jewish tradition in a period in which Levinas was becoming more and more familiar with, and involved in, Jewish interpretive and scholarly traditions himself. The myriad references to Isaiah in *Otherwise Than Being* testify to this familiarity.[11] If so, the placement of "The Glory of the Infinite" within *Otherwise Than Being* would not be radical or unique at all, but almost orthodox. Just as we go up to the heights for the holy and then down to earth for glory, just as we speak out the *Shema* but bless God's glory under our breath, so we come down from the central sections of *Otherwise Than Being* to the chapter subsection that seems almost an afterthought in which we encounter the glory of infinite.

This pattern of placement, though, is not unique in Levinas's writings. In "Loving the Torah More Than God" (1955), a piece not about our relation to the other in general, as in *Otherwise Than Being*, but more specifically about our relation to God, Levinas follows a similar pattern, with detailed discussion of adult religion as religion in the face of the absence of God, followed by a brief mention of the idea that, once one has gone through a process of taking in and accepting God's absence, we can then, finally, ask for a little bit of God's presence.

The essay is a response to Zvi Kolitz's "Yosl Rakover Talks to God," a fictional account of a last testament written, and put in a bottle for posterity, by a man named Yosl Rakover whose family members had died and who was himself about to die in the final days of the Warsaw ghetto uprising. His wife was dead. Two of his children died with her in the forest, two others searching for food outside the ghetto walls (the Nazis drilled holes in one's head, while the other lost her mind), another from tuberculosis on the day of his bar mitzvah, and one in the Rosh Hashanah roundup of children. Yosl, despite all the injustice visited on him and his family, retains his belief rather than becoming an atheist—his belief no longer in a God who gives him "gifts without end," but "in a God who has hidden his face from the world and delivered mankind over to its own savage urges and instincts" ("Yosl Rakover," 9). Even in his own case, he expects no miracle and does not "beg of him, my Lord, that he should take pity on me" (10–11). "I have followed Him," Yosl says, "even when he pushed me away. I have obeyed His commandments, even when he scourged me for it" (23).

Yosl, then, retains his belief in a God who is not manifest, though his nonmanifestation is not due to sins on our part ("For greater and better men than I are convinced that it is no longer a question of punishment for sins and transgressions," 9). Moreover, his belief is in a God who, though he does not make himself manifest by making justice reign in the world, is connected to us through his words in the Torah, words of law and commandment. Defiantly, Yosl says he loves the Torah more than God: "I love Him. But I love His Torah more. Even if I were disappointed in Him, I would still cherish His Torah. God commands religion, but His Torah commands a way of life—and the more we die for this way of life, the more immortal it is!" (18)

For Levinas, Yosl's religion is a religion for adults, with a God who is "not some kindergarten deity who distributed prizes, applied penalties, or forgave faults and in His goodness treated men as eternal children" (LT 81/190). Levinas interprets Yosl's obedience to commandment despite the nonmanifestation of God in terms of his own notion of fundamental human responsibility: "Because if Yosl exists in his utter solitude, it is so that he can feel all of God's responsibilities resting on his shoulders" (81/190). Suffering, Levinas says, "reveals a God who renounces any manifestation of Himself that would give succor, and calls on man in his maturity to recognize his full responsibility" (82–83/191). He understands Yosl's relation to God through Torah, not through another manifestation, as a relation between two minds: "a relation of minds mediated by instruction, through the Torah" (84/192). "It is," he goes on, "precisely the Word itself, not incarnate, that assures us of the living God among us" (84/192). It is this relationship through speech, Levinas's familiar idea of the importance of speaking to, that protects us from the "madness that comes from direct contact with the Sacred without the mediating power of reason" (84/192), reason that hears law: "God manifests Himself not by incarnation but in the Law" (85/192).

Finally, Levinas points out that Yosl, once he has accepted God's non-manifestation except through Torah and law, reproaches God to manifest himself a little, reproaches the veiled God to unveil himself and show his face. Levinas asserts, "Only he who has recognized the veiled face of God can demand that it be unveiled" (86/193). Yosl, he points out, says to God, "You should not pull the rope too tight, because it might, heaven forbid, yet snap" (19/193). "You have made our life such an unending and unbearable struggle that the weaklings among us were compelled to try to elude it" (19–20). In other words, once we have accepted that God is not manifest, and avoided the problem of thinking we can have the full presence of God on earth, then we can ask for some of God's presence. Once we have been on our toes enough, we can come back down to earth; once we have witnessed God's separateness, then and only then can we affirm God's glory.

The placement of "The Glory of the Infinite," then, is not surprising. It is echoed by Levinas's treatment of the manifestation of God in "Loving the Torah More Than God"—which itself interprets the treatment of it in "Yosl Rakover Talks to God"—and it echoes the strain of Jewish tradition discussed in the previous section of this chapter. Presence may be asked for and affirmed only if and when God's separation has been accepted and the connection to him has been found through just and responsible dealings with others. It is important to note that in the passage from Isaiah 58—the Yom Kippur *haftarah* portion discussed in the preceding chapter—God says that when you are just and merciful to others, then he will say, "Here I am." It is important to consider the passage again with that theme in mind:

> Is not *this* the fast that I have chosen:
> to unlock the shackles of injustice,
> to loosen the ropes of the yoke,
> to let the oppressed go free,
> and to tear every yoke apart?

> Surely it is to share your bread with the hungry,
> and to bring the homeless poor into your house;
> when you see the naked, to cover them,
> never withdrawing yourself from your own kin.
> Then shall your light break forth like the dawn,
> and your healing shall quickly blossom;
> your Righteous One will walk before you,
> the glory of the Lord will be your rear guard
> Then when you call,
> the Lord will answer;
> when you cry, God will say, *Here I am.*

In other words, when we are just and merciful, then and only then, can we have some of God's glory, some of God's presence. This passage is, of course, extraordinary in a Levinasian context since, in it, it is God who says, "*Here I am.*" Levinas is orthodox, then, not radical, in the way that he postpones and downplays, and then allows for, some glory.

3.

What, then, is glory for Levinas? It is, some would say, quoting Levinas, "immanent transcendence." But it is important to keep in mind that for Levinas, the transcendence of the other is an absolute transcendence, a transcendence that cannot be converted into immanence. "The order that orders me to the other," Levinas says at the beginning of the section on the glory of the infinite, "does not show itself to me, save through the trace of its reclusion, as a face of a neighbor" (*OB* 140/179). Moreover:

> Before this anarchy, this beginninglessness, the assembling of being fails. Its essence is undone in signification, in saying beyond being and time, in the diachrony of transcendence. This transcendence is not convertible into immanence (*OB* 140/179).

If the biblical passages I have cited are any guide, however, it is when we are just or responsible that God is in some way present: it is when you give your bread to the hungry and take the poor into your home that God says, "*Here I am.*" Moreover, as we have seen in scattered references throughout this book, Levinas does use terms like *surplus* (*TI* 27/xv, 97/70), *marvel* (*TI* 27/xv, 181/156, 292/269), and *teaching* (*TI* 171/146, 197/191), all of which suggest something we get, a presence for or in us.

How does this work? First of all, for Levinas, glory results from responsibility understood as a kind of passivity, specifically, a passivity beyond all passivity in a noncognitive responsiveness to the other. When we allow ourselves to be affected by the other, there is glory. When we are noncognitively vulnerable to the other, there is glory. One term for responsibility conceived in this way is *proximity*, specifically, proximity conceived as debit, not credit. I am near the other by a kind of breakup or rupture of everything that is, specifically, me. In an earlier reference to glory, Levinas says,

> The more I answer the more I am responsible; the more I approach the neighbor with which I am encharged the further away I am. This debit which increases is infinity as an infinition of the infinite, as glory (*OB* 93/119).

Glory, then, is a process—a process Levinas calls *infinition.* I tend to approach the other as a theme. I want to synchronize myself with the other, but I cannot. The approach to the other, Levinas says, "is a non-synchronizable diachrony, which representation and thematization dissimulate by transforming the trace into a *sign* of a departure, and then reducing the ambiguity of the face either to a play of physiognomy or to the indicating of a signified" (*OB* 93/119). The process of relating to the other is, then, as I said in chapter 5, a dizzying emptying-out process. I cannot help but represent, thematize, and signify the other, but the other eludes me, eludes every representation I make, every theme I propose, every signification for which I seek a fulfillment. My aiming at the other through a theme and then bracketing that theme over and over again is, in fact, the infinition of the infinite, or glory. The other "obsesses the subject without staying in correlation with him, without equaling me in a consciousness, ordering me before appearing, in the glorious increase of obligation" (*OB* 94/119). I direct myself again and again toward the other who, again and again, escapes the theme or sign by which I attempt to reach him or her. This process of direction and retraction is the infinition of the infinite or glory. "The infinite," Levinas says in the passage where he first refers to glory, "is non-thematizable" and "gloriously exceeds every capacity" (*OB* 12/14). This is the type of presence we have of the other, in a trace that cannot be made into "the appearing of a phenomenon" (*OB* 12/15). We cannot "bring it into immanence and essence" (*OB* 12/15). When we approach the other, there is a breakup of essence, a "breaking point where essence is exceeded by the infinite" (*OB* 12/15). The breakup, however, *is* also a "binding place" (*OB* 12/15). That is to say, there is a connection. There is glory. The binding or relation is called, by Levinas, *illeity,* coining a term from the French *il* (he) to indicate a way of relating to the other without thematizing the other. *Illeity* indicates "a way of concerning me without entering into conjunction with me" (*OB* 12/15).

Why, though, must my relation to the other without theme be preceded by relating to him or her by way of a theme? So far, the answer is not obvious. It becomes obvious when we take into consideration the next important point for Levinas about glory, namely, that it is found most of all in direct address, or what Levinas, in *Otherwise Than Being*, calls *the saying* (*le dire*). My relation to the other as other takes place most of all in the saying. But the saying always takes place in *the said* (*le disant*), that is to say, direct address always has some cognitive content. Hence the need for retraction, or what Levinas calls in an earlier section discussed in the preceding chapter, for reduction.

There are some forms of speech, however, that come close to having no content. These indicate to us what breakup of essence is like. Levinas is fascinated by them. One, of course, is "Here I am." What cognitive content does such a statement have, given that it is always true that I am here? What is the point of uttering it then? When I say, in response to direct address, "Here I am," I am making myself available or, to be more precise, I am indicating that I am available or, to be even more precise, indicating that I am making myself available. "Not the communication of a said," Levinas says, "which would immediately cover over and extinguish or absorb the saying, but saying holding open its openness, without excuses, evasions or alibis, delivering itself without saying anything itself" (*OB* 143/182). "Here I am" is as close as we come to a pure saying because it indicates no other content than the speaker's own making him- or herself available: "Saying saying saying itself [*Dire disant le dire même*]," Levinas calls it. "Here I am" is the exposure of exposure, a sign of the giving of signs, rather than being the exposure of some content or a sign of a signified. On the one hand, then, it is responsibility ("'Here I am' *means* 'send me,'" Levinas says in a gloss on Isa. 6:8)[12] while, on the other hand, it is sincerity: "Sincerity would then be saying without the said, apparently a 'speaking so as to say nothing,' a sign I make to another of this giving of signs, 'as simple as hello' (*bonjour*)" (*OB* 143/183), Levinas says, referring to another form of speech that comes close to having no content. Sincerity is, for Levinas, a directness in relation to another, a facing of an other without the armor of concepts or themes. Sometimes he calls it *droiture,* in French, or *temimut,* in Hebrew. What am I saying when I say "*bonjour*"? Am I really saying that the day (*jour*) is good (*bon*) or wishing you to have a good day? Not exactly. Instead, I am making myself available to you—or, even more, giving an indication that I am making myself available to you. "Hello" is, then, both sincerity and responsibility.

Sincerity, then, "refer[s] to the glory of infinity" where glory is conjunction without appearance (*OB* 144/183). And, to come to our last important point about glory, "Glory is but the other face of the passivity of the subject" (*OB* 144/184). The dizzying process through which I make myself available is the glory of the infinite. In this process, I have a connection to the other without the other becoming a phenomenon, without the other becoming something with which I can synchronize, without the other becoming something that I can recollect. This provides the best explanation of the term I mentioned at the beginning of this section, "immanent transcendence." The term, rightly understood, does not indicate a transcendence that *can be made immanent.* Instead, for Levinas, transcendence is absolute and cannot be converted into immanence. Instead, it indicates that for Levinas the far and near collapse into one. The near, that is, glory, is simply our awareness—in proximity, responsibility, sincerity, saying—of the far or transcendent.[13] Just as the *mishkan* is holy because, through it, we make ourselves aware of God, so glory is the dizzying emptying-out process by which we are made aware of the infinity of the other.

Levinas, then, utilizes two key relational terms for fundamental metaphysics, *the holy* to designate transcendence and *glory* to represent immanence—that fleeting kind of immanence the other, whether God or another human being, has for us when we relate to him or her as absolutely other. Glory as immanence is accessible but also problematic. It is accessible because it is that little bit of presence of the wholly other that we in fact do, in some sense, get, and it is problematic due to the problem of epistemological idolatry that constrains us to treat that presence carefully and not make it too central.

But Socrates is not unaware of similar issues. More specifically, like Levinas, Socrates is aware that the most accessible good can easily draw us away from the ethical. Beauty, which for Socrates is the most accessible good, can lead us to cover over or deny our vulnerability, lack, or neediness and, as a result, keep us from remedying it. For Socrates, awareness of our ignorance is what spurs us to inquire and come to know. And, since virtue is knowledge, admission of such lack is crucial to attaining virtue. Similarly, because of beauty's fundamental connection to appearance, our love of beauty can lead us toward what seems good or to a surface good rather than what is good or to a deeper good. This is another way that beauty, the accessible good, can lead us away from the ethical. Because of these problems, Socrates, like Levinas, often downplays the role of the accessible good—beauty—in our lives. In the *Phaedrus,* Socrates has to be forced to discuss it. The ecstatic palinode in which he describes our soul as a chariot pulled aloft to view a radiant vision of the highest forms is a speech he resists giving. Phaedrus has to threaten him, playfully, with violence to keep him from going away instead. But, in that speech, and in some other places, like Levinas, Socrates actually gives the accessible good its due. In the end, for Socrates, the beautiful and the good are not in conflict. Desire, though associated with beauty, aims at what is best and, rightly informed and developed, helps us attain that aim. Desire is like reason, for Socrates, in aiming at what is best, and only needs appropriate rational development to attain it. According to Socrates, the beautiful, appropriately understood, is the cause of the good.

4.

> Beauty, as we said, shone bright among the other beings! And now that we have come down here, we grasp it, shining most clearly, through the clearest of our senses. For sight is the sharpest of our bodily senses, although it cannot see wisdom—how awesome would be our love if an image of wisdom came through sight as clearly as beauty does—nor can it see any of the other loved things. Beauty alone has this fate, to be what shines forth most and is most loved. (*Phdr.* 250c8–e1)

Beauty shines brightly. Any of us can see it. It is the most accessible of the highest forms. It not only shines, but shines *forth* most (*ekphanestaton*). Socrates is motivated by it when he is young, as we see from the fact that, as a young man in the *Parmenides,* he does not want to extend the application of his newly discovered idea of form to such entities as hair, mud, and dirt. Likely to test Socrates, Parmenides describes hair, mud, and dirt as ridiculous, least honorable, and most base. Socrates takes the bait and concurs—though he confesses that he sometimes has at least some inclination to grant that there is a form of them, but that when he does, he flees "for fear of falling ruined into a pit of nonsense" (*Prm.* 130d6–7). Parmenides thinks Socrates has this reaction due to the fact that he cares how he appears. When he is older and more philosophic, Parmenides avers, Socrates will no longer dishonor such things:

> "For you are still young, Socrates" Parmenides said, "and philosophy has not yet taken hold of you as hereafter it will take hold of you, in my opinion. Then you will dishonor none of these things. But now, due to your age, you are still concerned with how you seem to people (*pros anthrōpōn doxas*)" (*Prm.* 130e1–e4).

Parmenides, of course, is right that when Socrates is older, he will come to care less about how he appears to people. We see this in numerous examples in the dialogues. For example, in the *Gorgias,* when Socrates and Callicles discuss justice, Callicles maintains that justice is nothing but the advantage of the strong or superior person, and Socrates uses as examples to think about Callicles's claim a doctor, a weaver, a shoemaker, and a farmer. Callicles complains to Socrates about the examples, saying, "By the gods, you simply never stop talking about cobblers, clothiers, cooks and doctors," mechanical artisans Callicles would not even consider as examples of strength or superiority (*Grg.* 491a1–3). By the time of the *Gorgias,* then, Socrates has changed. He is not embarrassed by homely examples.

Similarly, in the *Symposium,* Alicibiades points out that generally Socrates's speeches appear ridiculous at first because the words and phrases in them are rough like a hybristic satyr's hide (*Sym.* 221e1–4). Alcibiades complains about Socrates there that "he talks of packasses, blacksmiths, shoemakers and tanners" (*Sym.* 221e4–5). Again, Socrates is not wary of, but even known for, his homely examples.

We see the adequacy of Parmenides's diagnosis of Socrates's character even more in Socrates's choice of a simple, earthenware pot as example of the beautiful in the *Hippias Major.* We have discussed the example previously, in chapter 3, section 3. The type of pot Socrates mentions, a *chytra,* is an ordinary cooking pot, a round earthen pot used for everyday cooking and serving.[14] Hippias is contemptuous of such an example. He considers it base or vulgar and the person who uses it uneducated or a boor (*Hipp. Maj.* 288d1–3). Socrates responds that such a person—and we know he is referring to himself—is "not refined but trashy, caring for nothing but the truth" (*Hipp. Maj.* 288d4–5). By the time of the *Hippias Major,* as well, then, Socrates has changed. He is not embarrassed by but quite at home with—and even makes a point of—mundane or lowly examples.

If the interpretation I have given of the *Hippias Major* is right, though, in that dialogue, we see Socrates change again. Though he continues in the dialogue not to care how he seems—and even makes a point of being trashy—nonetheless, he comes to see the importance of appearance. Beauty *is* appearance for Socrates, as I have argued. It is the appearance of form. It is the transcendent aspect of all being. As such, it is what makes all knowing and communicating possible—and, since virtue is knowledge, it is as such a source of the ethical.

At the same time, beauty leads us astray. It is a problem for us. Our love of beauty often leads us to cover over whatever is ugly. It especially leads us to cover over what is ugly or deficient about ourselves, an overestimation of self that keeps us from pursuing wisdom. Such overestimation and lack of openness to the real is for Plato what epistemological idolatry is for Levinas: in each case, the accessible good leads us away from the ethical through the overestimation of self.

Beauty as a mere covering is a common theme in Plato's dialogues. Cosmetics is unflatteringly contrasted with gymnastics in the *Gorgias,* for example. Cosmetics deals with bad or ugly aspects of the body by covering them, while gymnastics instead aims at bringing the body into good condition through exercise. Cosmetics is "malicious, deceitful, petty and servile" so that people "take on an alien beauty instead of their own beauty that comes through gymnastic exercise" (*Grg.* 465b5–6). Cosmetics covers lack rather than making us aware of it. As a result, we have no spur to overcome the lack, no spur to become better. The discussion sets up an analogy to the soul. Sophistry, on the analogy, is cosmetics of the soul: sophistry makes speeches look good without being good. Sophistry prettifies the soul, as well, without engaging it in the kind of mental exercise that really would make the soul better.

Similarly, in the *Hippias Major,* after refuting Hippias's definition of the beautiful as a beautiful maiden, Socrates restates the core of the issue about what the beautiful is as what is "that by which all other things are ordered [*kosmeitai*] and appear beautiful" (*Hipp. Maj.* 289d2–3). Hippias's answer, as we saw previously, is gold. One might think he is not responsive to Socrates's effort to move their discussion of what the beautiful is away from substances. Instead, I believe that what happens in the interchange is that Socrates and Hippias interpret the word *kosmeitai* differently. Related to cosmetics, *kosmeitai* can be translated correctly either as "is ordered" or "is adorned." Presumably, Socrates means to imply that things in good order are beautiful. Hippias, instead, takes Socrates to mean that things are beautiful when they are adorned in a certain way. Much of the drama and the teaching of the dialogue stem from this difference in approach, with Socrates connecting beauty with good order and Hippias connecting it to surface covering.

For another example, in the *Symposium,* Alcibiades performs the conflict between surface and intrinsic beauty when, having come to the drinking party to wreathe Agathon the wisest and most beautiful, he finds himself unknowingly seated between Agathon and Socrates: "Alcibiades sat down next to Agathon, in between Socrates and the latter, for Socrates had made room for Alcibiades when he saw him. On sitting down, Alcibiades embraced Agathon and wreathed him" (*Sym.* 213a7–b3). After doing this, he sees Socrates. Having wreathed Agathon, he is loathe not to wreathe Socrates as well. "Otherwise," he says, "he will reproach me because I wreathed you but not him although he conquers all human beings in speeches not only recently as you did, but at all times" (213e2–5). Turning from Agathon to Socrates, Alcibiades cannot decide. Whom shall he love? Agathon's speech is beautiful on the surface: at one point, he extemporaneously breaks into verse—but empty of content—a vacuous listing of good human qualities. Socrates, to the contrary, is described by Alcibiades as like a satyr on the outside (215b3–4) but entirely beautiful within (*pankala,* 217a1). His speeches initially strike one as ridiculous according to Alcibiades, as we saw before, but by showing us our need, they show us the way to beauty. Alcibiades says that Socrates makes him realize he is in need of much and chastises him because he neglects himself (216a4–6). Only Socrates, he says, can make him feel shame (216b2). When drunken Alcibiades sits between Agathon and Socrates on the couch looking from one to the other, the choice is clearly delineated, between surface beauty and beauty within.

5.

The dialogues on love belie the starkness of this contrast, however. For, in both the *Phaedrus* and the *Symposium,* beauty is portrayed as the highest form, and our love of the beautiful as a passion that can lead us to the highest things. Even more, love of the beautiful is portrayed in these dialogues as a passion that has no fundamental conflict with the highest things, as we have seen in chapter 1. Let us review.

Phaedrus is carrying a speech written by Lysias in praise of nonlovers. Socrates criticizes the speech and rewrites it to make its presuppositions clear. In this first Socratic speech, Socrates brings out Lysias's presupposition that eros or love is a form of hybris. That, according to Socrates, is why Lysias can argue that a nonlover is preferable to a lover. The prior presupposition on which the claim that eros is a form of hybris rests, according to Socrates, is that there are two sole sources of human action (*Phdr.* 237d6–7), an innate desire for pleasures and acquired opinion that aims at what is best (237d9–e1). On this account, sometimes desire and opinion have the same goal, but sometimes they do not since desire and rational opinion have no intimate connection. Desire is not shaped by reason but is irrational and has its own natural goal while opinion has no intimate connection with desire and, when rational, comprehends what is good or just. In cases in which desire and opinion do not have the same object, one can control or master the other, and then the one in control is the source of our action. Moderation (*sōphrosynē*) is one type of mastery or control, specifically, control by rational opinion that guides us toward what is best. *Hybris* is the other kind, rule by irrational desire that drags us toward pleasures. Love, for Lysias according to Socrates, is a specific case of such *hybris* in which the desire involved is eros or love, which has to do with the pleasures of beautiful bodies (Socrates's euphemistic way of referring to sex). In love, Socrates says on Lysias's behalf, the desire for sex masters opinion that has an impulse toward what is right (238b7–c4). According to Socrates, it is as a result of these presuppositions that Lysias can conclude it is better to have a relationship with a nonlover than a lover since the nonlover will control his desires and aim at what is good.

Socrates's second speech on love, the one he resists giving, the palinode in which he takes back what Lysias said and instead expresses his own views, does not include the idea of human self-sufficiency or control on which Lysias's conclusions rest. Instead, Socrates strikingly associates love with lack of control and being outside yourself. This is a crucial point for this book's discussion of Plato as a philosopher of the other. For Plato's Socrates, "the greatest good things come to us by the way of madness when, that is, it is given by the divine" (244a6–8), and love is one example of such divine madness. Socrates, in other words, thinks of us as fundamentally directed outside ourselves. He associates love with being *moved* (as Levinas thinks of the ethical as passivity), with being *enthused,* that is, with having a god within (as Levinas thinks of the ethical as having the absolute other within), with *awe,* with *humility,* and, generally, with madness (*mania*) or being out of your mind. The helmsman or governor of the soul, who is identified with reason (*nous*), falls on his back at the sight of the beloved and then loves him and serves him. He is knocked out and no longer in the things of himself (as Levinas thinks of our ethical state as denucleation) (250a6–7). For Socrates, then, eros is a divine madness that pulls you out of your self (ecstasy) and draws you up (transcendence). Moreover, though eros is madness, it is not irrational. Instead, in eros, two lovers together cognize beauty. They cognize what really is. As I have said before, in chapter 1, the ecstatic madness of eros leads the lover to the most important kind of rationality, a responsive rationality that is a simple beholding of what is.

In his image of this responsive rationality, the two winged horses represent spirited and erotic passions, and the winged charioteer represents reason (*nous*). When the lover sees a beautiful youth, there is a conflict between the erotic and spirited horses. The erotic horse pulls them all forward so he can have sex with the youth, but the spirited horse due to shame refrains from going forward and pulls them all back. They struggle again and again until the erotic horse wins out and leads them to the boyfriend whose face flashes like lightning. But that is not the end of the story of the struggle. If it were, a control model would in fact be Socrates's model of the soul and of human action and virtue. If it were the end of the story, then Lysias in fact would be justified in his rejection of eros, and Levinas would be right that, for Plato, knowledge and virtue are a return to the self. For eros then simply would be satisfaction of one's own desires.

Instead, Socrates believes that when we see beauty in the world, sensual beauty, we discern its likeness to the eternal beauty we saw before we were born. We want to fly upward and see that beauty, the very form of beauty. When the horses have concluded their struggle with the victory of the erotic horse—with the erotic horse controlling and overcoming the spirited horse and leading them to the beautiful boyfriend—the charioteer sees the bright boy, remembers beauty itself, and in fear and awe, falls on his back (254b7–8). He is knocked out and no longer in the things of himself (250a6–7). He restrains the unruly horses until they cease to be unruly, and the erotic horse is humbled and follows the charioteer's forethought (*pronoia*).

In other words, at this very point, Socrates makes it clear that a soul can surpass virtue as control and achieve virtue as knowledge. As the three-part soul of the *Republic* is not Socrates's final account of the soul and the control model that accompanies it not the final model of virtue, so the image of virtue as control by the charioteer/reason over two unruly horses/passions is not Socrates's final account of virtue in the *Phaedrus*. Instead, the final account, the account of virtue in its strongest sense, is the account according to which reason and passion go in the same direction. The erotic horse follows the charioteer's forethought (*pronoia*), Socrates says. That is, eros ceases to be controlled by reason and, instead, simply follows it. And, even more, this state is not merely an erotic state or an erotic-cognitive state, but also an ethical state. For at this point the soul of the lover follows the beloved with shame and fear and serves the beloved's needs. Eros, in other words, is not self-directed and brute. Instead, it is open to reason and to being and, as a result, it is ethical. The shared vision of beauty makes the soul good. Virtue, in other words, is knowledge.

What is implied here, as I argued in chapter 1, is that passions are cognitively intentional. They may function as brute when they are underdeveloped or underinformed, as we see in the *Phaedrus* and in the *Republic*. There in fact is a stage in which passions function as if brute. In the *Republic,* it is the stage, described in book 4, in which the reason is calculative, not contemplative, and the reason involved is convention-engendered opinion rather than knowledge. Such a situation is unstable. For, in it, reason is not secured. It is not, to use the image of the *Meno,* chained down. In other words, reason is unstable because its conclusions are not based on argument, on grasp (*nous*) of forms or first principles, or on the combination of the two, that is, on argument that originates in a grasp of forms or first principles. When it is not chained down in that way, it is easily dislodged, as the decline of the regimes suggests. For example, a young man whose father did not increase his and his family's substance because he refused to seek office or engage in bad activities in an unjust regime might easily be dissuaded by a beautiful or charismatic interlocutor. "Why be good?" such a person might ask. "Look where it got your father" (*Rep.* 8.549c2–550b7). What if such a person were Alcibiades? What if the issue were expansionist war? What if he filled his listeners' eyes with visions of wealth and power? Views of justice accepted merely because they are conventional might easily disappear under such circumstances. Such, I maintain, is the longer account of what Socrates means when he argues that true opinion is not as good as knowledge for virtue. Only knowing for yourself what is good will withstand such beautiful speeches. Conventional views are not strong and secure enough.

In addition, if virtue is not to be fundamentally unstable—and we know, of course, that thinkers such as Hobbes and Freud believe it is deeply unstable—its arguments must be based on first principles or forms. It is not enough even to have one's own arguments if the arguments are not themselves secured. For Socrates, as for Aristotle after him, they are secured when they stem from first principles that cannot themselves be argued for but can only be grasped in contemplation. The term for the faculty that engages in such contemplation is *nous.* When we grasp the beautiful or the good, we love it. And, when we do, we simply are good. Our passion and our reason have the same object. We are, in a unified and secure way, virtuous. The charioteer, Socrates says, seeing the bright boy, remembers beauty itself. In other words, the encounter with a particular youth who is beautiful gives us a grasp of the form of beauty. This grasp of the universal in the particular is recollection. The lover's reason remembers beauty itself, Socrates says. That is to say, seeing the beautiful youth, the lover grasps and is informed by beauty and, as a result, becomes beautiful himself. In fear and awe before the form of the beautiful, the charioteer or *nous* falls on his back, Socrates says, giving us an unforgettable image of a type of reason that is not turned in on itself. As a result of this whole experience, the soul of the lover does not jump on the beloved but instead follows the beloved with shame and fear and serves the beloved's needs.

Similarly, for Diotima in the *Symposium,* eros for the beautiful is not contrasted to passionate bodily eros. Instead, it begins with it. Correct erotic development, according to her, in fact begins with bodily love. "One who is to go about this matter correctly must begin while young to go to beautiful bodies," Diotima says (*Sym.* 210a4–6). He begins by loving one beautiful body. He moves from there to loving all beautiful bodies, seeing that the beauty of all bodies is one and the same. Then he comes to love beautiful souls—decent souls—even more, then beautiful practices and laws, then beautiful knowledge, and, finally, the beautiful itself (210a6–211d1).

It is important, of course, in each of these two descriptions, as well as in the discussion of the divided line and cave in the *Republic,* that not everyone gets to the absolutely highest visions. Not everyone ascends out of the cave. Not everyone sees the beautiful itself in the *Symposium.* And not everyone is a philosopher in the *Phaedrus* where some are described as being more divine than others. In order of descent the possibilities are a philosopher, lover of beauty, musician, or lover; a lawful king, warrior, or ruler; an athlete, trainer, or physician; a prophet or mystery priest; a poet or another of the imitative artists; an artisan or farmer; a sophist or demagogue; a tyrant (248d2–e3). Socrates is willing to countenance different abilities of ascent in different people.

But our point is a slightly different one in this section. Our question is about desire, and whether it leads away from or toward what is best. Socrates makes it clear in each of the three ascents—to the beautiful in the *Phaedrus* and *Symposium* and to the good in the *Republic*—that ascent is a process of pulling out what is implicit in the low. The high is implicit in the low, we could say on Plato's behalf. What we see when we are lovers who see a beautiful body in fact is the beautiful—but it is the beautiful as exemplified by or found in a particular bodily instance. As things are images of the forms in the *Republic,* so the form of beauty is implicit in a youth's beautiful body. Bodily desire is not in fundamental conflict with desire for the beautiful because the beautiful is implicit in every beautiful body. It is because not everyone will move from beautiful bodies to the form of beauty implicit in them that Socrates is cautious about stressing beauty as much as the good. It is not because of a supposed fundamental conflict between desire and what is best for us. For Socrates, desire points us toward what is best for us, if only we will follow in the direction it points.

6.

We have seen that one problem with beauty is that it can lead us to care about surface beauty rather than deeper beauty. We have also discussed the fact that not everyone ascends from instances of bodily beauty to less bodily and more generalized or formal types of beauty. We have the resources now to see as well that, in fact, these two problems are the same! Beauty motivates all of us, but we do not all see it in its most stand-alone form. Alcibiades's ambivalence about whom to wreathe as wisest and best is a paradigm of the issue. It is so easy to love Agathon's speech, beautiful in form, dramatic in its extemporaneous virtuosity, in its accomplishment of on-the-spot poetic form. It is harder to love what Socrates does. His examples are mundane. He requires us to rethink our most cherished opinions rather than simply utilizing them and starting from them in our speeches and our deeds. Socrates is an irritant, like a fly buzzing around and biting you when you try to swat it away. He is always buzzing around your most vulnerable places where you least want him to be. He will not be swatted away.

For there lies the more serious problem with beauty, that the transcendent quality of beauty can lead us away from confronting our human condition. Eros, Diotima says, is the son of *Poros* and *Penia* (Resource and Need). Socrates, according to the oracle at Delphi as interpreted by Socrates, is aware of his ignorance. Human being is in between utter capacity and utter lack, variously described, as these passages suggest. Awareness of lack is uncomfortable. The beautiful can give us a respite from what makes us uncomfortable. That is the grace and charm of beauty, that it raises us above the least pleasant aspects of our ordinary lives, from irritants like an insect bite, to deeper irritants such as our own human failings or, on the graver end of things, the inevitability of death.

For example, in the *Hippias Major*, as previously discussed, when Hippias's first two definitions of beauty—as a beautiful maiden and as gold—are refuted, he provides a definition referring to death as his third:

> I say that always, for everyone, and everywhere it is most beautiful for a man who is wealthy, healthy and honored by the Greeks, having arrived at old age and having beautifully arranged the burial for his own parents when they have reached their end, to be beautifully and magnificently buried by his own offspring (*Hipp. Maj.* 291d9).

A beautiful funeral hides the inevitability, and possible nobility, of death. In fact, the very idea of a beautiful funeral is from a certain standpoint bizarre. Central to any funeral is a corpse, that is, a material entity, specifically, a body losing its form. What could be uglier? And, inevitably, we all at some point will be one, so to speak. A beautiful funeral, in one sense anyway, is a paradigm of beauty as a covering over what is ugly and, even more, as an event that can take the bite or the sting out of our inevitable, human fate.

Moreover, as Socrates's refutation of the definition shows, to see this as the paradigm or as the definition of beauty is to deny beauty to gods and heroes. For the gods do not die, and heroes, paradigmatically, risk early death for the sake of important ends. In Greek one even says about them that they died for the sake of the beautiful. That is, one says that their dying before their parents for something important is what makes them beautiful. Socrates mentions Achilles in his argument by counterexample (along with other heroes and gods)—Achilles who died to avenge his beloved friend, Patroclus. We can call to mind as well Socrates—who in the *Apology* compares himself to Achilles and who dies for his friend, wisdom—actually becoming a corpse in the *Phaedo.*

The reference to corpses and rot are made even clearer when Hippias responds to Socrates's suggestion that gods and heroes might not be beautiful. In fact, Socrates is only saying that Hippias's definition would make gods and heroes not be beautiful, but the allusion to the very idea that they might not be beautiful strongly bothers Hippias. "Go to blessedness!" he says euphemistically (293a2). The phrase is a euphemism for "Go to the crows!"[15] That phrase is similar to our "Go to the dogs!" or "food for crows" and is a reference to death and, even more, to the corruption of our bodies, since the idea is that the crows will eat you! What is this thing called a human being? It ranges from blessedness—being close to the gods—to being food for crows. Our lives range from blessedness or prosperity to being ground up in an animal's mouth. We range from divinity to dirt. It is hard, in thinking of this euphemism, not to think, as well, of the hierarchy discussed in the *Parmenides,* from forms such as the one, the beautiful, and the good all the way down to mud, dirt, and hair. The sweep is found in our human nature.

What, though, if beauty in general came out of what is ugly? A beautiful human body contains ugly guts and feces. Perhaps the body is the ultimate euphemism for us since it is, from one standpoint anyway, nothing but a beautiful covering over ugly guts and feces.[16] But this idea, that the beautiful results from or supervenes on what is ugly or plain, is one Hippias just cannot entertain, as we saw in chapter 3. After the third definition fails, Socrates wants the two of them, who lack knowledge, to inquire together in order to find it. Socrates exhorts Hippias to "look-for-it-with-me" (*suzētei*) (295b3). If they did inquire together, the beautiful, knowledge, would come out of the ugly, ignorance. If Hippias looked for it with Socrates and they then found it, that would be the most beautiful thing according to Socrates! The most beautiful thing is two together seeking and attaining wisdom (295b4). However, Hippias does not want to inquire together. He wants to say what he has already thought out and prepared when by himself. He says that if he were to go off and seek the beautiful himself, he would be able to say what it is precisely—more precisely even than any preciseness: "I know well that if I were to go into seclusion for a short time and investigate it by myself, I could tell it to you more precisely than all precision" (295a4–6). Hippias is ashamed for his ignorance and ugliness to be manifest in public. But if the two ignorant ones pooled their resources together, knowledge might come out of it. For both together might be more than each separately. Hippias's shame keeps him ignorant. It prevents him from becoming better.

This, then, is how beauty leads us away from what is best according to Socrates. It leads away from what is best if we cannot ever allow that we are besmirched by what is ugly. It leads away from what is best if we cannot admit our own lack, need, or vulnerability. Hippias, for example, cannot find beauty because he cannot admit that he is in part ugly. Socrates presents himself as the paradigm of how to find it through admission of not having it since he admits to or is aware of his own ignorance. If we let our ignorance be manifest, we have the resource to remedy it. If we let our ignorance be manifest together with another, we have perhaps even more resources to remedy it, since both together are different than each separately.

Even worse is when we prey on others' tendency to feel shame at their own lack. Socrates, the gadfly, does not do this, but Hippias, the sophist, does. He says what people want to hear not what benefits them. Near the beginning of the dialogue, he makes it clear that he thinks his wisdom is far above that of the ancients but that he does not say so "fearing the wrath of the dead" (282a7–8). In addition, since Spartans do not allow education that is contrary to established custom, Hippias does not teach them beneficial new ideas that he has. Instead, he teaches them ancient history, reciting genealogies of heroes and people and the founding and settlement of cities, since this is what they want to hear. Socrates accuses him of simply telling pleasing tales, like an old woman entertaining children with stories they like to hear: "the Spartans use you the way children use old women, to tell stories pleasantly" (286a1–2). Hippias, then, both is uncomfortable allowing his own deficiencies to be manifest and also preys on the similar tendency in others by saying what they want to hear. They flock to him as a result, but on Socrates's behalf we can ask whether they become better. Using Hippias's relation to the Spartans as an example, we can say that they do not. He is so far from making them more fine that he cannot even say what the fine is, and he is unwilling to undertake the personal revelations he would have to undertake in order to find out. Hippias perhaps does not hear the irony in Socrates's opening line greeting to him, "Hippias, the beautiful and wise" (281a1). Socrates, to the contrary, came in his life to the awareness of his own lack. According to himself, he learned it at least in one case from Diotima who taught him his human, all-to-human, state of being more like a daimon than like a god. She tells Socrates, you think Eros is the loved one rather than the lover. Instead,

Eros is the lover and love, because it is a kind of desire and desire is a kind of lack. Socrates, personified as Eros in the *Symposium,* progresses over time. He does not remain in a shame-governed state all his life. He learns to let his need be his resource, his awareness of ignorance be the spur to overcoming ignorance, and thus becomes Socrates, the paradigmatic philosopher we have come to know.

To summarize, beauty has the power to help us see and be motivated by the highest things while at the same time it is problematic in two important ways. Beauty's power is the power to point us toward what is most important for us, namely, the beautiful and good. Beauty points us in the right direction and, if we go far enough in that direction, we will see the first principles or forms the awareness of which can suffuse our lives and motivate us always to do what is best. The beautiful, then, is not problematic due to a supposed natural or eternal conflict with desire. That, according to Socrates, is Lysias's view of desire and beauty. Instead, beauty is problematic because, though we all see beauty, it being the most accessible of the evaluative forms, we do not all see it fully and so may prefer a surface beauty over a deeper one. Even more problematic is the fact that, under the spell of the beautiful, we may deny our human vulnerability. A beautiful funeral hides the inevitability, and possible nobility, of death. A beautiful tale can flatter the young by telling them what they want to hear rather than what they need. A beautiful political speech given by a beautiful, compelling speaker can lead a city to disaster.

Plato, then, has drawn for us a Socrates who is aware of the same type of problem about the accessible good that Levinas is, namely, the problem of overestimation of the self that leads away from the ethical. The problem delineated by Plato's Socrates is not, of course, exactly the same problem Levinas delineates. For Levinas, the issue is what I have called epistemological idolatry. The job of the philosopher is to loosen the grip of being, Levinas says, so that no one said, no one human perspective—especially not our own personal perspective—will become identified with the final or whole truth about things. To do so is to allow the hypostasis of an eon to become an idol, according to him. Even more, it is to see a perspective, our own perspective, and therefore ourselves, as being perfect, a form of idolatry, since idolatry is seeing what is not perfect as perfect. It is important for Levinas as a result that we accept that the other exceeds us and accept that we never quite get the other whole or pure. Put differently, it is important for Levinas as a result that we reinterpret glory not as immanence ordinarily understood but as just the other side of our responsiveness: "Glory is but the other face of the passivity of the subject," Levinas says (*OB* 144/184). Glory is an attenuated immanence. It is our recognition of the distance between the other and ourselves.

Socrates, too, is concerned with his most accessible good not causing us to overestimate ourselves. He, of course, does not call doing so idolatry. Nonetheless, much of his work is about the same general problem, the problem of not wanting to know our own limitations. Dialogues are full of examples of this. In the *Meno,* when Meno has been refuted time and again, his way of managing the pain of negative self-awareness is to attack Socrates. That is why he gives the image of Socrates as an ugly stingray fish, a fish that numbs those with whom it comes into contact (*Meno* 79e7–80b2). Meno, in other words, when faced with recognizing his own lack and seeing himself not as beautiful but as deficient and ugly, projects his own ugliness onto Socrates to relieve himself of the pain. Hippias, true perhaps to his nature as a diplomat, when in the same situation of having been soundly refuted, wants to run away and be by himself where he can devise a beautiful speech to give to Socrates—beautiful, but probably not true. For Socrates, this tendency we have to avoid recognizing our limitations, our lack, our vulnerability, leads away from the ethical. And most powerful among such motivations is the beautiful since it is the most powerful of all the evaluative forms. It is most accessible and can, as a result, either most powerfully lead us to the highest things or most powerfully lead us to cover over our needy human condition thereby denying us the resources we need to become good.

With this comparison, our discussion of similarities and differences between Plato and Levinas comes to a close.

Conclusion

What does the presence of an other hold out for us? Whether it is Phaedrus, anxious about his lovers, or Sartre, ashamed before a keyhole, the stakes of this question are high. For Phaedrus, the question is whether to open himself to others or shut himself off in fear. For Sartre, the issue is whether the presence of an other is a risk to his very self, a self that is a self by making others objects. For us, the question poses a challenge to some of the dominant thought of the cultures that have shaped us. Levinas's answer to the question is that fraternity is ipseity, that I am a self by being in relation to other—but that, adding his own proviso, I relate to others while remaining my self. In fact, the self is a self by relating to others while absolving itself from the relation and remaining itself. Striking about Levinas's idea of the relation is, first, that it is a relation in which I bracket all my own interests, desires, and presuppositions in order to relate to the other as such—as the singular other before me, the person before me no matter what their properties may or may not be at any one time—and, second, that though I am constituted by the other, I retain myself in that constitution. Levinas is between Heidegger, for whom I am fundamentally in the world, and Descartes, for whom I am fundamentally turned in on my self. It is this that makes Levinas an important transitional figure between those who define us by inwardly turned subjectivity and those who make subjectivity fundamentally an artifact of something outside itself—or, to use a common set of terms, between moderns and postmoderns.

Levinas, however, as I have shown, is not alone in critiquing the self-sufficient self and creating a philosophy of the other. Plato, his frequent contrast figure in *Totality and Infinity* for his own approach to the self, is a philosopher of the other. He describes and delineates a similarly fundamental and disruptive directedness of self to other. The similarities include the figuratively violent nature of the relation of self to other, the freeing quality of being in a relation to an other, and the fundamental vulnerability we experience in being in such a relation. In addition, their philosophies of the other each include a movement from disruption to service, from simple to complex freedom, and from personal desire to the active promotion of the futures of others.

With these similarities noted, the differences in each philosopher's view of the nature of relations to others stand out. In fact, one of the goals of this book has been to make them stand out and, in so doing, to alter how we see Levinas in the history of thought and how we understand what is most unique about him, and as well to open our minds to the idea that there is more than one fundamental way to be for or be affected by the other. Levinas is preceded by Plato, among others, in seeing self as fundamentally, metaphysically in relation to other. Levinas, then, is one of a number of twentieth-century philosophers to turn to premodern thought for a critique of the self-directed self found in Enlightenment thought, based in part on his acceptance of a fundamentally Enlightenment, as well as phenomenological, idea of the active aspects of knowing. But the premodern sources to which Levinas turns lead him to a strikingly different understanding of being for the other, as different from Plato's as the new is from the eternal, as glory is from beauty, and as relating to someone as singular is from the responsive beholding of that other's qualities. Two very different kinds of response. Two very different kinds of philosophy of the other. Each with its own importance, and each with its own very specific, and lasting, appeal.

NOTES

Introduction

1. Translations of works by Plato and Aristotle are my own. Translations of all other texts are by the cited translator. Page references separated by a slash are first to the English, then to the French text. The Socrates referred to throughout is the Platonic Socrates of the dialogues not the historical Socrates. As a result, some views that originated with Plato will be referred to as Socrates's views since they are views attributed to Socrates in the dialogues.

2. Compare Matthew Abbott, "Epistemological Humility: Knowledge After Levinas's Radical Separation."

3. For similar treatments of the history of Levinas's references to Plato, see Adriaan Peperzak, "Platonism of Emmanuel Levinas," and Naas, "Lending Assistance."

4. For discussion of the summary, see Peperzak's, "Platonism of Emmanuel Levinas."

5. For external support for this interpretation, see Aristotle, *Nicomachean Ethics* 1.6, where, after a short discussion of metaphysics—about the equivocity of the good—Aristotle similarly does not go to the most fundamental metaphysical level. He states that further precision on the topic belongs to another part of philosophy (1096b30–31). I argue the other part of philosophy is the discussion of being as potentiality and actuality in *Metaphysics* 9. Achtenberg, *Cognition of Value,* 44–49.

6. See Achtenberg, "Review of *The Philosophical Sense of Transcendence.*"

Chapter 1

1. I was fortunate to hear Stewart Umphrey discuss the *Symposium* in 1980 and was influenced by his approach and ideas. My approach to the *Phaedrus* shares a stress on human vulnerability with Martha Nussbaum's interpretation of them in *The Fragility of Goodness.*

2. That this vulnerability, figuratively understood as violence, is not violence in an ordinary, concrete sense, is clarified by a comment Levinas makes to an audience member during an interchange at the University of Leyden in 1975: "By vulnerability, I am attempting to describe the subject as passivity" (*OG* 133/83).

3. The view that Levinas thinks openness brings something good to the one who is open is counter to the more common assumption that, for Levinas, my responsible relation to the other fundamentally does violence to me. It is my view, counter to this, that for Levinas, though my relation to the other is all about the other, nonetheless it brings a good also for me. This view of his is more evident in *Totality and Infinity,* with terms like *marvel, new dimension,* and *teaching,* but also found in *Otherwise Than Being,* specifically in the concept of *glory,* despite the later work's greater emphasis on responsibility and its backgrounding of desire, a term central to *Totality and Infinity.* The concept of glory, in a Hebraic register, denotes a type of immanent good. Why Levinas emphasizes responsibility and backgrounds glory is one of the main topics of chapter 7, "Glory and Shine." The chapter also discusses a parallel foregrounding and backgrounding found in Levinas's

"Loving the Torah More Than God," where acceptance of the withdrawn God is in the foreground but gives one the standing to ask for a little of God's presence, and maintains that a similar pattern is found in one interpretive strain in Jewish thought, a strain in which the holy is emphasized and glory mentioned in hushed tones to de-emphasize it.

4. There are other frames. One of Derrida's ways of expanding Levinas's legacy is by utilizing many frames. I shall leave delineation of that extraordinary set of expansions to other discussions.

5. This chapter refers to Levinas's treatment of ideas in *Totality and Infinity*, the earlier of his two major works.

6. *Hybris* has a variety of meanings all suggesting a disposition to overstep limits: wantonness, arrogance, insolence, insult, violation, assault. The verbal form, *hybrizein*, can mean to rape someone.

7. At 246b1–2, Socrates refers to the charioteer as the ruler of the soul: "the ruler holds the reins of the pair [*ho archōn synōridos hēniochei*]." At 247c7–8, he calls *nous* the soul's governor or helmsman: "really existing being, visible alone to reason, governor of the soul [*psychēs kybernētēi monōi theatē nōi*]."

8. Since I see Socrates making one-to-one comparisons—moderation and shame to *hybris*, genuine reputation to boasting, driven by commands and speech alone to deaf and barely yielding to whip and goads—I translate *alēthinēs doxēs* (253d7) as "of true reputation." Love of honor (*philotimia*) is left out of the comparison due to the fact that Socrates is describing the virtue of the good and bad horses so that the sense is: though he is a lover of honor, nonetheless he has moderation and shame.

9. Though this comes from a slightly earlier part of his speech, in it, Socrates is talking about a lover (249e4).

10. Regarding the boy, Socrates refers to "the flow of beauty going back into the beautiful one through the eyes" (255c4).

11. In chapter A.2, Lingis translates *rupture* as *breach* (*TI* 35/5) while in the second reference given here, he translates it as *rupture* (*TI* 278/255).

12. See also *TI* 197/171.

13. As noted before, Levinasian absolute transcendence is distinct from Plato's transcendence of a whole over its parts.

14. The French "*le creuse*" could have a stronger meaning than "deepens it" such as "hollows it out" or "excavates it."

15. This calls to mind the other who threatens my integrity in Sartre's *Being and Nothingness* and in the lordship and bondage section of Hegel's *Phenomenology*.

16. *Fecundity* can be read as Levinas's response to Heidegger's being toward death and can instructively be read together with *natality* in Hannah Arendt's *The Human Condition* as another such response and with Derrida's *survival* (*survivre*) or *legacy*.

17. For ecstasy, see also *TI* 48/18 where Levinas states that metaphysics "excludes the implantation of the knowing being in the known being, the entering into the Beyond by ecstasy." In a similar vein, Levinas rejects apostasy of the self: "But faced with this alterity the I is the same, merges with itself, is incapable of apostasy with regard to this surprising 'self'" (*TI* 36/6).

18. The contrast is with Hegel's universal identity that negates the heterogeneous. Levinas quotes Hegel: "but this which is distinguished, which is set up as unlike me, is immediately on its being distinguished no distinction for me" (*TI* 36–37/6–7). In "Love and Filiation," Levinas says that in contrast to "knowledge which is suppression of alterity and

which, in the 'absolute knowledge' of Hegel, celebrates 'the identity of the identical and the non-identical,' alterity and duality do not disappear in the loving relationship" (LF 66).

19. As we will see in chapter 6, in *Otherwise Than Being,* Levinas refers to a "good violence" (*OB* 43/56).

20. As Sartre would maintain who, according to Levinas in his interview with Richard Kearney, interprets the other fundamentally as a threat. Levinas, "Ethics of the Infinite," 182.

21. In *Otherwise Than Being,* being is adverbial.

22. Thanks to Antonio Calcagno for helpful comments on a previous version of this chapter.

Chapter 2

1. Gorgias states that rhetoric is the greatest good for human beings because it brings freedom and the power to rule over others in one's own city (*Grg.* 452d5–8).

2. When Socrates directs the slave to draw an additional figure inside the original one, all the slave has to do to solve the geometrical problem of finding the double square is see that the new figure drawn is, in fact, the double square. Seeing that could, however, be understood to be an example of recollection as described in the *Phaedrus* where, as we have seen, it is defined as understanding what is said according to form, moving from multiple perceptions to what is gathered into one by reasoning (*logismōi*) (*Phdr.* 249b6–c4). Recollection, in other words, is, roughly, movement from perception to the conception or idea that is implicit in it. That is all the slave needs to do, make explicit what is implicit in what he sees.

3. When the topic of the sophists comes up, Meno begins to express some personal questions about which he would like to inquire: he admires Gorgias for not claiming to teach virtue but simply to make people clever speakers; he cannot tell whether the sophists are true teachers; and he wonders how good men ever come to be and whether there really are any. Meno's genuine questioning about what really matters to him—how to get virtue—enables Socrates to argue that knowledge, since it is more lasting, is superior to true opinion (97c11–98a4). The discussion then devolves into a mush of statements, some of which contradict claims they have made before that pass Meno by without notice, for example, the claim that if virtue is wisdom, then it can be taught (98d10), and the claim that since virtue cannot be taught, it is not knowledge (99a7–8), when they had agreed that knowledge was achieved through recollection. Just about nothing of the argument has stayed, in a lasting form, in Meno's mind. Meno remains the same. So the dialogue ends with the conclusion that virtue is true opinion and must come by divine allotment or fate, since it cannot come by knowledge. This parallels what Socrates probably thinks at the end of the dialogue about Meno himself, that if he is to achieve virtue, he would get it as a kind of divine gift and not through achieving knowledge, since he remains averse to or by disposition incapable of thinking for himself, that is, of recollecting.

4. Plato, like Homer, is fond of puns and wordplay. In the *Meno,* he plays on the similarity between the sound of Meno's name and the word for remembering (*mnēmōn, Menōn*) to make fun of the fact that Meno is someone who remembers what he has heard rather than thinking. The title of the *Meno* means *remaining,* which is what Meno does—remain the same, not change at all in his tendency to say what he has heard rather than thinking for himself—as pointed out by Jacob Klein, *A Commentary,* 44, 186. The title of the dialogue on friendship, a kind of relationship, is "breaking up" or "dissolution" (*Lysis*).

5. More specifically, one would suppose, the form of the good, since if virtue is knowledge of forms, it would have to be knowledge of evaluative forms not just of any kind of form since Socrates makes it clear at 88a–b that he distinguishes the type of knowledge that virtue is, wisdom (*phronēsis*), from intelligence or quick thought (*eumathia*). Virtue, for Socrates then, is wisdom not mere intelligence or intellectual ability.

6. The claim that virtue is the ability to get good things is refuted by the claim that it would only be the ability to get good things justly, moderately, or piously. But Socrates says to Meno about the definition, "perhaps you speak well" (78c3–4), suggesting the definition is correct. What ability would be the ability to get good things? The answer would be knowledge or wisdom. The passage, thus, indicates Socrates's own answer to the question, what is virtue.

7. "What is the subject most argued about by Chrysippus himself and Antipater in their disputes with the Academics? The doctrine that without assent there is neither action nor impulse, and that they are talking nonsense and empty assumptions who claim that, when an appropriate appearance occurs, impulse ensues at once without people first having yielded or given their assent." Plutarch, *Self-Contradictions* 1057A, in Long and Sedley, *Hellenistic Philosophers,* 317.

8. In *Otherwise Than Being,* I become a hostage to the other (6/6), substitute myself for the other (6/6), am wounded by the other (15/18), am penetrated by the other (49/64), etc.

9. Translation amended.

10. More literally, no longer inside the things of himself.

11. See chapter 1, note 7 in this volume.

12. Socrates does say that all nature is akin (*Meno* 81c9–d1).

13. Rousseau, "Sciences and Arts," 6.

14. Emerson, "Self-Reliance," 28.

15. He goes on in the passage to say that freedom is courage—a difference from Socrates according to whom it more centrally is wisdom.

16. Socrates's point is similar to the views of Anglo-American philosophers who associate freedom not simply with the ability to act on our desires or evaluations but on our decisive commitments (Frankfurt) or strong evaluations (Taylor). See Stalley, "Plato's Doctrine," 149–51.

17. The phrase is preceded by an *if,* but the affirmation of the antecedent is assumed.

18. Translation mine.

19. Punctuation mine.

Chapter 3

1. See also *TI* 292/268; GP 67–68/112; EI 188.

2. Another answer, not discussed in this chapter, is found in Levinas's critique of what he takes to be Plato's understanding of need as mere lack.

3. The idea of creation is discussed also in *Otherwise Than Being* where it is connected to a variety of central concepts taken up and developed in that book such as absolute passivity. In that work, Levinas draws a contrast between the Aristotelian idea of prime matter as pure potentiality and Levinas's idea of absolute passivity that, according to him, is related to the idea of creation (*OB* 110/140). This contrast between prime matter and absolute passivity is relevantly similar to the one stressed in this chapter between the eternal and the new.

4. In *Totality and Infinity,* Levinas speaks of openness—for example, of transcendence as "openness *par excellence*" (*TI* 193/167, my translation)—while in *Otherwise Than Being* he speaks of *anarchy.* The resonances of *openness* that are missing in *anarchy* (a term with its own resonances that *openness* lacks) are a good example of the benefits of not passing too quickly beyond *Totality and Infinity* in discussions of central Levinasian ideas.

5. For pregnancy, see Halperin, "Diotima a Woman," 117, 137–42.

6. In the *Phaedo,* Apollodorus's weeping at Socrates's death causes everyone present but Socrates to break down (117d3–5).

7. Cantarella, *Bisexuality,* 17–27; Davidson, *Courtesans and Fishcakes,* 167–82 (contra Dover, *Greek Homosexuality,* 100–109, and Halperin, "Diotima a Woman," 124).

8. Dover, *Greek Homosexuality,* 124–28.

9. Kirk and Raven, *Presocratic Philosophers,* 24.

10. With Kirk, reading *palintonos* in Fragment 51. Kirk and Raven, *Presocratic Philosophers,* 193.

11. A similar distinction is made by Renaissance Jewish philosopher Leone Ebreo (Judah Abravanel), who in his *Dialogues on Love* has Philo argue that truer and more unalloyed desire and love does not involve lack and gives as among his examples God's love for his creatures and a father's love for his child. Ebreo, *Philosophy of Love,* 180, 250–52. See also the new translation by Rossella Pescatori, forthcoming.

12. The interpretation I give of the good beyond being is my own. It is influenced by Klein's discussion of the divided line (*A Commentary*) and by Seth Benardete's discussion of the beautiful ("Introduction").

13. To associate form only with *eidos,* the fourth level of the divided line, though useful for making verbal distinctions in this essay, is somewhat misleading since the mathematicals (third level), the *eidē* or forms (fourth level), and the idea of the good (beyond the line) are all broadly speaking formal for Plato.

14. Achtenberg, "What Is Goodness," 148.

15. Achtenberg, "What Is Goodness," 149.

16. The interpretation of the *Hippias Major* that I give here is my own and has not been published elsewhere. Some other important recent interpretations are Paul Woodruff's in his translation and commentary, *Plato: Hippias Major* (1982); David Sweet's "Introduction to the *Greater Hippias*" (1987); Drew Hyland's "The Question of Beauty in the *Hippias Major*" (2008); and Seth Benardete's interpretation in the introduction to his book *The Being of the Beautiful* (1984). I read a version of Benardete's interpretation before the book was published and am influenced by Benardete's interpretation. I believe my interpretation is compatible with his though it develops most of the key ideas differently than he does. Woodruff's and Sweet's interpretations contain important ideas from which I have benefited, though my particular discussion of the dialogue's drama is not found in their work. My interpretation importantly differs from Hyland's about the role of definition in the dialogue. I see the dialogue as having an answer to the question, what is the beautiful. Hyland, to the contrary, doubts that Socrates "has as his serious goal in these dialogues to succeed in discovering an unimpeachable definition" (7–8) and thinks the *Hippias Major, Symposium,* and *Phaedrus* "give us good reasons to conclude that there *cannot be* an adequate articulation of the 'essence' of beauty itself" (17). Where Hyland maintains that there are difficulties in finding a comprehensive definition of beauty and so Socrates does not define it, I would say that Socrates has a definition that includes the central difficulty

about beauty—the central *aporia*—within it. There is something fundamentally puzzling about Platonic transcategorials, but the *aporia* does not make giving a definition impossible. Hyland also says that Plato's topics are occasioned by an existential situation. I agree, but I think that is compatible with giving actual definitions. As stated in the introduction to this book, I take the dialogues to be combinations of *logos* and *ergon*—argument and action—and see no reason why drama precludes successful definition. That is not to say, of course, that every dialogue that attempts to give definitions is successful, but I do think that some of them are, for example, the *Meno* on virtue, the *Phaedrus* on eros, and the *Republic* on justice.

17. Sweet, "Introduction," 350.

18. Benardete, "Introduction," xxxiv, Sweet, "Introduction," 350.

19. Daniel Gebhardt suggested this idea to me.

20. The doubling here is important and gives the reader an indication of what makes the form of beauty different than some other forms. Hippias cannot simply say "a maiden is beautiful" because some maidens are not. Nor can he simply say that something beautiful is beautiful without a mere redundancy. The forced doubling implies that beauty is not identical to the properties of a maiden nor are those properties wholly irrelevant to beauty in this case. The beauty of a maiden is in and through the maiden's properties, but it is not simply identical to those properties or reducible to them. Beauty is in and through those properties but surpasses them, we could say, foreshadowing a point Socrates will hint at later in the dialogue.

21. For Hippias, according to Sweet, "Beauty is any beautiful thing." "Introduction," 345.

22. This is exaggeration since a good cosmetician will bring out what is already there not just hide some of what is there, but I am following Socrates's understanding of cosmetics in the *Gorgias*.

23. Thanks to Silvia Benso and James D. Hatley for reading and critiquing a draft of an earlier version of this chapter.

Chapter 4

1. See Kirk and Raven, *Presocratic Philosophers,* 269, for this translation of fragment 3.

2. Translation emended.

Chapter 5

1. Derrida famously writes *difference* with an *a: différance.*

2. For "epiphany of the face," see *TI* 22/51, 48/75, 145/171.

3. See, for example, 1081a14, a23, b21, etc. For discussion of the indeterminate dyad, see Benardete, *Encounters and Reflections,* chapter 7; Klein, *Greek Mathematics,* 80–83.

4. Benardete used to say the most important word in Aristotle's *Metaphysics* was *pōs* (somehow).

5. I discuss this passage further in Achtenberg, "What Is Goodness," 116–18.

6. I discuss this passage further in Achtenberg, "What Is Goodness," 129.

7. Uniqueness, as a translation of *unicité,* is meant to convey singularity not possession of a set of properties possessed by nothing else.

8. For *dénucléation,* see *OB* 64/81, 141/180, 181/228.

9. See, for example, *TI* 43/13–14, "to receive nothing of the other but what is in me" (regarding Socrates); 43/13–14, "to receive nothing, or to be free" (regarding Socrates); 51/22, "to *receive* from the other beyond the capacity of the I."

10. Translation emended.

11. For similar comments, see Lingis, introduction to *Otherwise Than Being,* xxxii.

12. Translation emended (substituting *Lord* for *Eternal*).

13. Translation emended.

14. This remark presages Levinas's extended discussion of the glory of the infinite in chapter 5.

15. See, for contrast, Husserl on retention and protention in internal time-consciousness.

Chapter 6

1. For the proportion, see Klein, *A Commentary,* 118–19.

2. Chaining true opinions down by "reasoning about why they are true" is one way of interpreting "*aitias logismōi*" (*Meno* 98a3–4).

3. Klein, *A Commentary,* 36–38.

4. Aristotle's use of *phronēsis* to mean *practical wisdom* is a later development, though it is foreshadowed by the use of it in the *Republic* to mean knowledge of the good.

5. Or, at least, as *an* Athens is to *a* Jerusalem, as I indicate in what follows.

Chapter 7

1. Translation emended.

2. Translation emended to follow the note and *Holy Scriptures.*

3. Steve Reich's translation in "Tehillim, Three Movements" (liner notes).

4. Robert Alter, *Book of Psalms.*

5. Translation emended.

6. Translation emended.

7. Chananya ben Teradyon, second century C.E., was head of Sichnin yeshiva in the Galilee.

8. Rabbi Shimon bar Yochai, a student of Rabbi Akiva, lived in the second century C.E.

9. Translation and spelling emended. Proof texts rescinded.

10. Malbim, *Remazei Hamishkan,* in Plaut, *The Torah: A Modern Commentary,* 614. Rabbi Meir Leib ben Yechiel Michael Weiser, called Malbim, was a nineteenth-century Volhynian rabbi.

11. For discussion of the Isaiah references, see Eisenstadt, *Driven Back,* chapter 2.

12. *OB* 199/186n11.

13. Hence Levinas, in *Otherwise Than Being,* can refer to the other interchangeably as near or far, hither or beyond. As mentioned in chapter 6, if to relate to the other as other is to relate to him or her without a mediating term, relating to the other as other is relating to an other who is far, because not connected to us by any term, and near, because not separated from us by any term.

14. Woodruff, *Plato's* Hippias Major, 53n73.

15. Benardete, "Introduction," xxxiv.

16. Thanks to Christopher Anderson for discussion of the idea of the body as a covering.

BIBLIOGRAPHY

Abbott, Matthew. "Epistemological Humility: Knowledge After Levinas's Radical Separation." M.A. thesis, University of Nevada, Reno, 2006.

Achtenberg, Deborah. "Aristotelian Resources for Feminist Thinking." In *Ancient Philosophy and Feminism,* 95–117. New York: Routledge, 1996.

———. *Cognition of Value in Aristotle's Ethics: Promise of Enrichment, Threat of Destruction.* Albany: State University of New York Press, 2004.

———. Review of *The Philosophical Sense of Transcendence: Levinas and Plato on Loving Beyond Being* by Sarah Allen. *Notre Dame Philosophical Reviews* (2010).

———. "What Is Goodness? An Introduction." Ph.D. diss., Graduate Faculty, New School for Social Research, 1982.

Allen, R. E. *Plato's Parmenides: Translation and Analysis.* Minneapolis: University of Minnesota Press, 1983.

Allen, Sarah. *The Philosophical Sense of Transcendence: Levinas and Plato on Loving Beyond Being.* Pittsburgh: Duquesne University Press, 2009.

Alter, Robert. *The Book of Psalms: A Translation with Commentary.* New York: W. W. Norton, 2007.

Arendt, Hannah. *The Human Condition.* Chicago: University of Chicago Press, 1958.

Aristotle. *De Anima.* Edited by David Ross. Oxford: Clarendon Press, 1986 [1956].

———. *Metaphysics.* Edited by W. Jaeger. Oxford: Clarendon Press, 1978.

———. *Nicomachean Ethics.* Edited by I. Bywater. Oxford: Clarendon Press, 1975 [1898].

———. *Physics.* Edited by David Ross. Oxford: Clarendon Press, 1973.

———. *Poetics.* Edited by Rudolf Kassel. Oxford: Clarendon Press, 1988 [1965].

Benardete, Seth. *The Being of the Beautiful: Plato's Theaetetus, Sophist, and Statesman.* Chicago: University of Chicago Press, 1984.

———. *Encounters and Reflections: Conversations with Seth Benardete.* Edited by Ronna Burger. Chicago: University of Chicago Press, 2002.

———. "Introduction." In *The Being of the Beautiful: Plato's Theaetetus, Sophist, and Statesman,* xi–xlviii. Chicago: University of Chicago Press, 1984.

Bolotin, David. *Plato's Dialogue on Friendship: An Interpretation of the* Lysis *with a New Translation.* Ithaca, N.Y.: Cornell University Press, 1979.

Cantarella, Eva. *Bisexuality in the Ancient World.* Translated by Cormac Ó Cuilleanáin. New Haven, Conn.: Yale University Press, 1992.

Davidson, James. *Courtesans and Fishcakes: The Consuming Passions of Classical Athens.* New York: St. Martin's Press, 1998.

Derrida, Jacques. "Différance." In *Margins of Philosophy.* Translated by Alan Bass. Chicago: University of Chicago Press, 1982.

Dover, K. J. *Greek Homosexuality.* Cambridge, Mass.: Harvard University Press, 1978.

Ebreo, Leone. *The Philosophy of Love (Dialoghi d'Amore).* London: Soncino Press, 1937.

Eisenstadt, Oona. *Driven Back to the Text: The Premodern Sources of Levinas's Postmodernism.* Pittsburgh: Duquesne University Press, 2001.

Emerson, Ralph Waldo. "Self-Reliance." In *The Essays of Ralph Waldo Emerson,* 27–51. Cambridge, Mass.: Harvard University Press, 1987 [1841].

Ferguson, Alfred R., and Jean Ferguson Carr. *The Essays of Ralph Waldo Emerson.* Cambridge, Mass.: Harvard University Press, 1987.

Goldin, Judah. *The Fathers According to Rabbi Nathan.* New Haven, Conn.: Yale University Press, 1983 [1955].

Gonzales, Francisco J. "Levinas Questioning Plato on Eros and Maieutics." In *Levinas and the Ancients,* 40–61. Indianapolis: Indiana University Press, 2008.

Gourevitch, Victor, ed. and trans. *Jean-Jacques Rousseau, The First and Second Discourses Together with the Replies to Critics and Essay on the Origin of Languages.* New York: Harper & Row, 1986.

Halperin, David M. "Why Is Diotima a Woman?" In *One Hundred Years of Homosexuality and Other Essays on Greek Love.* New York: Routledge, 1990.

Hegel, Georg Wilhelm Friedrich. *Phenomenology of Mind.* Translated by J. B. Baillie. New York: Harper and Row, 1967.

Homer. *Iliad.* Translated by Richmond Lattimore. Chicago: University of Chicago Press, 1967 [1951].

———. *Odyssey.* Translated by Richmond Lattimore. Chicago: University of Chicago Press, 1967 [1951].

Hyland, Drew A. *Plato and the Question of Beauty.* Indianapolis: Indiana University Press, 2008.

———. "The Question of Beauty in the *Hippias Major.*" In *Plato and the Question of Beauty,* 7–26. Indianapolis: Indiana University Press, 2008.

Jewish Publication Society. *The Holy Scriptures According to the Masoretic Text.* Philadelphia: Jewish Publication Society, 1945 [1917].

———. *Tanakh: A New Translation of the Holy Scriptures According to the Traditional Hebrew Text.* Philadelphia: Jewish Publication Society, 1985.

Kearney, Richard. *States of Mind: Dialogues with Contemporary Thinkers.* New York: New York University Press, 1995.

Kirk, G. S., and J. E. Raven. *The Presocratic Philosophers: A Critical History with a Selection of Texts.* Cambridge: Cambridge University Press, 1957.

Klein, Jacob. *A Commentary on Plato's* Meno. Chicago: University of Chicago Press, 1965.

———. *Greek Mathematical Thought and the Origin of Algebra.* Translated by Eva Brann. Cambridge, Mass.: MIT Press, 1972 [1968] [1934].

Kolitz, Zvi. "Yosl Rakover Talks to God," 1999 [1995]. Translated by Carol Brown Janeway. In *Yosl Rakover Talks to God,* 3–25. New York: Pantheon, 1999.

Kravitz, Leonard, and Kerry M. Olitzky. *Pirke Avot: A Modern Commentary on Jewish Ethics.* New York: UAHC Press, 1993.

Lauterbach, Jacob Z. *Mekhilta de Rabbi Ishmael.* Vols. 1–2. Philadelphia: Jewish Publication Society, 2004 [1933].

Lehrman, S. M. *Midrash Rabbah. Exodus.* London: Soncino Press, 1983.

Levinas, Emmanuel. "*Aimer la Thora plus que Dieu,*" 1993 [1955]. In *Difficile Liberté,* 1995 [1963], 189–93. Translated as "Loving the Torah More Than God." In *Difficult Freedom: Essays on Judaism,* 142–45. Baltimore: Johns Hopkins University Press, 1990.

———. *L'au-delà du verset: Lectures et discours talmudiques.* Paris: Les Éditions de Minuit, 1982. Translated as *Beyond the Verse: Talmudic Readings and Lectures* by Gary D. Mole. Indianapolis: Indiana University Press, 1994.

———. *Autrement qu'être ou au-delà de l'essence.* Dordrecht: Martinus Nijhoff, 1991 [1974]. Translated as *Otherwise Than Being or Beyond Essence* by Alfonso Lingis. Pittsburgh: Duquesne University Press, 2000 [1981].

———. *Collected Philosophical Papers.* Translated by Alphonso Lingis. Pittsburgh: Duquesne University Press, 1998.

———. *De Dieu qui vient à l'idée.* Paris: Librairie Philosophique J. Vrin, 1998 [1982]. Translated as *Of God Who Comes To Mind* by Bettina Bergo. Stanford, Calif.: Stanford University Press, 1998.

———. *De l'évasion.* Montpellier: Fata Morgana, 1982 [1935]. Translated as *On Escape* by Bettina Bergo. Stanford, Calif.: Stanford University Press, 2003.

———. "Dieu et la philosophie." In *De dieu qui vient à l'idée,* 93–127. Paris: J. Vrin, 1986. Translated by Bettina Bergo as "God and Philosophy." In *Of God Who Comes to Mind,* 55–78. Stanford, Calif.: Stanford University Press, 1998.

———. *Difficile liberté.* Paris: Albin Michel, 1995 [1963]. Translated as *Difficult Freedom: Essays on Judaism* by Seán Hand. Baltimore: Johns Hopkins University Press, 1990.

———. *Ethics and Infinity: Conversations with Philippe Nemo.* Translated by Richard Cohen. Pittsburgh: Duquesne University Press, 1985.

———. "Ethics of the Infinite." In *States of Mind: Dialogues with Contemporary Thinkers,* 177–99. New York: New York University Press, 1995.

———. *Humanisme de l'autre homme.* Montpellier: Fata Morgana, 1972. Translated as *Humanism of the Other* by Nidra Poller. Urbana: University of Illinois Press, 2003.

———. "Love and Filiation." 1982 [1981]. In *Ethics and Infinity: Conversations with Emmanuel Levinas,* 63–72. Pittsburgh: Duquesne University Press, 1985.

———. "La philosophie et l'idée de l'infini," 1967 [1957]. In *En découvrant l'existence avec Husserl et Heidegger,* 2e éd., 229–47. Translated as "Philosophy and the Idea of the Infinite" by Alphonso Lingis. In *Collected Philosophical Papers,* 47–59. Pittsburgh: Duquesne University Press, 1998.

———. "Résumé de *Totalité et Infini.*" "*Annales de l'Université de Paris*" *La Société des amis de l'Université* 31, no. 3 (1961): 385–86. Translated as "Summary of Emmanuel Levinas, *Totalité et Infini*" by Adriaan Peperzak. In *Platonic Transformations,* 120–21. Lanham, Md.: Rowman and Littlefield Publishers, 1997.

———. "La signification et le sense." *Revue de Métaphysique et de Morale* 69, no. 2 (1964): 256–66. In *Humanisme de l'autre homme,* 17–63. Montpellier: Fata Morgana, 1972. Translated as "Meaning and Sense" by Alfonso Lingis. In *Collected Philosophical Papers,* 75–107. Pittsburgh: Duquesne University Press, 1998.

———. *Le temps et l'autre.* Montpellier: Fata Morgana, 1983 [1947]. Translated as *Time and the Other* by Richard A. Cohen. Pittsburgh: Duquesne University Press, 1987.

———. *Texte du traite "Yoma" (85a–85b).* 1968 [1965]. In *Quatre lectures talmudiques,* 29–64. Paris: *Les Éditions de Minuit,* 1968. Translated as *Toward the Other,* 1994 [1990]. In *Nine Talmudic Readings,* 12–29. Indianapolis: Indiana University Press, 1994 [1990].

———. *Totalité et infini: Essay sur l'extériorité.* Dordrecht: Martinus Nijhoff, 1993 [1961]. Translated as *Totality and Infinity: An Essay on Exteriority* by Alfonso Lingis. Pittsburgh: Duquesne University Press, 2000 [1969].

Long, Anthony, and David Sedley. *The Hellenistic Philosophers.* Vol. 1, *Translations of the Principal Sources, with Philosophical Commentary.* Cambridge: Cambridge University Press, 1990 [1987].

Naas, Michael. "Lending Assistance Always to Itself: Levinas' Infinite Conversation with Platonic Dialogue." In *Levinas and the Ancients,* 79–102. Indianapolis: Indiana University Press, 2008.

Nemo, Phillipe. *Ethics and Infinity: Conversations with Emmanuel Levinas.* Translated by Richard A. Cohen. Pittsburgh: Duquesne University Press, 1985.

Nussbaum, Martha C. *The Fragility of Goodness: Luck and Ethics in Greek Tragedy and Philosophy.* Cambridge: Cambridge University Press, 1986.

Pangle, Thomas L. *The Roots of Political Philosophy: Ten Forgotten Socratic Dialogues.* Ithaca, N.Y.: Cornell University Press, 1987.

Peperzak, Adriaan Theodoor. *Platonic Transformations: With and After Hegel, Heidegger, and Levinas.* Lanham, Md.: Rowman and Littlefield Publishers, 1997.

———. "The Platonism of Emmanuel Levinas." In *Platonic Transformations,* 113–20. Lanham, Md.: Rowman and Littlefield Publishers, 1997.

Plato. *Crito.* In vol. 1 of *Platonis Opera.* Edited by John Burnet. Oxford: Clarendon Press, 1985 [1900].

———. *Euthyphro.* In vol. 1 of *Platonis Opera.* Edited by John Burnet. Oxford: Clarendon Press, 1985 [1900].

———. *Gorgias.* In vol. 3 of *Platonis Opera.* Edited by John Burnet. Oxford: Clarendon Press, 1974 [1903].

———. *Hippias Major.* In vol. 3 of *Platonis Opera.* Edited by John Burnet. Oxford: Clarendon Press, 1974 [1903].

———. *Laws.* In vol. 5 of *Platonis Opera.* Edited by John Burnet. Oxford: Clarendon Press, 1984 [1907].

———. *Lysis.* In vol. 3 of *Platonis Opera.* Edited by John Burnet. Oxford: Clarendon Press, 1974 [1903].

———. *Meno.* In vol. 3 of *Platonis Opera.* Edited by John Burnet. Oxford: Clarendon Press, 1974 [1903].

———. *Parmenides.* In vol. 2 of *Platonis Opera.* Edited by John Burnet. Oxford: Clarendon Press, 1973 [1901].

———. *Phaedo.* In vol. 1 of *Platonis Opera.* Edited by John Burnet. Oxford: Clarendon Press, 1985 [1900].

———. *Phaedrus.* In vol. 2 of *Platonis Opera.* Edited by John Burnet. Oxford: Clarendon Press, 1973 [1901].

———. *Philebus.* In vol. 2 of *Platonis Opera.* Edited by John Burnet. Oxford: Clarendon Press, 1973 [1901].

———. *Republic.* In vol. 4 of *Platonis Opera.* Edited by John Burnet. Oxford: Clarendon Press, 1972 [1902].

———. *Seventh Letter.* In vol. 5 of *Platonis Opera.* Edited by John Burnet. Oxford: Clarendon Press, 1984 [1907].

———. *Symposium.* In vol. 2 of *Platonis Opera.* Edited by John Burnet. Oxford: Clarendon Press, 1973 [1901].

———. *Theaetetus.* In vol. 1 of *Platonis Opera.* Edited by John Burnet. Oxford: Clarendon Press, 1985 [1900].

———. *Timaeus.* In vol. 4 of *Platonis Opera.* Edited by John Burnet. Oxford: Clarendon press, 1972 [1902].

Plaut, W. Gunther, ed. *The Torah: A Modern Commentary.* New York: Union of American Hebrew Congregations, 1981.

Plutarch. *On Stoic Self-Contradictions,* 1057A. In *The Hellenistic Philosophers,* 317. Cambridge: Cambridge University Press, 1990 [1987].

Reich, Steve. "Tehillim, Three Movements" (liner notes). New York: Elektra Nonesuch, 1994.

Rousseau, Jean-Jacques. "Discourse on the Sciences and Arts." In *The First and Second Discourses Together with the Replies to Critics and Essay on the Origin of Languages,* 1–27. New York: Harper & Row, 1986.

Sartre, Jean-Paul. *Being and Nothingness.* Translated by Hazel E. Barnes. New York: Washington Square Press, 1992 [1956] [1943].

Schroeder, Brian, and Silvia Benso. *Levinas and the Ancients.* Indianapolis: Indiana University Press, 2008.

Staehler, Tanja. "Getting Under the Skin: Platonic Myths in Levinas." In *Levinas and the Ancients,* 62–78. Indianapolis: Indiana University Press, 2008.

———. *Plato and Levinas: The Ambiguous Out-Side of Ethics.* New York: Routledge, 2010.

Stalley, R. F. "Plato's Doctrine of Freedom." *Proceedings of the Aristotelian Society* 98, no. 2 (1998): 145–58.

Sweet, David R. "Introduction to the *Greater Hippias.*" In *The Roots of Political Philosophy: Ten Forgotten Socratic Dialogues.* Ithaca, N.Y.: Cornell University Press, 1987.

Thucydides. *Histories.* Edited by Henry Stuart Jones and John Enoch Powell. Vol. 1. Oxford: Clarendon Press, 1942 [1902].

———. *The Peloponnesian War.* Translated by Steven Lattimore. Indianapolis: Hackett Publishing Company, 1998.

Woodruff, Paul. *Plato: Hippias Major; Translated, with Commentary and Essay, by Paul Woodruff.* Indianapolis: Hackett Publishing Company, 1982.

INDEX